A Critical History of Southern Rhodesia

A Critical History of
SOUTHERN
RHODESIA

Gardner Thompson

LYNNE
RIENNER
PUBLISHERS

BOULDER
LONDON

Published in the United States of America in 2024 by
Lynne Rienner Publishers, Inc.
1800 30th Street, Boulder, Colorado 80301
www.rienner.com

and in the United Kingdom by
Lynne Rienner Publishers, Inc.
1 Bedford Row, London WC1R 4BU
www.eurospanbookstore.com/rienner

© 2024 by Lynne Rienner Publishers, Inc. All rights reserved

Library of Congress Cataloging-in-Publication Data
Names: Thompson, Gardner, author.
Title: A critical history of Southern Rhodesia / Gardner Thompson.
Description: Boulder, Colorado : Lynne Rienner Publishers, Inc., 2024. |
  Includes bibliographical references and index. | Summary: "A provocative
  history of British colonial rule in Southern Rhodesia, from the first
  colonial settlements in Mashonaland to the establishment of the
  country's sovereignty as Zimbabwe"— Provided by publisher.
Identifiers: LCCN 2023034616 (print) | LCCN 2023034617 (ebook) | ISBN
  9781685859886 (hardcover) | ISBN 9781685859893 (ebook)
Subjects: LCSH: Zimbabwe—History.
Classification: LCC DT2925 .T46 2024 (print) | LCC DT2925 (ebook) | DDC
  968.91—dc23
LC record available at https://lccn.loc.gov/2023034616
LC ebook record available at https://lccn.loc.gov/2023034617

British Cataloguing in Publication Data
A Cataloguing in Publication record for this book
is available from the British Library.

Printed and bound in the United States of America

The paper used in this publication meets the requirements
of the American National Standard for Permanence of
Paper for Printed Library Materials Z39.48-1992.

5 4 3 2 1

*In memory of Michael Twaddle (1939–2023),
mentor and friend*

Contents

Preface   ix

1   Why a New History of Southern Rhodesia?   1
2   The Founding of Southern Rhodesia   9
3   The Settler Colony   17
4   Winds of Change   47
5   Liberal Dawn?   73
6   Turn to the Right   103
7   Cul-de-Sac   137
8   Legacy: Zimbabwe   169
9   Judging Empire   189

Timeline   221
List of Acronyms   223
Sources   225
Index   231
About the Book   245

Preface

WHEN I FIRST WENT TO AFRICA AS A YOUNG TEACHER, IT WAS to Uganda. That experience of a former British protectorate led me back to university, research, and return visits to East Africa. The provenance of this book is comparable, in that it arose from personal experience of Zimbabwe—three visits between 2011 and 2018—which stimulated questions about the country's past as a White settler colony: a very different story from that of Uganda. Being in what was formerly Southern Rhodesia, I was reminded of earlier times. I could remember, rather vaguely, news references in my youth to the Central African Federation, Roy Welensky, and Garfield Todd—and more clearly, televised coverage of Ian Smith and his Unilateral Declaration of Independence in 1965. How had the Southern Rhodesia of Garfield Todd given way to the Rhodesia of Ian Smith? And how in turn had Rhodesia yielded to the Zimbabwe of Robert Mugabe and Emmerson Mnangagwa? Here was a new project . . . one sustained, furthermore, by the coincidental outburst of soul-searching about Britain's imperial past prompted by Black Lives Matter and Rhodes Must Fall. *A Critical History of Southern Rhodesia* would occupy me through Covid-19 and beyond, and perhaps inform judgments emanating from this lively, at times contentious, ongoing debate.

I would like to thank innumerable friends and relatives who patiently listened to me talk about this plan and kindly offered comments, suggestions, or simply support—three people in particular. Sally Field and I discovered that we had been contemporaries at Cambridge, but by what different routes had we arrived there! She was most generous with her advice and her time, describing what it was like to be the daughter of the prime minister of Southern Rhodesia in the early 1960s. I thank Cleophas Lunga for his reflections on Rhodesia, for his insights into Zimbabwe, and for steering my research fruitfully toward the religious arm of European colonialism. I am also most grateful for a long association with Michael Twaddle, who I am sad to say died in March 2023. As both teacher and mentor, he supported and guided me in all my academic endeavors; his final contribution was to recommend me to Lynne Rienner as a possible publisher of this book.

"The past is a foreign country: they do things differently there." Novelist L. P. Hartley's line is much quoted, but its import is not always acted on: that we must allow for context—of place and time and culture—when we summon individuals from the past to the court of today's public opinion. But this is not to absolve every one of them from every wrongdoing. We are entitled to judge influential historical figures who, when faced with moral choices in their own context, committed themselves to courses of action that had harmful consequences, foreseeable and foreseen.

1

Why a New History of Southern Rhodesia?

"THERE IS SOMETHING UNFORGETTABLE ABOUT A CAMP-FIRE at night under the clear, sparkling skies of Africa." So wrote Judith Todd about her visit in 1964 to a barren, malaria-infested detention camp in Southern Rhodesia. This was Gonakudzingwa: "Where the banished ones sleep." Her father, prime minister Garfield Todd, had lost power in 1958. The new premier, Ian Smith, had recently dispatched a number of dissident Africans to this remote place. Among them was Joshua Nkomo, former president of the banned African National Congress. There is perhaps no better picture than Todd's of how, within half a dozen pivotal years, the Whites of this settler colony had taken a decisive fork in the road:

> I thought as we sat there that night, how this place above all others illustrated the way in which the government mocks the values they use to justify the things they do to the people of Zimbabwe. The glowing fire picked out the faces of teachers and students, chiefs, scholars and businessmen, old men, young boys and women, evangelists and farmers—people who themselves represented the various facets of the Christian and the civilised standards Smith so endlessly talked about."[1]

* * *

This history of Southern Rhodesia is a response to three current interests in Britain and the United States.

Map 1.1 Southern Rhodesia (1890–1980)

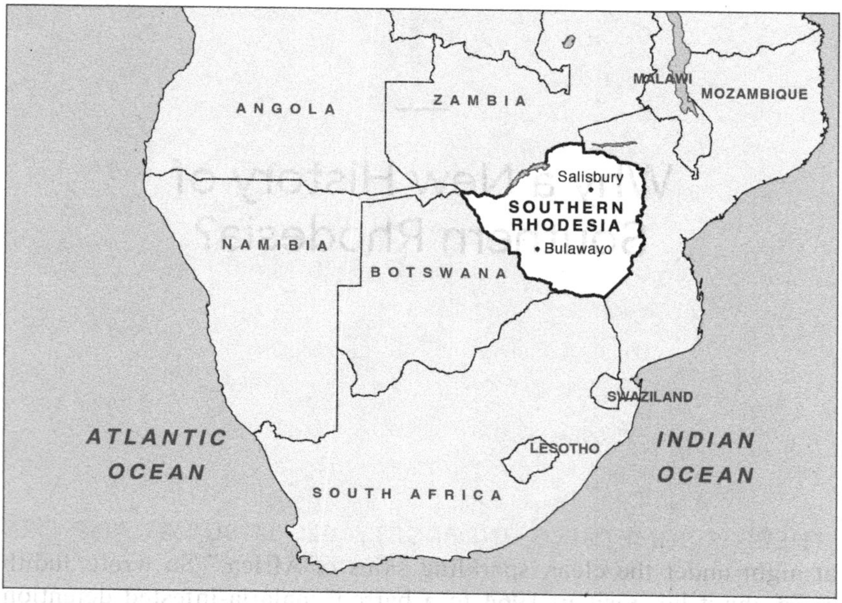

Note: Southern Rhodesia in the context of modern Africa.

First, an understanding of the former colony's history—especially the final two decades of reactionary White supremacist rule—throws light on the plight of twenty-first century Zimbabwe: on its spectacular descent "from breadbasket to basket-case"; on the personality and rule (up to 2017) of Robert Mugabe, widely demonized as an archetype of capricious postimperial African dictatorship (and of Emmerson Mnangagwa since then); and on the fate of Zimbabwe's remaining White inhabitants, still regarded by many in Britain as "kith and kin." Above all, this review of the country's past shows how the strategic political/moral choice of direction made by the White settler regime in the late 1950s and early 1960s—to consolidate, rather than to dilute, a regime of racial domination—had consequences for subsequent generations in Zimbabwe. Rhodesia outlived other British African possessions by almost two decades of going it alone: years of political reaction which intensified racial division and led eventually to liberation war. As a result, this colonial impact was particularly damaging.

Second, recent years have seen renewed discussion of empire in general—sparked by events, campaigns, and arguments on both sides of the Atlantic. Weighty evidence-based volumes have also contributed. Priyamvada Gopal's 2019 *Insurgent Empire: Anticolonial Resistance and British Dissent* and Nigel Biggar's 2023 *Colonialism: A Moral Reckoning* represent two competing, and incompatible, assessments. Discussion has been hindered by generalizations rendered suspect by the subject's very complexity. Yet, in his classic critique of belief in laws of history, Karl Popper implored us to recognize that "history is characterised by its interest in actual, singular, or specific events, rather than in laws and generalisations."[2] What follows is indeed a study of singular and specific events—albeit a study that closes by offering a means of making value judgments on any period of the past.

This British colony covered an area of Central Africa that was half as large again as Great Britain, its notional imperial ruler, between 1890 and 1980 (later as simply Rhodesia). It was just one of the forty or so territories, diverse in size and character, that were defined and appropriated across Africa by European powers scrambling for raw materials and markets—and for strategic purposes, too—in the closing decades of the nineteenth century. Here in Southern Rhodesia, we encounter full-blooded colonialism: a White settler colony, as distinct from a protectorate such as Uganda, where the British administered with a relative lightness of touch and where settlers were all but unknown. This case study offers material for further informed discussion of imperialism. For this reason, its primary focus is on the territory's Europeans: what they did, why they did it, and what were the consequences. This is not to imply that Africans were passive, let alone mere victims. Within the colonial framework, they were makers of their own choices and agents of their own destiny.

This was not slavery—that age had largely passed—but a history of Southern Rhodesia under White control can highlight relations between European rulers (never more than 5 percent of the population) and the Africans they ruled, as well as examine the extent to which attitudes and forms of racial interaction changed over time. Understandably, more academic attention has been paid to the African politics of this era (before and after 1980) than to the nature and lasting significance of ninety years of White minority rule. Forty years on, it is time for a fresh consideration of yesterday's men.

Third, this book proposes a framework for making fair judgments about the past, and past historical figures. I thus consider not only judgment by outcome—such as the impact of White rule on what followed—but also judgment by values. Chapter 9 provides a template for answering a general nagging question of our time, while concentrating on the specific case of the Whites in Rhodesia: How may we, now, reasonably make moral judgments about colonialism—and colonists—then?

* * *

Two "great men" are most closely associated with the late nineteenth-century burst of British enterprise in Central Africa and the colony's origins. David Livingstone, a medical missionary and explorer, died in 1873. Cecil Rhodes, an immensely wealthy businessman and political zealot, died in 1902. Yet these two may be regarded as the influential advocates of two lasting, contrasting, future roles for Europeans—and for race relations—in Southern Rhodesia. Livingstone's vision arose from what he saw as the needs of Africans, while Rhodes's vision was founded on the interests of his fellow Europeans. Livingstone was famed for the respect in which he held the Africans whom he came across, and for his regard for them as human beings of equal standing under God. He had explored the area some decades before Rhodes's pioneer settlers arrived. On his travels, he came across the slave trade. He wrote of its horrors and argued that it could be ended only by a European presence. He advocated commerce, Christianity, and civilization. Rhodes, however, while subscribing to "the three C's," repeatedly professed the superiority of his own race and the benefit of others being ruled by Anglo-Saxons.

Personifying the spirits of their age, Rhodes and Livingstone had much in common. Neither person doubted that Africans would profit from British rule, and Rhodes no more questioned the benefits of "civilization" than Livingstone had done when he saw its absence firsthand. Even so, the first decades of the twentieth century may be viewed as a time when two traditions, those associated with Livingstone and with Rhodes, competed for mastery in Southern Rhodesia. Though this was a period of considerable consensus among Europeans in the colony regarding the acceptability of imperialism, there were some indications of the open disputation that was to come. Unsurprisingly, most of the first White colonists and later generations saw themselves as successors of Rhodes. Yet, there was always a minority of liberals moved by a more Livingstonian tradition.

In the transforming wake of World War II, these two strands came into sharper contrast and sustained a debate among Southern Rhodesia's settler rulers. My focus will thus be on the 1950s. Large numbers of new White immigrants arrived from Britain and South Africa. Growing numbers of Africans found employment in the expanding White economy.

Many of these became politicized, partly in response to the creation of the Central African Federation (CAF) in 1953 as a superstructure for sustaining White rule across the region. In Southern Rhodesia, with imperialism coming under attack from many quarters and the Cold War dominating international relations, it became clear during the 1950s that the White minority had to make a choice—moral as much as political—as to the course they wanted to take. The settler society and state that had emerged over the previous half-century was beginning to look unsustainable. An emergent middle class of educated Africans, who were in part products of the White man's "civilizing" mission and were aroused by political developments elsewhere in Africa, asked more insistently than previously for their admission into the White man's world and the opportunity to share in its future as equals.

It is therefore natural to see the 1950s primarily as the decade of rising African nationalism. To be sure, rural as well as urban Africans did much to shape the debate among Whites and to influence its outcome. But to understand what happened, we must examine those in power in government and dynamics and arguments within the dominant White minority. The defining feature of Southern Rhodesia was White privilege; consequently, political dialogue regarding the future was dominated by issues of race. Settlers with conservative views were now challenged by liberal Europeans who acknowledged the African case and, to an extent, spoke on their behalf. The latter proposed a shift in political direction, in which the colony's Africans would gradually advance through the removal of social discrimination, and their leaders would become engaged in a multiracial political partnership. In short, one option was to suppress emergent African nationalism—to retain White racial supremacy—and the other was to respond to African aspirations, promote African advancement, and seek a multiracial future through dialogue and accommodation.

A range of contemporaries wrote analyses at the time or memoirs later, providing us with a rich seam of source material, including Southern Rhodesians, both European and African, and outsiders, mostly academics and journalists who observed the unfolding situation. This raises the question: Do we see a problematical situation more clearly from inside or outside? Conservative Rhodesians insisted throughout the period of White minority rule that only they could see things clearly, and that the views of outsiders were skewed by ignorance and prejudice. Expressing a then widely held view among Whites, Roy Welensky (second prime minister of the CAF) once admonished his critics, saying, "You must give us credit for knowing the African a little better than people in London."[3] Rejecting that self-serving view, the academic Philip Mason, a visitor who knew the self-governing colony well, argued in 1958 that "no-one who has not made his home in a country can understand it; true, but it is also true that no-one can understand a country [which] he *has* made his home."[4] Surely Doris Lessing was right to value both perspectives, while putting more faith, in the end, in that of the experienced outsider. She wrote: "To understand a place like Rhodesia, it is no good looking coolly from the outside. You have to experience the paranoia, the adolescent sentimentality, the neurosis. Experience—*then* retreat into a cool look from outside."[5]

Lessing brought a Marxist's eye to her analysis of Southern Rhodesia. This approach to the study of history famously eschews value judgments, guided as it is by the fundamental view that human history unfolds according to laws pertaining to class struggle. To this extent, Marxist philosophy is amoral: people behave in the only ways open to them, given their class interests. This, however, is not a theoretical straitjacket for which non-Marxists have much sympathy, and it is most interesting to note that Lessing could not stop herself from breaking free of it. "I am bored with my own contradictions," she wrote in 1957, adding:

> If, as a Marxist, I say certain kinds of people are bound to behave in a certain kind of way, according to the type of society they live in, or what part of that society they are, then there should be nothing emotional about this; it is certainly no theme for moral indignation. One can and should be morally indignant about the form of society, but not about the behaviour of the people in it. Yet these comfort-loving, pleasure-satiated white settlers make me angry and disgusted. And the way the Africans are forced to live makes me angry and miserable because of the waste and stupidity of it.[6]

In the following chapters, sympathy will be detected with Lessing and the small band of Whites in Southern Rhodesia whose progressive standpoint in the 1950s reflected the nobler aspirations of that postwar generation. The historian Robert Blake declared a similar interest toward the end of his magisterial *History of Rhodesia*, which he completed in 1977 while the liberation war raged and the destiny of Rhodesia remained unknown. The concluding sentences, which display a nuanced tolerance of empire, deserve to be quoted at length:

> Cecil Rhodes and his successors managed against all the odds to build up a flourishing colony in which the standard of living for Africans as well as Europeans improved out of all recognition. It is

sad that the multi-racialism which genuinely inspired some of the makers of Rhodesia should have ended in a bleak and seemingly irreconcilable confrontation between black and white—sad but not perhaps wholly surprising.[7]

However, even in the Rhodesian Front (RF) period, Blake could add: "Although Ian Smith has regularly won every European seat, a solid core of 20 to 25 per cent of the electorate has consistently voted against him. . . . Their hope of a multi-racial society is not likely to be realised, but their aim was neither foolish nor ignoble." It would be the RF whose aims could be described as both foolish and ignoble. Blake concluded with a forecast:

> The historian of Zimbabwe in the year 2000 will probably forget their existence or, if he remembers it, sneer at their political ineffectiveness. . . . It would be a pity, however, to disregard those who tried to soften the acerbity of conflict and to provide some bridge between the polarised extremes towards which race relations have been moving.[8]

But those relatively liberal Whites who recognized the legitimacy of African aspirations, and who proposed a progressively close political association in Southern Rhodesia of the European minority and African majority, will not be forgotten or sneered at here.

* * *

In the pages that follow, Chapter 2 examines Cecil Rhodes, the man who founded the colony and inspired many generations of settlers, though he died in 1902. This short portrait of Cecil Rhodes helps to contextualize the history of Southern Rhodesia that is the focus of this book.

Chapter 3 provides an overview of the first half century or so of settler rule: how it was established, the nature of European society, the range of African responses, and the institutionalized segregation of the races.

Chapter 4 highlights changes in the global context brought about by World War II. It examines the changing postwar nature of Southern Rhodesian society, White and Black, and the significance for the colony of the 1953 establishment of the CAF.

Chapter 5 focuses on the premiership of Garfield Todd at a time of challenging developments in African society and deepening divisions among Europeans: a schism that led to the defeat of those who represented the Livingstonian tradition by those who considered themselves to represent the path of Rhodes.

Chapter 6 asks why, between 1958 and 1962 and continually thereafter, most Whites chose to continue racial discrimination and to limit African advancement; and how Ian Smith and the diehards of his RF illegally came to declare Rhodesia independent of Britain.

Chapter 7 moves beyond 1965, examining the rhetoric and realities of illegal RF rule following Rhodesia's Unilateral Declaration of Independence (UDI), the consolidation of White privilege within the colony, spasmodic searches for a settlement with Britain, and the gathering intensity of a liberation war. It concludes by weighing the factors that led to a conference of all interested parties at Lancaster House in London toward the end of 1979.

Chapter 8 assesses the consequences of that preceding settler rule for Zimbabwe from 1980 onward. The argument here is that while previous exercises elsewhere in decolonization had been problematical, the legacy in Zimbabwe was especially damaging. The RF years had harmed the country—if not beyond repair, then beyond the capacity of Robert Mugabe's successor government to make good.

Chapter 9 introduces a framework for making value judgments about people in the past. This is applied, primarily, to the generations of Whites who settled and governed Southern Rhodesia between 1890 and 1980—especially those in power in the 1960s and 1970s—though it also considers the reputation of Cecil Rhodes as its founder.

Notes

1. Todd, *Rhodesia*, 84.
2. Popper, *The Poverty of Historicism*, 143.
3. Quoted in Keatley, *The Politics of Partnership*, 473.
4. Mason, *The Birth of a Dilemma*, 9. Italics in original.
5. Lessing, *Going Home*, 238. Italics added.
6. Lessing, *Going Home*, 129.
7. Blake, *A History of Rhodesia*, 411.
8. Blake, *A History of Rhodesia*, 411.

2

The Founding of Southern Rhodesia

ABOUT ONE HUNDRED AND TWENTY YEARS AFTER HIS DEATH, Cecil Rhodes remains a hugely controversial figure. In Oxford in 2020, a Rhodes Must Fall campaign—started five years earlier in a brief echo of student protests at his statue at Cape Town University (which he never attended)—was given fresh, impassioned impetus by the Black Lives Matter movement on both sides of the Atlantic. A statue of Rhodes had stood at Oriel College, Oxford, since 1911. When the twenty-year-old Rhodes returned to England from South Africa in 1873 for his higher education, having made enough money in three years from growing cotton and acquiring claims in the Kimberly diamond fields to fund it, he applied to University College. Its Master turned him down but passed him on to Oriel, telling the would-be student that Oriel would be less particular. Rhodes spent just one term at Oriel, as poor health and business affairs in South Africa's burgeoning diamond industry kept him away. He was finally able to spend several terms in the college, 1876 to 1878, before being awarded his B.A. in 1881.

This history of Southern Rhodesia is not the place for further analysis of this much commented on and ongoing issue. But, in this inescapable context, it must begin with reference to Rhodes, because he not only founded the colony but helped to shape the lives and attitudes of numerous settlers, during his lifetime and later. We need to know why and how the founding of Southern Rhodesia came about, so we begin with the background to Rhodes's association with Central Africa.

* * *

Although English by birth, Cecil Rhodes's financial and political power base was South Africa. By the late 1880s, South Africa's diamonds and gold had brought him immense wealth; furthermore, he was an influential member of parliament in the Cape Colony, of which he was shortly to become prime minister. In South Africa at that time, the British (who formally acquired the territory in 1815 for its critical location on the sea route to India) remained heavily outnumbered by Boers/Afrikaners (originally Dutch settlers who had started to colonize the area in the seventeenth century). Rhodes, a shrewd politician, maintained good relations with Afrikaners in the Cape; he even chose a predominantly Afrikaner constituency through which to enter parliament in 1881. But he could not tolerate the claims to independence of the Orange Free State and the Transvaal (also known as the South African Republic), which some of the Boers most hostile to British rule had established as land-locked republics in the interior. Rhodes's hostility to the independent Transvaal and its indomitable leader, Paul Kruger, intensified when in 1886 the discovery of huge gold deposits on the Witwatersrand threatened to make its capital, Johannesburg, the richest spot on earth and, in time, to place Afrikaners in control of South Africa's destiny.

Here lay the origin of Rhodes's ambition. While he dreamed of extending British imperial influence from the Cape to Cairo, more immediately pressing was the need to limit the Transvaal's expansion and influence by any means available to him, and to find another Witwatersrand to reestablish and confirm British regional hegemony: hence the expedition that he sent north of the Limpopo River in 1890.

His pioneers had to deal with two main Indigenous African peoples, each a cluster of subgroups. The Mashona had lived in the region for centuries; the ruins of their "Great Zimbabwe" testified to a period of prominence and prosperity long since passed. The Ndebele were relative newcomers. Not only in Europe and America was this an age of migration, conquest, and subjection of Indigenous peoples. The Ndebele were recent arrivals from southern Africa, exiles from the tumultuous Zulu wars. Though concentrated to the west and south in Matabeleland, the Ndebele held sway over the region of the Mashona too—though the Mashona were twice their number (a contemporary estimate was 300,000)—and periodically raided them.

There were two steps to Rhodes's preparation for sending his would-be settlers northward. The first was to negotiate with Lobengula, king of the Ndebele. In February 1888, Rhodes won the king's promise not to give rights away to any other foreign power without first consulting the British. Eight months later he secured a more formal treaty. In October 1888, in return for funds, guns, and a gunboat, the king conceded in a written agreement with Rhodes's business associate, Charles Rudd, "complete and exclusive charge over all metals and minerals" in his kingdom, and "full power to do all things that they may deem necessary to win and procure the same." There was no reference to the occupation of land. Lobengula received only oral promises that no more than ten White men would prospect in his territory, and that they would abide by his laws and be under his authority.

The Rudd Concession served the second step of Rhodes's plan handsomely. He used it to persuade the British government to charter his newly formed British South Africa Company (BSAC). The BSAC was now licensed to move into a loosely defined area (the size of Germany and France combined) and to establish effective occupation and governance in Britain's name. The British prime minister, Lord Salisbury, wanted to protect "Zambezia" from Germans, Transvaalers, and Portuguese, primarily on behalf of ambitious Cape colonists in South Africa. And Rhodes's company would preserve the area from foreign rivals "at no cost whatever to the British taxpayer."[1]

As we have seen thus far, David Livingstone and Cecil Rhodes were the two key figures who drew Britain into the region and bequeathed contrasting approaches to dealings with Africans. It is interesting to note that the man behind Lobengula's first concession in 1888 (which opened the way for Rudd) was John Moffat, the missionary son-in-law of David Livingstone. However, when he learned of the duplicity of Rudd's dealings with Lobengula, Moffat disowned the Rudd Concession (as it came to be known); and he fell out with Rhodes himself when shortly afterward the latter provoked Lobengula into fighting a war against the BSAC forces, which the Ndebele could only lose. Here were early indications, in events and relationships of the years around 1890, of what can be seen as an enduring tension among Whites, over time, regarding the ethical priorities for race relations.

* * *

While still a young man at Oxford in 1877, Cecil Rhodes produced a short article titled "Confession of Faith," which guided him for the remaining twenty-five years of his life. Imbued with widely shared assumptions, it assists us in understanding what drove him, and it offers one means by which to measure his achievements. Much of the article is taken up by advocacy of a secret society that would drive and guide a global empire (a society modelled on the Jesuits, though Rhodes had just joined the Masons). But the core aspiration lies in these three sentences:

Of the Anglo-Saxons: "I contend that we are the finest race in the world, and that the more of the world we inhabit the better it is for the human race."

Anglo-Saxon hegemony would bring an end to all wars, and it would end barbarism too, by "bringing the whole uncivilised world under British rule."

"Africa is still lying ready for us; it is our duty to take it."[2]

It is not hard to see why views such as these—suffused with imperial arrogance and racism—were commonplace in the last quarter of the nineteenth century. Never had Great Britain been so powerful, its navy supreme. A quarter of the world's population was (already) under British imperial rule, and it might have been more: Rhodes bitterly regretted the loss of America and dreamed of a resumed union with the United States. Britain's Industrial Revolution had led the world; the British advocated free trade, knowing that, in a world without protective tariffs, British manufacturing and commerce would dominate. In Africa, pre-wheel technology confronted Europeans' mechanized firepower. This empire was (nonetheless) professedly Christian, committed to the abolition of the slave trade. And Anglo-Saxons prided themselves on having developed a unique model of constitutional representative government, now under a benign, long-lived queen. This was already copied in the dominions; a version of it might, in time, be exported further.

In 1897, the sixtieth anniversary of Queen Victoria's accession was marked, in the words of the biographer of Lord Salisbury (the prime minister), "by a populace bursting with legitimate pride at the longevity of their Queen and the breadth of her Empire."[3] Many British subjects who were more knowledgeable and influential than "the populace" agreed, as a matter of course, with the essence of what Rhodes had expressed in "Confession of Faith." The influential writer and philosopher John Ruskin, one of young Rhodes's lecturers at Oxford, asked his students, with Shakespearean flourish, "Will you, youths of England, make your country again a royal throne of Kings, a sceptred isle, for all the world a source of light, a centre of peace. . . . This is what England must do or perish: she must found colonies as far and as fast as she is able . . . seizing every piece of fruitful waste ground she can set foot on."[4] Among Britons, the self-serving assumption was approaching universal: that this was not only the most extensive but also the most beneficent empire the world had seen. One country or another had to assume the burden. As Lord Rosebery, the prime minister, put it in March 1893, shortly before the Ndebele war, "We have to consider that countries *must be developed* either by ourselves or some other nation, and we have to remember that it is part of our heritage to take care that the world, as far as it can be moulded by us, shall receive an English-speaking complexion, and not that of other nations."[5]

Moreover, the occupation of what became Southern Rhodesia happened at a time when the spread of empire, formal and informal—the former involving the acquisition of territory, the latter involving preeminent political and economic influence—was a global phenomenon. Americans were fulfilling their Manifest Destiny by moving west, Russians were spreading east, and European Zionists were planning to colonize Palestine. European states had the means and the inclination to spread their influence—if not also the need, as Marxists have argued, to acquire raw materials and markets overseas (or at least to deny their rivals possession of them). In Africa, Britain became involved in a keen rivalry—primarily with France and Germany—to reaffirm pre-existing (largely coastal) claims and to secure them via expansion into their hinterlands.

In the British case, expansion into Africa in the late nineteenth century did not merely follow slavery but was to some extent a reaction against it. The British slave-trade was abolished in 1807, and slavery itself in all British territories in 1833. In 1865, a British parliamentary assessment of Britain's scattered possessions in Africa concluded that, apart from the Cape in South Africa, they should all be abandoned—except for Freetown, west of the Gold Coast, because that was the base for Britain's anti-slave trade naval patrols. It was at this time that David Livingstone was appealing for trade in legitimate goods to be developed in Central Africa. Such a change, he believed, would have two urgently needed outcomes. Africans who were involved in the slave trade would be weaned from it, and the Arabs' slave trade in East and Central Africa would wither and die. Many in Britain responded. There were individual critics of "empire," to be sure; but by the late 1800s slavery and the slave trade were anathema to all, Rhodes included.

As a capitalist and imperialist (and philanthropist), Rhodes was representative of his age. Even as harsh a critic today as Priyamvada Gopal observes that although "a small but distinct body of dissident discourse developed" in nineteenth-century Britain, even the 1857

Indian uprising "did not constitute a crisis that forged anything like a critical consensus on the downsides of empire."[6] Moreover, there was more to the reputation of imperialism than the black-and-white alternatives of being for or against it. The academic Philip Mason in the late 1950s wrote that there existed at that time "broad division between those who were hostile to an increase or even a continuance of British responsibility, and those who were not; [but] each of these broad divisions was again divided into two bands of clear colour with a broader belt of mixed colours in between." He concluded that, among the innumerable supporters of empire at the end of that century, "those who combined a theoretical altruism with a practical business instinct were probably the most numerous."[7] We might number Rhodes among those supporters.

However, Rhodes's views were distinctive in two respects, which have a bearing on what follows. First, he did what he could to resist the metropolitan authority of Britain. He believed that political power should reside locally, with the elected representatives of White settlers—as in South Africa. He collaborated closely with British governments, but his relations with them were uneasy, and he tended to regard their involvement in the affairs of the regions under his sway (first Cape Province, then the Rhodesias) as unwarranted interference. Half a century after his death, a majority of White settlers in Southern Rhodesia chose to detach themselves from the British government. Rhodes did, nevertheless, recognize that Salisbury, a somewhat reluctant imperialist, was ultimately responsible for the security of British personnel and territory and had the authority to determine Britain's strategic overview. Salisbury, in turn, valued this "gentleman with some considerable force of character" but treated him with "detached scepticism and caution," viewed him as primarily self-seeking, and completely repudiated Rhodes's visionary scheme of building a railway from Cairo to the Cape.[8]

Second, Rhodes's imperialism owed little or nothing to Christianity. He was the son of an Anglican vicar—he may even have considered the priesthood—but as an adult he was disenchanted with Christianity. His "Confession of Faith" expressed commitment not to the missionary goals of his time but to the secret society he sought to create, which he pointedly described as "a Church for the extension of the British Empire." Rhodes was not alone in casually supposing that a world order dominated by Anglo-Saxons would have the moral purpose of spreading "civilization," and Christianity had its place within that broad aspiration. But the sometimes uneasy relations between settlers and the churches in Southern Rhodesia, considered in the next chapter, would to some extent reflect the secular priorities of its founder.

* * *

Rhodes's ambition and dynamism distinguished him. So, too, did his luck. The great mineral deposits in South Africa gave him the opportunity to make his fortune at just the time when Africa was on the verge of being partitioned by European powers. "It is no use having ideas without the money for putting them into practice," Rhodes once observed.[9] A ruthless self-made entrepreneur and financier, he used his staggering wealth from diamonds and gold first to achieve political power in Cape Colony, then to wield that power in an attempt to realize the two related visions of his "Confession of Faith." Of those visions, one was fantastic: the founding of a brotherhood among Anglo-Saxons (including Americans and, for a while, Germans) which would one day rule the whole world for its own good. The other vision was conventional: the extension of British imperial influence in Southern and Central Africa (thereby checking the Boers, Germans, and Portuguese), and he threw all his energies into it. Rhodes was perhaps above all a man of action, a man in a hurry: suffering from ill health throughout his life, he expected to die young, and in 1902 he did, at age forty-nine.

By the time of his death, Rhodes was already regarded as the epitome of the imperialist, by admirers and critics alike. Though he could be described as "a rather mediocre person" and "an unlikely vehicle for greatness," his influence in his time was momentous, and his impact on the course of subsequent events was considerable. In the period between two world wars, "respectable or disgraceful, according to taste, Rhodes remained the Englishman's symbol of the empire builder."[10] Rhodes sought immortality, and with over fifty biographies to date—ranging from hagiography to debunker—he may be said to have achieved it.

What follows is a single case-study of empire, culminating in an unapologetically racist regime. It focuses on approximately three generations of expatriate Whites who, like their benefactor, have recently come under the spotlight. Southern Rhodesia was the preeminent settler colony within Britain's African Empire (which Rhodes founded), whose many thousands of settlers he inspired (for the most part) over several decades.

The centenary of his birth in 1953 was marked in Bulawayo by a huge celebratory exhibition. Here in Southern Rhodesia, the White minority professed loyalty to the Crown but rejected, as Rhodes had done, "imperial interference." Meanwhile, for over half a century, the Whites honored Rhodes's mantra of "equal rights for all civilized peoples"—though they manipulated the common voting roll as a means of excluding, not including, significant Black political participation. Moreover, with Southern Rhodesia at its heart, the Central African Federation (CAF), launched in 1953, was very much in line with Rhodes's vision. It was intended by its architects to become a settlers' dominion, with a constitution modeled on Westminster but dominated by the region's White minority, independent of metropolitan control.

It collapsed. A decade or so later, the White settlers of Rhodesia made their Unilateral Declaration of Independence (UDI) from Britain. Though they were outnumbered by more than twenty to one by Indigenous Africans, their country now flew its own green-and-white flag, and from 1970 onward it was a republic. According to Rhodes's many latter-day admirers there, this illegal state was for several years an embodiment of the founder's vision. The extent to which Rhodes himself might have endorsed the UDI—indeed, whether he should be held responsible for anything that occurred in the colony, decades after he died—is discussed in Chapter 9. But there can be little doubt that Rhodes's settler-borne legacy extended into the era of independent Zimbabwe.

Notes

1. Fieldhouse, *Economics and Empire*, 353, 354.
2. Rhodes, "Confession of Faith."
3. Roberts, *Salisbury*, 665.
4. Quoted in Maurois, *Rhodes*, 43, 44.
5. Quoted in Eldridge, *Victorian Imperialism*, 192. Italics added.
6. Gopal, *Insurgent Empire*, 45, 81.
7. Mason, *The Birth of a Dilemma*, 126.
8. Roberts, *Salisbury*, 533, 535.
9. Quoted in Maurois, *Rhodes*, 59.
10. Flint, *Rhodes*, xiv, xviii, 234.

3

The Settler Colony

IN 1890, A PIONEER COLUMN OF WHITE ADVENTURERS ENTERED the region between the Limpopo and Zambezi rivers, moving northward from South Africa. Numbering around 200, these were settlers: fearless, determined, and ruthless men at the sharp end of global European imperialism in its golden, or not so golden, age. As states competed for distant lands, innumerable individual Europeans left their homes for the more promising of those faraway places. Zambesia was one such region. "White frontiersmen were bound to make their way into the interior; they could no more be stopped than could the pioneers who opened up the American West."[1]

It was not David Livingstone who inspired the pioneers. They acted on behalf of Cecil Rhodes; they were his men, in part selected by him. While Rhodes (and the British government) had strategic goals for this initiative, the pioneers sought for themselves mineral wealth, land for settlement and farming, and homes. The first White settlers were, in the words of one of their number, Major Leonard, "such a mixed lot I never saw in my life." He was just one among "all sorts and conditions, from the aristocratic down to the street Arab, peers and waifs of humanity mingling together like the ingredients of a hotch-potch."[2] Ethnic backgrounds were as varied as they were social—here were Germans, French, and Afrikaners, as well as Englishmen. But they had much in common. Many had origins in South Africa; most had some military experience; all were drawn by the lure of gold; all had come to stay.

The diary of Frank Oates, a young naturalist who had explored Central Africa a few years earlier, gives us a good idea (couched in the racist language and assumptions of his day) of how these pioneers would have regarded the Africans among whom they settled. Oates met the Ndebele king, Lobengula: "The picture of a savage king, just as one might have imagined"; by contrast, a European mission station was "one of the last outposts of civilisation." His description of relations between the Ndebele and the Mashona was stark. "Some of the Mashonas are subject to the Matabele [sic]. Those that refuse allegiance are mercilessly hunted down. . . . They fall an easy prey." He recorded, in another matter-of-fact entry on the plight of the Shona, that "lately . . . a kraal was taken, the young men killed . . . and the old men and women burnt to death. The young women and children were made slaves of, and the cattle taken."[3] Twenty years earlier, the missionary, Robert Moffat, writing to his wife, had described the Ndebele as a people who worshipped "the god of war, rapine, beef-eating, beer-drinking and wickedness."[4] Moffat, and subsequently Oates, depicted an African way of life (and death) that numerous men of his day had no inhibitions against bringing under Britain's sway.

Tens of thousands more Whites would settle in the colony of Southern Rhodesia, seized and held by the pioneers in the 1890s. They would exercise authority over themselves and millions of Africans whom, like Oates, they looked down on as inferior. They were for the most part ordinary men and women. But in the 1950s, in the context of unprecedented local and global change, they would bear extraordinary responsibility for determining the colony's future—and the destinies of all its peoples.

* * *

The pioneers were wary of Lobengula, whom Charles Rudd had deceived, and of his warriors, many of whom were frustrated at their king's apparent accommodation with Rhodes. So they skirted Matabeleland and settled first among the Mashona without significant conflict, and they established Fort Salisbury, in their midst, as a base for their search for gold. However, relations with the Ndebele quickly deteriorated, and open conflict in 1893 led to the military defeat of Lobengula and to the settlers' occupation of the capital, Bulawayo. Thereafter, multiple grievances led to widespread revolt against the White newcomers in 1896 by both Mashona and Ndebele. This was suppressed only in 1897.

As in numerous comparable engagements at this time, African losses in the suppression of the 1896–1897 revolt were heavy, and disproportionately so. This was in part a reflection of weaponry; the Maxim machine gun and the Martini-Henry rifle were devastating against men armed with spears. It was also a reflection of mentality. The killing during the revolt of around 500 Europeans—roughly 10 percent of the total, including women and children—outraged White settlers. According to Frederick Selous, who had led the pioneers into Mashonaland, some "vowed a pitiless vengeance against the whole Matabele race."[5] Acts of atrocity were committed, amid violence on a major scale, for which Rhodes and his colleague, Jameson, bear responsibility. The cautious if shocking conclusion of Alois Mlambo of Pretoria University is that "there are no statistics of African casualties . . . but they probably amounted to many hundreds of people."[6] Toward the end of the revolt, Rhodes himself famously went unarmed to parley with Ndebele chiefs to bring about peace, defying other White authorities' "reluctance to accept an arrangement that was not marked by sensational hangings and other severities."[7] Though there was unquestionably a genocidal mood among Rhodes's men during the suppression of the revolt, the strategic goal of the BSAC was to dominate, not to destroy. Once cowed, Africans were to be taxed into working in mines or on farms.

By the end of the 1890s, the settlers were firmly in control. In 1898, Orders in Council in London established the terms and conditions for the company's future administration of "Southern Rhodesia" and its now conquered peoples. Around this time, the British Colonial Office had taken on both "Northern Rhodesia" (beyond the Zambezi and its magnificent falls named after the Queen Empress) and Nyasaland to the northeast (where Livingstonia, a town founded in 1894 by missionaries of the Free Church of Scotland, was evidence of origins beyond White settler ambition).

The company invested heavily in railway building. It expropriated much African land and seized many cattle too. But the pioneers' hopes of mineral riches in Mashonaland were disappointed. Many turned to farming, though they were for the most part not farmers. As the years passed, the settlers became increasingly critical of the BSAC's control over their affairs. For its part, by the 1920s the company was ready to abandon its administrative responsibilities, if the price was right. Having been unable to pay its shareholders any dividends, it wanted only to secure an adequate return on invested capital. The British government offered the settlers a choice as to what would replace it. Southern Rhodesians could choose either to join the Union of South Africa, as its fifth province—as Rhodes had once envisioned—or to become a separate, self-governing colony under the British Crown.

Who was entitled to make this momentous decision? Up to a point, the territory enjoyed representative government, and there was a common electoral roll on which Blacks as well as Whites could register. But qualifications ruled out all but a tiny number of the former. It was London, rather than Salisbury, which had decided to adopt this franchise, modeled on that of Cape Province in South Africa. It was too much for some settlers. As a senior colonial administrator in Southern Rhodesia noted in 1906, "There is no doubt that [White] public opinion is practically unanimous in condemning the grant to natives of any right to the franchise."[8] The Whites had little to worry about, however. Along with a literacy test, the qualifications were set high: property worth £150, or an income of £100 per annum. Around 20,000 of the European population of 35,000 were on the voters' register, as were just sixty Africans. Although these represented no threat to the Whites, in 1917 it had been officially stated that if the qualifications "should be in danger of being reached by Africans," they could be raised again.[9] It is evidence of the effectiveness of these tests, in excluding all but a tiny number of Africans from voting, over several decades, that no substantial changes were deemed necessary, by the exclusively White government, before 1951.

In October 1922, the electors of Southern Rhodesia made their choice. By a small margin, they opted to remain separate from South Africa—8,774 chose "responsible government" (i.e., legal authority over the people of the territory, Black as well as White, while ultimately answerable to the British government), and 5,989 chose union with their great southern neighbor. The following year, on October 1, 1923, the territory was formally annexed to the Crown.

By this time, World War I had brought imperialism into question. In the wake of it, the League of Nations—of which Britain was a leading member—instated mandates for former German colonies (such as German East Africa and South West Africa), wherein the interests of the native peoples were supposedly prioritized. Consistent with this modified imperialism, in the same year as Southern Rhodesians' historic choice (1923), the White settlers in Kenya were denied the "responsible government" that they sought for themselves. The British declared that the interests of the native peoples were "paramount." Against this background, there was perhaps something anomalous about Britain's readiness to offer the tiny White minority in Southern Rhodesia almost unlimited authority and power.

Simple political and economic realities explain this outcome. Settlers had already secured a majority in the territory's legislature in 1911 while it was under company rule. And the British were happy to transfer the responsibility and burdens of administration. As long as the White settlers could administer the colony without making financial demands on the British government, they would be more or less free to determine its future. Winston Churchill had expressed concern about conceding self-government to the settlers. In 1921, while holding the role of colonial secretary, he said of Southern Rhodesia's future: "It will be an ill day for the native races when their fortunes are removed from the impartial and august administration of the Crown and abandoned to the sea of self-interest of a small white population. Such an event is no doubt very remote. Yet the speculator, the planter and the settler are knocking at the door."[10] Not so remote.

We may pause here to consider an observation on colonialism made by Ronald Hyam of Cambridge University: "It is easy to condemn the extension of Western rule as sheer acquisitiveness. But the brutal alternative would have been rule by *irresponsible* European adventurers, armed with all the resources of their civilisation to work their selfish will as they pleased, without any superior control at all."[11] In this light, Southern Rhodesia appears to be something of a hybrid; "superior control" handed these "adventurers" all the authority and powers they sought.

In two respects, however, this was not a fully self-governing colony. First, there was no element of self-government for the Africans. Their lives were governed by White Native Commissioners (NCs) who headed the Native Affairs Department. Second, White self-government was formally subject to a constitutional limitation. Proposed legislation regarding African affairs had to be approved by the British government which, after 1923, retained its right to challenge or amend it. In the event, however, this reserved power was never exercised, in part because informal discussions between Salisbury and London preceded any controversial legislation. Such dialogue could lead to the blocking of a colonist's proposal. Thus, for example, ethnic cleansing measures were not endorsed. In July 1934, when Colonel C. L. Carbutt, the chief native commissioner, advocated transferring "advanced natives" across the border into Northern Rhodesia so that the colony "would be freed of the embarrassing necessity to consider native interests," London was not supportive.[12] Even so, a convention developed whereby a British parliament never legislated for Southern Rhodesia except by agreement with, or at the request of, its settler-dominated government. The constitutional limitation thus meant far less in practice than it did in theory and law. The colony's legislative assembly was allowed to pass laws for the whole population. It was fitting that, when the British government separated a dominions office from the colonial office in 1925, the affairs of Southern Rhodesia were transferred to the former—alongside those of Canada, Australia, New Zealand, South Africa, and the Irish Free State.

Nonetheless, when looking at the decades that followed 1923, we may conclude that Whites' acquisition of all but complete authority in that year proved not a blessing for them, but a curse. In hindsight, it looks as though what the Whites needed as a small minority in possession of all the power were constitutional provisions that required them, over time, to increase political participation by Blacks. Instead, the Whites manipulated the common roll in their own short-term interests to preclude such involvement. The Whites ruled on their own. There was little remarkable about such an arrangement in the early days, but over the decades the settlers became accustomed to exclusive power. When their own world and the wider world beyond was changing in the mid-century, they could not adjust. At that time, the prominent liberal Hardwicke Holderness noted his fellow Whites' collective failure to recognize that, having been given virtually total power in 1923, "we had to find a way of sharing it," thereby "putting ourselves in direct touch with the people we were supposed to be dealing with."[13] No such way was sought.

Like Cecil Rhodes before him, Godfrey Huggins went to southern Africa partly for his health. He arrived in Salisbury in 1911, a twenty-eight-year-old surgeon in need of a well-paying job. Like so many other immigrants after him, he easily found one; he was offered a partnership in a local medical firm that paid six times what he had earned in London. Not all were so fortunate. The lives of the early settlers were tough and demanding, and levels of both suicide and emigration remained high into the early 1920s. But Huggins remained and was prime minister of the self-governing colony for twenty years, from 1933 to 1953. When he was interviewed in 1952, his recollection of this early period was concise and uncomplicated: "There was no native problem then. The Africans were nice old souls. You lost one, you got another."[14] Views set in such a manner, before 1923, came to regard actual or prospective change, especially in their relations with natives, as alarming if not dangerous. A collective attitude of mind—a mixture of paternalism, disdain, and apprehension—proved a handicap when, twenty-five years later, a generation of educated Africans wanted a fair share of the White man's world.

The newly constituted self-governing colony was a highly qualified parliamentary democracy, with a legislative assembly for thirty inevitably

White elected members. What were the settlers' priorities now? How did they use their authority and power; in whose interests; and with what intended and unintended consequences for the various races? Answers lie in three particularly important laws, enacted during the first twenty years or so after 1923. They formed what historian Robert Blake identified as "the tripod" that held up White supremacy.[15] The colonists' domination would rest securely, almost unquestioned, on this tripod into the 1950s.

The first leg of the tripod, in time and significance, was the Land Apportionment Act of 1930. In the beginning, Europeans had little interest in using the land they had acquired, because they had placed their ambitions on finding minerals. During those early days Africans were allowed to stay—as tenants, paying rent in labor—on land which they had lost to the settlers. But when it became clear that Whites searched for a new Witwatersrand in vain, and thus moved from mining to farming, they wanted land for their exclusive use. From around 1910 onward, Africans were moved off land designated "European" and into native reserves. These had been created at the turn of the century as a provisional, pragmatic means of protecting vanquished Africans from wholesale expropriation, which enabled many to continue to live in their customary way; when overcrowded in later years, they also generated a cheap, migrant labor supply for White mines and towns. By 1925, 60,000 Africans were transferred to reserves, approximately 10 percent of the territory's African population.

Some chose to move. But once resettled in a reserve, by order or by choice, Africans found they had exchanged one form of subjection for another. The father of Joshua Nkomo, for example, lived in an area alienated to Europeans. There, Nkomo senior came under multiple pressures: the hut tax, demands for labor, restriction of areas where Africans could farm as "White areas" filled up, and restriction of cattle numbers, as well. In 1923 he decided to leave. But in moving to a reserve, he found he was not free there, either. "In the reserves the natives were just occupiers, not free owners. The white administrators, the Native Commissioners, controlled everything that mattered."[16] This large influx soon put pressure on the reserves. As early as the 1920s, there were reports of overstocking, of land overuse, and—establishing a pattern for later years—of Africans having to leave the reserves to seek work on White farms, in the mines, or in the White man's towns. There was an evident, if not urgent, need to examine the land question closely. In 1925, the colony's governor appointed an experienced colonial administrator, Morris Carter, to chair a commission of inquiry into the issues of land ownership and occupation in Southern Rhodesia. But the creation of the

Carter Commission owed more to settlers' demands, and especially to their resentment of Africans buying land close to the properties they themselves had acquired, than to African complaints. White proprietors did not welcome Black farmers as neighbors.

Given the significance of the Land Apportionment Act to which the 1925 Carter Commission Report gave rise, it is helpful to look at the core land division adopted in acres: 21.6 million to existing native reserves; 7.5 million as native purchase areas; and 49.1 million for Europeans (of which nearly two-fifths were available, not yet alienated).[17]

The act was, of course, welcomed by the Europeans; one White farmers' leader frankly acknowledged that they did "not need anything like" what they had acquired.[18] Initiated by their own parliament, it gave the settlers what they wanted. Indeed, over time it assumed for some the status of a Magna Carta, a historic cornerstone for the continuing dominance of the minority White community. It gave political, even ideological, shape to what had previously been an ad hoc segregation. The division was iniquitous, and it remained so. The Whites awarded themselves over 49 million acres, about 62 percent of the whole land area; native areas would total 29 million acres, about 37 percent of the total. At the time, the European population numbered about 50,000, the African around 900,000. By the mid-1950s, these same lands were divided between a European population of 180,000—of whom only about 8 percent were farmers—and an African population of around two million, of whom the vast majority were farmers. After an amendment in 1961, the Europeans still owned more than a third of the land—in the hands of 6,400 White farmers and another 1,400 tenant farmers—though they were only one seventeenth of the population. Yet only 3.5 percent of the usable European land was under cultivation.

A novelty of the act was the designation of protected areas for African purchase only. These might release pressure on the existing reserves and, given that the act ended any notional right of Whites to purchase *anywhere*, identified those places where aspiring African farmers alone could buy land in the future. But so few chose or could afford to buy a freehold in the native purchase areas that by 1939 only 893 farms had been established by Africans within them (among whom were veterans of the police force of Southern Rhodesia and immigrants from outside its borders). For the Ndebele, these areas had no appeal. The superintendent of natives in Bulawayo noted that local areas set aside for African purchase were "almost useless," adding that "every native to whom they have been offered has declined to live on them."[19] Across Mashonaland, lands for purchase were short of water or far from communications; here, moreover, Africans were less interested in buying land than in exploiting a system of communal tenure in the reserves that allocated land to those able to use it rather than to those who needed it most. Nonetheless, this clause in the act could later win it the backing of a relatively liberal White leader committed to African advancement. Garfield Todd, prime minister in the 1950s, acknowledged that "it had seemed a completely sensible and natural provision when it was introduced," and "if there had not been a Land Apportionment Act there is no doubt that Europeans, with their capital resources, would long ago have bought up most of Southern Rhodesia."[20]

Overall, the main limitation of the act was that it could not foresee or legislate flexibly for the future. As population numbers increased among Europeans and especially Africans, the proportion of land allocated to each seemed increasingly unsustainable. And as the number of Africans working in the towns increased too, a deep flaw in the act was exposed. Bulawayo and Salisbury and the other smaller towns were all in areas designated European. The Carter Commission had assumed that Africans in towns were merely migrant laborers who would eventually return to their reserves and thus neither want nor need to own urban land. This assumption soon proved short-sighted. The number of Africans employed in the towns would rise from 45,000 in 1936 to 200,000 in 1956. Barred from owning urban property, growing numbers of these African workers had to depend on housing provided by their employers or live in locations designated by the municipal authorities (a provision for the most part for single men only, not for families). Neither provided any security.

Reginald Reynolds, a traveling Quaker with experience of India, observed in 1953 some consequences of the inadequacies of the act: "There was hardly an African in any of the larger towns who could not be evicted at short notice, refused another place in which to live, and forced back to his reserve." And while staying on the estate of one White farmer, Reynolds observed that "across the Rusapi river, where hundreds of African families had once lived, land had been alienated and these Africans removed to make room for two European families." "People who remembered such things," he added, "felt bitter."[21] In such ways, the full consequences of the implementation of the act were experienced long after 1930, during and especially after World War II. The act provided for the continued removal of Africans from any European areas into the reserves, which in turn became inadequate to contain them. This widespread disruption to African lives had huge significance for the White colonial state, as we will see shortly.

Between 1931 and 1941, a further 50,000 Africans were moved; between 1945 and 1959, 85,000 more were moved to make space for postwar White immigrant settlers.

Meanwhile, Whites did not all think as one. A singular contribution to the discussion of land issues was made by Arthur Shearly Cripps, an ascetic Anglican missionary devoted to the well-being of the Africans among whom he lived. In 1927, he supported complete segregation of Africans and Europeans (as protection for the former).[22] But—and this was for him the crucial measure—Africans must have enough land to develop on lines of their own choosing. "Let us awake to the fact that a million Rhodesian acres go a very small way in the provision of huge cattle-ranching estates for European colonists, but go a very great way in the provision of room-to-plough for African peasants."[23] Cripps was not alone in this belief. Remarkably, the secretary of the Rhodes Trust at that time agreed: Africans must be awarded enough land "above all to preserve that peculiar self-respect and freedom which comes from being independent owners of the soil, owning no man as master."[24] Cripps condemned the enforced transfer of Africans from one area to another, as African religion was rooted in the soil, and Africans were attached to the particular lands where their deceased parents and chiefs lay buried. He was highly skeptical, moreover, of his fellow Whites' self-serving view that it was necessary to remove Africans from the land so that they could enjoy the civilizing effects of employment as unskilled wage laborers for White masters. A little later, Doris Lessing's verdict on the Land Apportionment Act was unequivocal. It was "not so much a piece of legislation as an octopus," which had been "growing, spreading, burgeoning" over the years.[25]

The second leg of the tripod was the Industrial Conciliation Act of 1934. This positive-sounding legislation formalized an industrial color bar. It safeguarded the futures of White artisans, and it kept the towns largely White. Unskilled Blacks—around 99 percent of the African labor force—fell outside the provisions of the act. Its central concern was conciliation procedure between White employers and registered White employees through their trade unions. Africans were deemed not ready to be unionized and thus were omitted from the definition of "employee." Meanwhile, employers were required to pay identical wages to skilled European and skilled African workers. While this appeared fair, the provision did not serve potential African workers, as previously the only reason to employ Africans rather than Whites was so they could pay them less. Furthermore, by obstructing the emergence of a skilled African working class, the act put pressure on successive settler governments to attract increasing numbers of immigrant White workers from overseas.

The third leg of the tripod came a little later with the Native (Urban Areas) Accommodation and Registration Act of 1946, a further consolidation of segregation and White supremacy. A principal purpose of this act was to control the lives of Africans in urban areas, whose numbers had grown rapidly during the war years. Local authorities were empowered to remove unemployed Africans seeking work and to return them to the increasingly overcrowded rural reserves. Indeed, this was the core of the act: by making White employers responsible for paying the rent of African employees, any African who for whatever reason and duration found himself out of work could be summarily evicted from both lodgings and town.

In 1946, every African working in a "European" town was still officially regarded as no more than a temporary visitor, so that even when native urban areas were provided by local authorities, there was permission only to occupy properties, no right to own. Though the act required employers and local government authorities to provide basic housing for African workers in the towns, not enough accommodation was provided in practice even for single men (one room was considered adequate space for four), let alone for wives and families. Many Africans, employed and unemployed, had to lodge illegally with relatives or sleep out on peripheral land.

Movement of Africans from rural to urban areas was from now on to be even more rigidly controlled in the wake of 18,000 prosecutions for "pass law" offenses in 1942 alone. Africans were required to carry passes as identification if they went to the towns (since all remained designated White) and if they hoped to be employed there. Psychologically as well as physically, the pass laws were crippling. They were, for Africans, a continuing and depressing stigma of defeat. The retrospective verdict of the Zimbabwean economist and politician Bernard Chidzero was withering: pass law legislation was introduced "not so much to avoid urban overpopulation (why otherwise should Europeans not need passes also?) as to ensure a steady supply of cheap labour on European farms and, more and more in recent years, to ensure police control."[26]

The three acts of the tripod were the consolidation in legal form of established day-to-day practice. While it formalized temporary dominance, this legal apparatus can also be seen as an instrument of defense—a discriminatory bulwark against full African participation in the social and economic life of the territory. Taken together, the acts stood at the heart of a system, which lasted until the late 1950s. Continuing belief in racial hierarchy, and fear of the alternative, were at their heart. The lives of Africans were "made the subject of authoritarian direction by officials up to a point that would be deemed intolerable, if applied to themselves, by the Europeans who heedlessly built up the system."[27] In time, as legislation led to prosecution, they became intolerable to the Africans too. It was these three laws above all others which Chidzero selected for direct repeal or reform when writing in 1960 of how to bring good government to Southern Rhodesia.

The Whites of Southern Rhodesia

Southern Rhodesia was a big country, but its White population was small. In the 1930s, a single English town such as Norwich or Reading could boast double the population. And a community small in number could also be described as small-minded. "Salisbury in the early 1950s was a provincial town whose politicians had the mentality and outlook of county councillors," wrote one stern nonresident White critic.[28] It was not until the 1930s that Salisbury was linked to London for the first time by air transport and telephone. It will be helpful, for our understanding of views held by Whites in subsequent decades, to note here that Southern Rhodesia's settlers evolved as a community while largely removed from social, cultural, and attitudinal shifts that matured beyond the colony's borders and overseas.

Politics reflected size, or lack of it. There were no sharp divisions between government and society. As late as 1959, Colin Leys could describe "a small white community in a relatively poor and undeveloped country.... Underlying an elaborate formal structure, there is also an informal one.... Public servants, politicians, and the leading figures in every walk of life are mutually acquainted to a degree which would be impossible in a country of similar size which drew its governing class from all strata of the population."[29] Formal, confrontational political parties such as those in Britain were unknown. There was a rather bewildering sequence of parties with changing labels and flexible membership arising from splits and fusions, but an overall political consensus prevailed, marked by the uninterrupted premiership of Godfrey Huggins from 1933 to 1953—a tenure that straddled the reigns of four British monarchs. Sociable informality and self-distancing, from the rest of the world and from the reality of life for the African majority, shielded the White community for many years from serious debate about the future of the country. This weakness was evident in the 1946 election. On that occasion, the so-called liberal party almost produced a shock victory for White racial diehards. Huggins only won on account of his political skill and personal following, not through having won a public debate on policy—because there had been none.

Several commentators highlighted the absence of important social ingredients: something, or someone, was missing. Looking back at the 1920s in the aftermath of World War I, the historian Lewis Gann observed that this "small backward community . . . totally lacked that cultural, self-questioning and hypersensitive group of literary men and artists whom war and the aftermath of war fired into bitter criticism of the established order in wealthier countries overseas."[30] The Canadian-born journalist Patrick Keatley wrote of the founding fathers of Southern Rhodesia that "it was not a cross-section of Victorian England that emigrated to Rhodesia: the intellectuals, the aristocrats and the social reformers stayed at home." This colony, in its formative first decade under British South Africa Company (BSAC) rule, had few of the figures that could be found elsewhere in the British Empire of that time (e.g., judges, elite civil servants, etc.), even in neighboring African protectorates. "Even the mellowing influence of the ordinary professional man was missing."[31]

Taken as a whole, the White community was an impenetrable hereditary caste. By 1940, it numbered a mere 65,000 but it dominated every aspect of the lives of 1,390,000 Africans. Whites had much in common with each other, as we shall see, but there were differences, embryonic tensions too, and any simple generalization would be wide of the mark. As for provenance, by the end of that decade, the Whites could be divided roughly into thirds: 33 percent had been born in Rhodesia, 31 percent in South Africa, and 30 percent in Great Britain. It is far harder to pin down their character. More than half lived in urban/suburban areas, primarily in the two centers first established in the 1890s: Bulawayo (in Matabeleland) and Salisbury (in Mashonaland). Latent class differences among the settlers would manifest later. For the time being, various occupations were associated with being part of, or outside, a White establishment. This comprised top civil servants and professionals, along with leaders in business, commerce, and finance. At its core were members of the Bulawayo and Salisbury clubs. Around 5,000 large-scale White farmers were a respected and influential "establishment" voice. Not included, according to this rough binary division, were the poorer farmers (among them a significant proportion of Afrikaners), along with lower-level civil servants, minor businessmen, shopkeepers, artisans, and unionized workers (on the railways, for example). Arising from these class distinctions were significant if still untapped differences regarding race relations. Members of the establishment had less to lose from African advancement than those outside it.

* * *

In parallel with the secular appropriation of African land by the pioneers and their successors, from the outset there was a religious expansion into Central Africa in the shape of Christian churches and missions. White missionaries, as we have seen, visited the area and played a part in proceedings before 1890; in 1891, the Church of England's Mashonaland diocese (which included Matabeleland) came into being.

Relations between the religious and secular arms of European enterprise in this remote and challenging location fluctuated in these early decades and were not always easy. The ambition of the first Anglican bishop, George Knight-Bruce, contrasted with that of Cecil Rhodes: the bishop wanted the English Church to occupy all Zambezia, ultimately linking the Church of the Province of Southern Africa (to the south) with the Universities' Mission to Central Africa (to the north and east). He originally wanted his diocese to be free of any settlers seeking land and gold. Settlers were for him no better than civilization's "degraded camp-followers" and thus something of a curse.[32] Knight-Bruce wanted "a purely native country"—one, moreover, in which Africans would be won to Christianity by African catechists.[33] Those hopes for the spread of Christianity were in large part fulfilled. South of the Equator, "although most of the pioneer mission stations were founded by whites, it was African catechists, teachers, traders and migrant labourers who assimilated the faith and initiated villagers, kinsfolk, workmates and strangers into this new identity."[34] Though Knight-Bruce came to accept the reality of land seizure and settlement, his longing to be rid of it indicates some ongoing tension between the differing visions of the late Livingstone and the now dominant BSAC.

The relationship between settlers and clergy would remain complex. In 1897, Knight-Bruce's successor, the bishop William Gaul, arranged for a Black priest to preach to a settler congregation in Salisbury on the sin of racial prejudice and the unacceptability of unfair working practices. He explained his motive: such sermons "ought to do good. . . . Educated natives, and especially Christian natives are . . . measuring us by our own bushel of the gospel and testing us by its standard."[35] Just a year after the suppression of the revolt, Gaul sensed that Africans, brought up in knowledge of Christian teachings, would in due course collectively hold Europeans accountable and find them wanting. When we look at the chorus of African criticisms and complaints in the 1940s and 1950s, we see how prophetic Gaul had been.

Subsequent senior Anglican clergy could also be stern in rebuking settlers when they went astray. Bishop Frederic Beaven was "at heart a colonial chaplain" who believed that the British Empire was "the world's greatest secular agency for good"; and during his enthronement sermon in 1911 he listed Cecil Rhodes as well as David Livingstone among his personal heroes.[36] During his time, however, he appointed a Black clergyman to serve in the diocese and gave Indigenous Christians a voice in the affairs of the church. Like his predecessors, he advocated justice, irrespective of color. The historian Pamela Welch observes that, although the majority of the settlers in this period were educated young Englishmen, "many discarded the habit of church-going once in Africa as they discarded other conventions"—and in so doing, we may add, freed themselves from having to listen to sermons criticizing the way they lived.[37] As for the other prong of the Church's work, numerous settlers were indifferent, if not hostile, to the missions. They wanted the Indigenous peoples subjugated and quiescent, not liberated by education. Most Europeans in the colony, Christian or not, were loath to accept Africans as equals. Many resented the expectations that the mission schools cultivated. A settler member of the legislative council (MP) in Huggins's time probably spoke for those who elected him when he said: "The native will continue to be honest if you leave him with his beads and blankets. . . . If we could clear out every mission station in this country and stop all this fostering of higher native education, we would much sooner become an asset to the Empire."[38] Lawrence Vambe quoted another settler who clearly did not regard Christianity as a tool of White hegemony. This farmer strongly disliked mission-educated "boys." He believed "that the real enemy of the black man was the white missionary with his religion and education, both of which were 'bad poison' to Africans."[39]

Nonetheless there was, inevitably, fellowship of clergy and laity in the territory; relations had to be pragmatic, and they could be warm. Knight-Bruce was realistic enough to accept the reliance of his church on the BSAC, not only for the establishment of order (he welcomed the reduction of Ndebele raids on the Shona following the setters' arrival in Mashonaland), but also for the provision of both infrastructure (roads and transport of supplies) and grants of land for churches and mission stations. He and his successors also acknowledged their dual responsibility: the clergy were to minister to White settlers as well as to reach out as missionaries to the Africans. The former role was readily adopted by Gaul, who wrote that he would miss "his good friends, the miners, railwaymen and police of Rhodesia, who always hit hard and straight themselves, and always take kindly to the Bishop's humble attempts from the shoulder. May God bless them all," he added, "men and women in their tussle with life and its trials, in the shaft, the workshop and the home."[40]

Clergy as well as laity rejoiced in the railways, described by Gaul as "carrying the religion and politics and commerce and enterprise and hopes and fears of the Empire . . . into and through the great, dark Central African continent," though together they suffered from construction delays and from subsequent high freight charges.[41] As for "the tussle of life," all suffered, in this period, dislocations from war and revolt, drought and disease (Knight-Bruce died of blackwater fever), along with shortage of labor, supplies, and income. Life was hard for Europeans, whatever their occupation or profession. Even thirty years after pioneers first entered the region, the missionary Edgar Lloyd had to undertake regular three-month journeys of five hundred miles on a donkey in order to visit all the members of his mission.

Overall, while the church was inextricably associated with colonization, it did represent a distinct White voice. For instance, where there was conflict between White and Black, notably in 1893 and during the revolt of 1896–1897, Anglicanism professed neutrality or, rather more positively, sought to act as a buffer, even mediator. It is not possible, of course, to calculate just how effective it was in softening settler attitudes or shaping their practices but, over time, the presence of the church could be seen as having attenuated darker aspects of colonization. Lawrence Vambe, born in Salisbury in 1917, wrote in 1972 that "the church deserves no small praise for its share in mitigating some of the evil effects of an economic, social and political order that took little, if any, account of the human and especially family interests of the working Africans."[42]

* * *

One characteristic of most Whites, whatever their religious leanings, social class, or ethnicity, was to a greater or lesser extent fearfulness. Below the bravado was the insecurity of a small but visible minority—albeit for now dominant—heavily (and increasingly) outnumbered by "uncivilized" Africans. The Whites knew the history of their colony, all of which was of course recent. They remembered or were taught that, shortly after the pioneers arrived, African revolt had resulted in hundreds of settler casualties. For the Africans, moreover, that revolt had not been in vain: the deal that Rhodes personally negotiated to end it included the recognition of rebel leaders as salaried chiefs and as spokesmen for their people, and the setting up of processes for complaint and redress. In this light, continuing African compliance could not be taken for granted. When the settlers proposed, in their new legislative council, to quadruple the hut tax from ten shillings to two pounds a year, the British resident commissioner blocked them. He believed that the tax increase would have "an unsettling effect on the natives, calculated to endanger security and good order in the country." The "governing consideration" he maintained, was "that there should be no risk of native disturbance."[43] The colonial secretary decided to raise the tax to just one pound per annum and to delay its implementation.

For years, Europeans of all types lived separately from the Africans. A distinguished French lawyer, Henri Rolin, who visited Southern Rhodesia during company rule in 1912, described how this social distancing had come about. The circumstances of the territory's birth, he argued, had shaped and determined the pattern of relations between the Whites and the Blacks thereafter:

> Society is composed, so to speak, of two societies, one superimposed on the other, almost of two castes: an aristocracy of white landowners and capitalists, a proletariat of blacks. The whites conquered the country in 1893. They are established there as masters, with the overwhelming superiority given them by their intellectual and moral heritage from Greece and Rome, from the achievement of Europe in science and mechanical invention, in industry and the art of ruling, in accumulated skill and capital. Below the whites, the blacks. . . . One has to see them, in their sordid villages, half-naked . . . to appreciate the immense distance which divides the victors from the vanquished.[44]

We find in these passages both the pride in empire and the casual racism that were typical of that age. We may pause at some of Rolin's language—and question, for instance, the extent to which members of the Pioneer Column had been the purveyors of classical civilization—but his focus was sharp. The events of the 1890s lived on in memory; they never passed into history. And "the immense distance" that divided the two castes persisted. To be sure, there were some exceptions, but for half a century and more relations between Whites and Blacks were characterized by remoteness—between numerous Africans whose daily lives and circumstances were those of a people vanquished, on the one hand,

and a small, self-conscious, and victorious (albeit insecure) master race, on the other hand.

Initially, social distancing was understandable, as was the legislative framework of the tripod. But in the longer run, White interests would be ill served by their own ignorance arising from the former, or by African grievances arising from the latter. Caution and conservatism marked the political consensus of the time. We may agree with Blake's dry summary that after 1923 "enlightened liberalism was not a cause which had much hope of success in the assembly."[45] Moreover, prevailing White supremacist assumptions became frozen in time, subsequently to be shared with and spread among tens of thousands of European newcomers in the late 1940s and early 1950s.

African Responses

Subjects of the British Empire were not, in all places and at all times, engaged in active opposition. Colonization did not directly provoke a protonationalist challenge. Rather, as has been pointed out by African scholars, the arrival of White settlers gave rise among Africans to a range of social struggles and identities, such as "the protean ethnic identities of the past, the ambiguities of missionary influences and imperial citizenship, the claims for a more respectable 'civilised' status from the tiny black elite, and the demands of early labour struggles." African responses to colonization were not simple alternatives of resistance and collaboration; they were, in short, "ambiguous and contradictory."[46] Indeed, following the suppression of revolt in the 1890s, and in the absence of a strong shared identity across the territory—and in the absence, too, of a clear vision of an alternative future—continual resistance was far less likely than numerous forms of accommodation.

During the more than two decades of BSAC rule following their defeat, Africans in Southern Rhodesia had neither the inclination nor the capability to resist White domination by force. It is worth bearing in mind, when we look at the staccato political stirrings of the decades before World War II, that many Africans even in, say, 1940, could recall seeing the first settlers arrive, had participated in the revolt of 1896–1897, and had experience of its failure. As we have seen, the pioneers sought land and, after defeating the Ndebele and the Mashona, they appropriated much of the land that these Indigenous peoples claimed as theirs. Among the Ndebele, whose kingdom had been beaten, but not crushed, there were campaigns for the reinstatement of their kingship and for home rule; but these longings could be, and were, ignored by the settlers. For the time being, the Shona, who were not (yet) suffering land alienation on the same scale, reluctantly accepted defeat.

However, the first generation of White administrators were under no illusions regarding the consequences of expropriation of African land by White settlers. In June 1920, the superintendent of natives in Bulawayo wrote on the land question to the chief native commissioner, relaying the grievances of the Ndebele. In doing so, we may note, he revealed that a single individual White official could be both an architect and a critic of imperial policy. The Africans' outrage penetrates his bureaucratic understatement. It is worth quoting at some length.

The Ndebele "now suffer from an ever-increasing sense of dissatisfaction with the provision made for them. Within a few months of the European occupation, practically the whole of their most valued region ceased to be their patrimony. White men of varied origins . . . become in a day their landlords, their overlords, with power to dispossess and drive forth. To an aristocratic race, the delegation of such power has appeared unseemly in many cases." The Ndebele had been mystified as well as shocked. "That land on which people live, and have lived for generations, can be purchased for money . . . is a matter hard to be understood." The authorities should be worried, because the Ndebele, "the formerly dominant tribe of this territory . . . must inevitably establish their major influence for good or bad in the future development and happiness of our natives."[47]

Ndebele were being evicted from their lands. The Mashona for the most part farmed land that was poorer, so less coveted by Europeans than that of the high veldt. Even so, Vambe could recall the impact of loss of land, and of freedom of movement, in his home region of Mashonaland:

> Now we had white farmers as neighbours. In the good old days . . . any member of the tribe could walk or travel . . . without let or hindrance, knowing that this was tribal property, any part of which he could use and share with his fellow men. But now every European who bought a part of this land put a stop to this freedom . . . and erected barriers, such as fencing, wire, gates, and regulations to deter African or animal trespassers. . . . Many farmers promised that they would shoot anyone wandering on their property. And if any confrontation came to court, there would be no sympathy from the magistrate, "for where black and white interests clashed, white men were still as much above the law as the members of the Pioneer Column had been."[48]

Remarkably, hundreds of Africans were allowed to testify to the Carter Commission, which preceded the passage of the Land Apportionment

Act. Chiefs and pastors, teachers and members of the Ndebele royal family, as well as the leaders of new associations, gave evidence. Resigned to a degree of subjugation—just thirty years or so from the defeat of their revolt—Ndebele spokesmen objected not so much to the principle of segregated land distribution as to the disproportionate allocations. In the year before its enactment, the bill was attacked by one Ndebele on the grounds that "this Bill does not show any security for the native land." Another critic appears to have spoken for many when he said "the bill is no good. It is all for the white man. Rhodesia is big. Let them cut the land in half and let us live on one side and the white man on the other."[49] Such a division would have awarded the Africans 48 million acres, not 28 million. Thirty years later there was, as noted, an adjustment in this direction, but it was not enough to meet expectations of a generation of Africans by now far more numerous and far less deferential.

During the 1920s and 1930s, although the countryside was outwardly calm, problems were brewing, and the more perceptive colonial officials knew it. Before the Great Depression, a "comprehension of the white system" developed that enabled African farmers to retain agency.[50] In groundbreaking work, the radical historian Terence Ranger stressed that, for the most part, Africans chose the peasant option to stay on the land and farm it rather than the alternative of working for White settlers—a choice that, of course, had an adverse effect on the Whites' labor supply. In the early days, even when facing famine, Africans refused to accept relief if it had to be paid for by their migrant labor. In these decades, such an option was practicable. Despite much dispossession, it was still possible for Africans to remain on alienated land; overall, there was enough land in the reserves, too. This determination to farm as they chose was "in many ways an adaptation to the colonial economy rather than resistance to it."[51] But it was adaptation on their own terms. Africans chose to migrate to where there were traders and transport links; they chose which crops to grow (mainly maize); and they chose whether to sell or not, when prices fell.

By the end of the 1930s, however, new grievances fed a consciousness of the unevenness of competition between farmers, Black and White. Controls that interfered with the marketing of grain were deeply resented. Before 1934, African peasant farmers could sell to the highest bidder among European traders, farmers, and miners. Thereafter, they had to submit their produce to government-appointed traders at fixed, depressed, prices: in short, their role was to be taxed, to subsidize and ensure the survival of White farmers. This practice extended to Matabeleland; not all the Ndebele were cattle herders. Meanwhile, steps were taken to strangle entrepreneurialism in Mashonaland, where many adopted the plough to bring more and more land under cultivation and increase their output. White farmers did not welcome competition, and administrators preferred "traditional" society to African class formation, but the main purpose of curbing the more prosperous and enterprising farmers was to keep as much land as possible available in the reserves for the future day when thousands of peasant families would be exiled from land allocated to Whites. Officially in the interest of conservation, redistribution of land in the reserves was imposed from above, and Africans who resisted this upheaval were subject to prosecution. This was "the beginning of the era of government interference in every detail of peasant life."[52] By the end of the 1930s, increasing numbers of Africans living on White, or White-designated, land were being moved to the reserves, putting pressure on those already living there to reduce their own land (and cattle) possession to accommodate them.

White colonial officials had predicted that maize controls would be widely unpopular. By 1937, the secretary for native affairs acknowledged that "what is asked for" by White farmers and the White colonial state (by enforcing maize controls and containing African entrepreneurialism) "is economic privilege on a colour basis." He went on to argue that "the direct or indirect repression of the production of wealth by the natives" could lead to demands for political representations and even provoke "racial antagonism," which was growing at that time in South Africa. Five years later, when some White officials were urgently advocating destocking (the enforced reduction in the number of African-owned cattle), the chief native commissioner fought to postpone such a measure: "You would fail to get co-operation," he insisted, "and that in my mind is essential. . . . I feel we have to keep the native contented."[53] Who was really in control of the countryside?

Perennial, unequal, competition for land and increasingly bitter disagreements over land use were the most divisive issues in the developing history of the colony. Thereafter, questions relating to the ownership and use of land were fundamental in contextualizing and defining relations between the races. As Nathan Shamuyarira, the Zimbabwean writer and politician, put it in the late 1960s, "No issue is of greater dimension and of deeper emotional appeal to Africans . . . than land shortage, in a motherland that has thousands of acres, abounds with fish, fruit and honey, but is occupied by foreign landlords."[54] After African nationalism took effective organizational shape in Southern Rhodesia in 1957, the Zimbabwe African People's Union (ZAPU) defined itself as "an association of people who have been dispossessed of their land."

The other high-profile issue, not for rural farmers but among educated Africans who had their own priorities, was the franchise. The 1920s saw the emergence of the Rhodesia Bantu Voters' Association (RBVA), founded in 1923. Ostensibly inclusive of all Africans, it was strongest in Matabeleland. The name of the organization proclaimed a readiness to accept the fact of White rule. But the RBVA claimed that Africans had a right to participate in the affairs of the colony, voting as equals of Whites. Owing much to Black South African leadership, with its members primarily from the urban, educated elite, this was the first Indigenous organization to focus on politics at the center. It encouraged Africans to use such votes as they had on the common roll and tried to persuade Whites to accept them as agents in the political process. As we have seen, since 1898 the franchise was officially colorblind, based on property, income, and educational qualifications. The RBVA sought to add ownership of cattle to the means of qualifying, which would have enfranchised the more prosperous freehold African farmers. But White settlers disliked any nonracial franchise. This particular African proposal to strengthen the African voice was blocked by the colony's first prime minister, Charles Coghlan.

The White regime ignored the RBVA; and when they were not listened to, they were powerless. Even so, the RBVA, by acquiescing in a qualified nonracial franchise, set a pattern for African political activity that lasted thirty years: of trying to push the door further open, not trying to knock it down. Given that after twenty years there were just 258 Blacks on the common roll alongside 48,000 Whites, this strategy is striking, either as a sign of Africans' principled commitment to gradualism or as an indication that there was no alternative open to them. For what may appear in hindsight to have been an extraordinarily long time, Africans in Southern Rhodesia sought to achieve their rightful place within a society dominated by the White minority, not to undermine or destroy it.

Some hopes remained of achieving peaceful change. In 1926, the Industrial and Commercial Workers' Union (ICU) was born. Though originating in South Africa, it may be regarded as Southern Rhodesia's first African mass movement. As an embryonic trade union, it primarily sought to improve the material and social condition of workers in the towns and to protect them from high levels of official harassment. But the question of land could not be ignored. As one ICU activist, Masotsha Ndhlovu, put it in 1931, "We must have land. This was our country once. Why is it divided by fences?"[55] Following the passing of the Land Apportionment Act, the ICU advised Africans against buying property in the native purchase areas on the emotionally powerful grounds that the land already belonged to them. Though more radical than the RBVA, the ICU, too, supported the extension of the qualified nonracial franchise as its political goal. But, again like the RBVA, its influence faded: through government intransigence, its own internal organizational weaknesses, and the onset of the Great Depression. Though it attracted large crowds to its meetings, it did not acquire the members (or membership fees) to enable it to organize effective strike action.

In the 1940s, the ICU was succeeded by a reformed ICU (RICU), led by the Roman Catholic mission–educated Charles Mzingeli. This differed in some respects from its predecessor. For example, RICU was largely concerned with urban issues in Salisbury on behalf of workers of all races, whereas the ICU had tried to be a national movement for Africans. This new organization was also committed to gradual constitutional change, but it was regarded by the White government as communist-inspired and dangerous. Its impact was limited. In retrospect, what catches the eye is the founding in 1934 of a Southern Rhodesia branch of the African National Congress (ANC), a movement formed in 1923 to unite South Africans of all races in resistance to White domination. In reality, this ANC lacked a dynamic core, but it provided a flicker of inspiration in subsequent years. Over two decades later, and after one or two other false starts, there was something of a rebirth when the Native (Urban Areas) Act was passed, and Prime Minister Huggins threatened to abolish the common roll. A regenerated Southern Rhodesian ANC would present itself in 1957 as a political movement that the White regime could not ignore.

***

How is the association of Africans with Christian missions best characterized? From the African point of view, missionaries were as much a part of their overall experience of colonialism as White farmers; but the former were Whites who had different priorities (saving souls rather than finding labor), and they had their own distinct impact and significance.

The missions came in many denominations: Methodist, Anglican, Roman Catholic, and others. Though they were accompanied by fellow European traders, soldiers, settlers, and administrators, and thus could be perceived as one arm of a multifaceted invasion, they enjoyed independent sources of finance, recruitment, and control, and could thus follow their own agenda. They had the potential to be more than mere agents of an alien religion deploying blandishments in the interest of colonizers and European cultural imperialism.

At the heart of mission schools lay the curriculum. Reading, writing, and arithmetic were taught alongside scripture, hymns, and the catechism. In addition, there tended to be practical subjects: training in carpentry, gardening, bricklaying, or printing, for example. In the case of girls, this part of the curriculum would comprise such skills as sewing, cookery, and nursery work. Mission schools thus cultivated among Africans a dual appeal of Christianity across the territory. One was religious. A factor here was the collapse of faith (temporary, in some instances) in the spirit mediums who had organized and sustained resistance to the Whites. Their god was discredited; Christianity was the new spiritual power. As Isaac Shimmin, among the first Methodists in the colony, put it, "They knew that this religion must be very good, for it was the creed of the superior strangers."[56] Christianity met ongoing concerns of life and death. Jesus and his disciples were healers of both body and spirit. This new religion attracted Africans in such large numbers that conversions threatened to overwhelm missions, which were often short of staff and funds. Bishop Gaul had found, shortly after the revolt, that his brand of Christianity suited the Ndebele, especially the elite. "They want the King's Church," explained an Anglican clergyman in 1911. "They do not like other bodies. They believe greatly in royal authority and command."[57] St. Columba's mission, founded in 1897, had to enlarge its church five years later to accommodate a congregation of 800.

The second appeal was more pragmatic. Literacy was a liberator, opening up new horizons, imagined and real. Through hundreds of mission schools, young Africans could gain access to the White man's world, if initially only its lower levels. Here lay the promise of income and status. Missions offered change: an invitation to shed past beliefs and customs. This loosening of adherence to tradition could, moreover, extend into other fields: for example, a break with inherited farming practice. The father of Bishop Abel Muzorewa was not the only American Methodist convert to take up entrepreneurial farming and put his hand to the plough.

Nevertheless, the missions were allied to the colonial project to an extent and could be perceived as such by Africans. While some missionaries approved of aspects of traditional cultures, and most sought to protect Africans from European vices, they generally regarded colonization as beneficial, not harmful. Beyond the religious conversion of Africans, they looked to the transformation of their lives, believing as they did in development, growth, and progress. These aspirations perfectly suited the settler economy; imbued in many cases with the Puritan work ethic, missionaries deplored what they regarded as idleness or sloth. As Bishop Gaul had argued, Africans needed to move from "the false dignity of loafing to the true dignity of labour."[58] It was widely accepted that obedience, discipline, hard work, and responsibility would be good for them, and countless potential White employers agreed. One Methodist missionary reported in 1899 that "nine out of every ten White men have a hateful prejudice against the uplifting and saving of the Blacks: the natives are beasts of burden and ought never to be thought of as anything else."[59] But by the 1920s and 1930s, mission-educated Africans were seen by some Whites less as rascals than as a comparatively contented and stable work force.

While the colonial economy needed literate and numerate Africans, and Africans wanted literacy, numeracy, and work, there was concern among Whites when Africans educated in Christian missions began to question and challenge the colony's racial stratification. In mission schools, Africans encountered freedom of thought, speech, and discussion. Political consciousness was not far behind. From the start, successive White minority governments were wary. Though the BSAC had introduced grants-in-aid for mission primary schools in 1910, there was no government school for Africans in Bulawayo before Mzilikazi Primary School opened in 1946. Meanwhile, mission schools provided some Africans with life-changing education. One ingredient was the Bible's message that history is progress, that time is linear not cyclical, and that individuals, guided by faith, bear responsibility for its course. There emerged over time a generation that not only questioned White supremacy but also exposed the hypocrisy of Whites who professed to be agents of a Christianity-centered civilization but acted otherwise.

Meanwhile, African restlessness in the 1930s sometimes found religious, rather than political, outlets in a range of independent church movements. Adoption of Christianity did not entail grafting a European theology on to an African tabula rasa. In subtle ways, foreign teachings interrelated with existing African beliefs, to the extent that not only did catechists spread Anglicanism (for example) but many inspired Africans organized their own religious blends and took them into the villages. Later, around the time of the rebirth of the Southern Rhodesian ANC in 1957, while some Christian missions and their converts were evidently at the heart of the movement, in other instances African disillusionment with the conservatism of the White man's church prompted a return to prophetism and spirit mediums.

Overall, were Africans liberated or oppressed by Christian missions in the colonial period? In the case of Southern Rhodesia, as elsewhere, there is no simple answer. It can be argued, on the one hand, that mission schools opened young minds, provided valued skills (and hence opportunities) in the new order, and freedom from the constraints of custom. On the other hand, the schools served, and taught subservience to, the White man; personified racial arrogance; and were agents of cultural domination. But there is a false dichotomy here: neither view is satisfactory on its own. The interrelationship between the missions and Africans was at least as complex as the Anglican Church's relationship with the White settler community.

It has been argued that, by the 1950s, "missionary education had become the Achilles' heel of colonialism."[60] But this view not only presupposes a somewhat negative view of colonialism but also makes sense only if one regards late nineteenth-century imperialism as a monolithic force. An alternative perspective enables us to see the arrival in Africa of a broad range of Europeans, some of whom were keener to save souls than to achieve wealth—or even to liberate rather than dominate. One may conclude that insofar as the religious and educational aims of White missionaries were narrow, even oppressive, their schools had considerable unintended consequences. It should be noted that in this field as in others, generalizations tend to break down. South Africans had a powerful influence on the character of Southern Rhodesia. In the 1930s, nearly 20 percent of the White population professed membership of the Dutch Reformed Church; earlier, the pioneers, many from South Africa, had been agents of conquest and subjugation. Yet it was the Dutch Reformed Church that founded the colony's first school for the blind, in 1927, and would open a school for the Deaf in 1946.

For some Africans at least, religion and politics were not worlds apart in the interwar period. The life of Thompson Samkange illustrates how Christianity did more than offer literacy (and prestige) and could feed into political commitment. As Samkange put it in 1942, "Some of our people think Christianity is a plan made by the advanced nations to tame us: they gave us the Bible and they take the land from us. . . . In spite of all this, the Church stands for Christian justice and fair play, this it has done and is still doing with good results."[61] These words can be applied to his own career. He was a beneficiary of the Methodist church's openness to the aspirations of Africans and their potential. Like the Anglican bishop Knight-Bruce, Methodists believed, as a report in

1893 put it, that "Africa is to be saved by Africans themselves"—a strategy likely to be cheaper and better manned, and perhaps more effective, than relying on White personnel.[62] Samkange led the Protestant ecumenical movement for twenty years, and in 1938 was selected to speak for all Southern Rhodesia's African Christians at an international missionary conference in Madras, India. A Shona who was at home among Ndebele, Samkange was actively involved with the RBVA and the ICU before assuming the presidency of the ANC from 1943 to 1948.

Through the 1930s and 1940s, an African middle class was emerging, many of them from a mission school education. It comprised clerks and teachers, preachers and social workers, doctors and nurses, journalists, businessmen, and lawyers; and insofar as it included, in addition, farmers (owners of land in the native purchase areas), it was not wholly urban-based. There was diversity of experience and response among these, of course. They no more spoke with a single voice than the Whites did. But this was a class nonetheless bound by common interests and purpose. These were Africans who for the most part rejected tradition and custom in favor of modernity and progress. In the 1870s, Lord Salisbury had darkly depicted the acquisition of Western education by the empire's subjects as a "deadly legacy."[63] For their part, twentieth-century Africans in Southern Rhodesia wanted to be educated in the White man's "wizardry," primarily as preparation "for life in their world."[64] As yet, this emerging class sought to reform, not to overthrow, the colonial state.

* * *

In the wake of conquest and the suppression of their revolt, Africans were clearly subjects of colonial rule, and some, like those evicted from their own lands, were obvious victims. But while there was resentment, there was also acquiescence—some passive, some more active. Segregation itself was not the primary concern. Even educated Africans at this time were not obsessed with race relations or with lining up against (or for) colonial rule. Rather, many of the products of mission schooling "built themselves lives to be proud of," attaining "positions of importance, respect and leadership" at a local level, and as they did they became "fundamentally different sorts of people from those conquered in the nineteenth century."[65] Some formed associations to challenge their White rulers, especially on the two issues of land and votes. But not all were alienated. When growing Black numbers put White institutions of control under strain after 1945, there were numerous educated and accomplished Africans with whom the more liberal Europeans among their colonial masters could, for a while, find common ground.

Notes

1. Gann, *Southern Rhodesia*, 80.
2. Quoted in Blake, *A History*, 68.
3. Oates, *Matabeleland and the Victoria Falls*, 74, 75 and 84, 85.
4. Quoted in Blake, *A History*, 22.
5. Quoted in Blake, *A History*, 125.
6. A. Mambo, *Zimbabwe*, 50.
7. McDonald, *Rhodes*, 214.
8. Quoted in West, *The Rise of an African Middle Class*, 127.
9. Quoted in Leys, *European Politics*, 19.
10. Quoted in E. Mlambo, *The Struggle*, 279.
11. Quoted in Biggar, *Colonialism*, 122, 123. Italics added.
12. Quoted in Palmer, *Racial Domination*, 195.
13. Holderness, *Lost Chance*, 234, 235.
14. Quoted in Gunther, *Inside Africa*, 591.
15. Blake, *A History*, 220.
16. Nkomo, *My Life*, 17.
17. Palmer, *Land and Racial Domination*, 185.
18. Quoted in Palmer, *Land and Racial Domination*, 194.
19. Quoted in Ranger, *Peasant Consciousness*, 111.
20. Quoted in Woodhouse, *Garfield Todd*, 117.
21. Reynolds, *Beware of Africans*, 250, 254.
22. Cripps, *An Africa for Africans*, 11. By 1950, Cripps had changed his mind, declaring "I do not believe that segregation is a righteous policy in a British colony." Handwritten note on opening page of author's copy.
23. Cripps, *An Africa for Africans*, 49.
24. Philip Kerr, in Preface to Cripps, *An Africa for Africans*, ix.
25. Lessing, *Going Home*, 240.
26. Chidzero, in Leys and Pratt, *A New Deal*, 180.
27. Tredgold, *My Life*, 154.
28. Verrier, *The Road to Zimbabwe*, 75, 76.
29. Leys, *European Politics*, 57.
30. Gann, *Southern Rhodesia*, 314.
31. Keatley, *The Politics of Partnership*, 78, 268.
32. Quoted in Welch, *Church and Settler*, 9.
33. Bernard Mizeki is one such example. He was killed during the revolt on June 18, 1896. Today his grave is a martyr's shrine, and Bernard Mizeki Day is celebrated annually by thousands of Anglicans in Zimbabwe.
34. Richard Gray, *Black Christians*, 81.
35. Quoted in Welch, *Church and Settler*, 48.
36. Welch, *Church and Settler*, 93, 94.
37. Welch, *Church and Settler*, 68.
38. Quoted in Keatley, *The Politics of Partnership*, 297.

39. Vambe, *An Ill-Fated People*, 216.
40. Quoted in Welch, *Church and Settler*, 46.
41. Quoted in Welch, *Church and Settler*, 48.
42. Vambe, *An Ill-Fated People*, 232.
43. Quoted in Ranger, in Gann and Duignan, *Colonialism in Africa*, 311.
44. Quoted in Mason, *The Birth of a Dilemma*, 245.
45. Blake, *A History*, 227.
46. Ndlovu-Gatsheni, in Raftopolous and A. Mlambo, *Becoming Zimbabwe*, xix, 74.
47. Quoted in Stokes and Brown, *The Zambezian Past*, 178, 179.
48. Vambe, *An Ill-Fated People*, 213, 214.
49. Quoted in Stokes and Brown, *The Zambezian Past*, 191–192.
50. Ranger, *Peasant Consciousness*, 40.
51. Ranger, *Peasant Consciousness*, 46.
52. Ranger, *Peasant Consciousness*, 74.
53. Quoted in Ranger, *Peasant Consciousness*, 86, 88.
54. Shamuyarira, *Crisis*, 90.
55. Quoted in West, *The Rise of an African Middle Class*, 137, 138.
56. Quoted in Zvobgo, *Methodist Missions*, 66.
57. Quoted in Welch, 59.
58. Quoted in Welch, 61.
59. Quoted in Zvobgo, *Methodist Missions*, 67.
60. Gray, *Black Christians*, 97.
61. Quoted in Ranger, *Are We Not Also Men?* 16.
62. Quoted in Zvobgo, *Methodist Missions*, 68.
63. Quoted in Roberts, *Salisbury*, 139.
64. Tsitsi Dangarembga, *Nervous Conditions*, 36.
65. Summers, *Colonial Lessons*, xv, xxvii, xxviii.

4

Winds of Change

AFTER 1945, SOUTHERN RHODESIA LOST ITS ISOLATION IN A world transformed. World War II brought forward serious, previously dormant questions as to the character and future of empires. Nazi genocide in Europe, along with atrocities committed by the Japanese in the Far East, had been a terrifying illustration of the depths to which racial division, fueled by fear and contempt, could descend. The two new superpowers, the United States of America and the Union of Soviet Socialist Republics, were critical of Europe's empires. They competed for influence in the United Nations (UN), a new international body in which all members were supposedly committed, in the words of Article 1 of its charter, to "the principle of equal rights and self-determination of peoples." Here were the makings of a challenge for even a relatively insignificant colony in the heart of Central Africa.

During the New Cold War, there was no doubting the loyalty to "the cause of freedom" of Southern Rhodesia's White community and government, nor was there any hesitation on their part in branding complaints from the Black African majority as communist-inspired. But Southern Rhodesia was no stronghold of equal rights or self-determination. However, the wider British Empire was in slow retreat, as illustrated by the independence of India in 1947 and the abandonment of Palestine in 1948. South of the Limpopo, the trajectory of political change was quite different. In 1948, South Africa took a decisive, reactionary, political turn. The White minority elected the nationalist party of D. F. Malan and adopted the party's program of complete separation of the races—apartheid.

It would not be long before the White regime in Southern Rhodesia would have to make a strategic decision of its own.

In Southern Rhodesia, society—Black and White—was changing. The growth of secondary industries in the 1940s entailed the permanent urbanization of Africans. This had never been envisaged in prewar White policy and practice. In October 1945, 2,400 African railwaymen went on strike for more pay. The reality of African discontent and frustration could no longer be disregarded, and neither could the raw reality of numbers. To be sure, tens of thousands more Europeans arrived to settle in the territory, but even this high rate of postwar immigration could not keep pace with a far faster increase in the number of resident Africans. While the European population more than doubled between 1946 and 1956, from about 83,500 to 178,000, the African population grew in that same period by half a million, from about 1,719,000 to 2,290,000. This changing ratio, alarming for White supremacists, formed part of the background against which all Whites would shortly have to make momentous choices.

The Central African Federation

By the end of the 1950s, the White politics of Southern Rhodesia would be in ferment. This proved to be a decade in which conventional conservative racial attitudes were challenged, and Europeans were presented with alternative, competing visions of the colony's future. These arguments were, for ten years, inextricably linked to the wider politics of the Central African Federation (CAF). Conceived in the late 1940s and inaugurated in 1953, this was a new political superstructure comprising Southern Rhodesia and its two neighboring British protectorates, Northern Rhodesia and Nyasaland. Questions about relations between Whites and Blacks lay at its heart, unresolved but inescapable. The story of the short-lived federation (it ended in 1963) is complex. It concerns us here primarily to the extent that its unfolding narrative and its political discourse proved powerful influences on the internal affairs of Southern Rhodesia.

Before World War II, nothing had come of discussions among White political leaders on the possible amalgamation of the two Rhodesias. But in the late 1940s there seemed to be a fresh need and opportunity to consolidate White supremacy in the region. Europeans anticipated sizeable economic benefits. These did indeed come about, and for some years benefited members of all races, if unevenly. "The federation brought a boom for colonists and commercial interests; capital and immigrants flooded in. Africans gathered crumbs from the rich man's table in improved social services and the spread of consumer goods."[1] But it was the political potential of federating that most excited the Whites: London would be persuaded to grant dominion status to this federation. There would follow full independence within the Commonwealth of Nations and thus complete freedom for Whites to regulate race relations, within those extensive borders, just as they pleased.

The British government had long since abandoned Southern Rhodesia to its settlers, and in the late 1940s it had neither the means nor the will to dictate to them. Given Britain's postwar political and financial dependence on South Africa, it was significant that the vast British dominion, governed from 1948 by D. F. Malan's unashamedly racist national party, should approve the CAF plan. With an eye to racial issues across Central Africa, Malan appears to have hoped that London and Salisbury together would continue to keep Africans north of the Limpopo submissive, without the necessity for active intervention. The overall British attitude to the CAF was lukewarm, but on balance it was favorable as long as costly Nyasaland was included. At first, even some Africans in Southern Rhodesia provisionally favored the new arrangement. Across the federation, Blacks would be an even higher percentage of the overall population and so might achieve more political influence over the Whites. But this sentiment was short lived, and it was outweighed by serious concerns among Africans in Northern Rhodesia and Nyasaland that the White settler outlook of Southern Rhodesia would infect their protectorates.

The CAF was launched as an exercise in partnership. This was a serviceable though cynical (if not entirely bogus) label. "Partnership" was open to many interpretations. Indeed, the term was acceptable to a range of White opinions just because it could not be defined. Even so, it was a hostage to fortune. Patrick Fletcher, conservative United Rhodesia Party (URP) minister for native affairs in Southern Rhodesia, condemned in July 1955 "those people who rush round the country ramming partnership down our throats." They were "a perfect nuisance." Even so, he added, "I am becoming hardened and quite immune to this poking finger of partnership."[2] It was Africans, though, who could not accept this kind of relationship. The infamous analogy offered by Godfrey Huggins, the first prime minister of the CAF, was that of rider and horse. To Africans such as Lawrence Vambe, this meant a relationship "in which the riding White man controls and decides what is good or bad for the horse, the African."[3] This derogatory definition did nothing to reassure African political leaders, who were increasingly impatient to throw off subjugation in exchange for a genuine partnership of equals. In the event, though many Africans benefited from the economic boom of the first years of the CAF, a lasting formula for the political progress of both races was neither sought nor stumbled upon by its White leaders. Huggins made his views clear in 1956: "We want to indicate to the Africans that provision is made for them to have a place in the sun as things go along. But we have not the slightest intention of letting them control things until they have proved themselves *and perhaps not even then*. That will depend on my grandchildren."[4]

It is no surprise that Southern Rhodesian Africans, who by this time were not content to have "provision made for them," were inclined to have more respect for Whites in South Africa who were completely frank about what they believed and what they were doing than for Whites in the CAF who said one thing and did another. Joshua Nkomo wrote: "On the personal level I, like most Africans, found the Afrikaners much easier to get on with. They expected black people to know their place, which was inferior. But once that was established, they could be friendly enough, and talk away freely. The English-speakers were theoretically more liberal, but when it came to social contacts they were much less free. If you tried to talk to them, they would get embarrassed and quickly find something else to do."[5] Such was the fruit of self-distancing. Certainly, there were some White liberals who ignored the prevailing social etiquette, but Africans were more familiar with those who professed commitment to cooperation but did not, or could not, deliver it.

The CAF was torpedoed by the politics of race, especially unresolved controversy regarding the place of Africans within its constitutional provisions. Early in the 1960s, Northern Rhodesia and Nyasaland were allowed to leave it (to achieve independence as Zambia and Malawi). If the CAF had actually institutionalized "partnership" through progressive constitutional evolution, it might have lasted longer. But Huggins and his colleagues were disinclined, or temperamentally unable, to adapt to changing times and expectations. Instead, the most elaborate constitutional contortions were resorted to regarding the federal franchise in order to produce a façade of broad-minded inclusivity while securing White supremacy. Africans saw through the devious complexity to conclude that their path to self-determination was being blocked. Significantly, the politics of the CAF severely damaged the reputation of White politicians in its political powerhouse, Southern Rhodesia.

"Who whom?" Lenin's question takes us to the heart of the matter. Who was deciding the future for whom, according to the federal constitution of 1953? The answer was clear in the franchise arrangements: the minority Whites would determine the future for themselves and for the Black majority. In their hands, moreover, the electoral process could be managed in order to perpetuate their own power, at least "for the foreseeable future." As Roy Welensky, the prominent Northern Rhodesian who was to be the second and last prime minister of the CAF put it in 1952, shortly before the federal experiment was launched: "If there is going to be domination, it is going to be my race that will dominate."[6] Huggins, the first prime minister, had refused to allow Africans to attend the 1949 Victoria Falls conference on the CAF. He conceded the presence of a "handful" in 1951, but he ordered them to be accommodated in huts and to be separated during meals from their White colleagues. This was not so much partnership as Whites treating educated African spokesmen as if they were servants. When the first federal parliament met in February 1954, Huggins refused to allow the handful of African members to appear in traditional dress, insisting that a Western parliament required European clothing.

The CAF's constitutional devices, like the dress code, were designed by Whites for Whites. Initially, the electoral system for the CAF was a hodgepodge; the franchise already in existence in each territory would apply. There would be thirty-five elected members of the federal parliament (MPs) in all, plus a Speaker. These would comprise three categories. The numbers were made up as follows: twenty-six Europeans were elected according to existing territorial franchises (fourteen for Southern Rhodesia plus eight for Northern Rhodesia and four for Nyasaland); six "specially elected" Africans comprised two for each territory; and three "specially elected" Europeans (to speak on behalf of Africans) comprised one from each territory. As far as Southern Rhodesia was concerned, there would be fourteen (plus one) European MPs and two African MPs. Regarding the latter, while only African candidates could stand in the two constituencies, Mashonaland and Matabeleland, it was a 99 percent White electorate that voted. Joshua Nkomo, who stood against Huggins's nominee in Matabeleland and lost could thus dismiss these as "token black seats."[7]

Partnership? These elaborate arrangements meant that from 1953, just six of the thirty-six seats (a sixth) were for Africans, and just nine (a quarter) for the sum of members representing African interests.

These were complicated constitutional provisions, in part because they had to be. Realistically, the CAF could be launched only if local, established voting arrangements in the colony and the two protectorates were adopted, for the time being at least. Beyond that, Britain's constitutional experts had to decide how to weigh representation across the three territories. But the greatest challenge was posed by the racial question: how to incorporate some Africans in a federation marketed as a partnership while ensuring that policies that served the White minority could be enacted and put into practice without obstacle. The fine tuning in this respect, which included Europeans as a third of those speaking on behalf of Africans, could be regarded as an admission that, after fifty years, the British Empire in Central Africa had failed in its "civilizing" mission. In reality, there was no shortage of Africans who could have been elected by their own people to speak for them. But the Europeans had no appetite for hearing what they had to say.

Arrangements became still more byzantine when, later in the decade, the federal government turned its attention to producing a new electoral system for 1958 that would apply uniformly for elections to the federal parliament across all three territories. For this task, they had to consider the primary question: Should there be a single common electoral roll for all races, or separate rolls for Whites and Blacks? This was a highly charged matter and one on which Whites were not all of one mind, the former practice being regarded as more liberal than the latter. Indeed, while the federal franchise was being reviewed, so too was that of Southern Rhodesia. When the respective revisions were published in late 1957, the CAF was seen to have opted for separate rolls, while the self-governing colony had decided to retain its common roll.

A common roll appeared to be more liberal through being nonracial. Anyone who met the qualifications, whatever their color or ethnicity, would be equally entitled to register and to vote. Moreover, it could be supposed that an increasing number of Africans would come to meet the qualification. To this extent the common roll allowed for eventual majority rule of Blacks by Blacks (unless the White minority continued to raise the qualifications bar whenever too many Africans proved able to clear it). Liberal and not-so-liberal Whites could profess that this franchise gave Africans a vote now and the prospect of power . . . one day. There was indeed equality here, insofar as qualifications were the same for all; the "equal rights for all civilized men" principle attributed to Cecil Rhodes was herein embodied. However, there was no equality, since the Whites were defining the qualifications and doing so in their own interests. In Southern Rhodesia in 1953, there were just 380 Blacks on the common roll.

Separate rolls did not offer Africans the prospect of future majority rule. Instead, they offered representation of Blacks by Blacks in the here and now—that is, Black MPs in the legislature. For Africans, separate rolls could be regarded either as a substantial acquisition of representation or as tokenism: an indicator of powerlessness in a constitutional dead end. And in this light, it is interesting to jump forward to 1980 when, after the liberation war and the end of White minority rule in Rhodesia, a separate roll for Whites provided them with the powerlessness and tokenism of 20 reserved seats out of 100 (and only for a time-limited period).

We may note here three aspects of importance in the revised federal system of 1958. First, and uncontroversially, the legislative assembly was enlarged from thirty-five seats (plus Speaker) to fifty-nine seats (plus Speaker). Second, MPs would be elected by voters on separate rolls. Third, there would again be a quarter of seats for MPs speaking for Africans (that is fifteen out of sixty, from nine out of thirty-six). Nine of these fifteen (African and European) would be elected as before. What caught the eye of many was the means for electing the additional six. Though this was the year when the Gold Coast protectorate in West Africa achieved its full independence from Britain as Ghana, in British Central Africa the additional members (Africans) would be elected by an overwhelmingly European electorate. The new federation-wide separate rolls announced in 1957 thus offered Africans of the three territories nothing beyond a voice, often secondhand, without power, once again.

It worked like this. Overall, the new franchise system involved two sets of electors with separate kinds of qualifications: a higher set, essentially European; and a lower set, overwhelmingly African. The higher list of voters would elect the forty-four ordinary members. But both rolls together would take part in elections for the additional African members. So, in practice, the six new African MPs would be elected by an electorate with a strong European element (except in Nyasaland). "The whole arrangement is complicated," wrote Philip Mason, somewhat superfluously. "It is difficult to explain on a public platform," he continued, implying that, as an exercise in democracy, it fell short. In the end, the details need concern us no longer. The whole arrangement was an exceptionally complicated insurance policy to protect Europeans in the legislature from unwanted representatives of the majority race. Africans were to be represented not by the people they chose as their leaders but by the people Europeans thought suitable to lead them. Robert Tredgold, who resigned as chief justice of the CAF in 1960, commented later that "it passes understanding how anybody who had any pretension to fair-mindedness could devise a system which has as a feature a provision that members supposed to represent one interest should be chosen by the opposed interest."[8]

Perhaps the CAF is best viewed through the lens of fluctuating African expectation and hope. From the start, federal franchise discussions stimulated political consciousness among the African majority in Southern Rhodesia; with both parliaments, territorial and federal, situated in Salisbury, it could hardly have been otherwise. For a few years, some politically conscious Africans in Southern Rhodesia hoped for equitable representation within the new federal superstructure. But by the late 1950s, conditional acquiescence yielded to disillusionment and then outright rejection. It was no coincidence that the new African National Congress (ANC) in Southern Rhodesia came into being in late 1957, as the government in Britain was making constitutional concessions to a White federal leadership doggedly opposed to equality, integration, and authentic political partnership. Tortuous deliberations over the new federal franchise, which clearly signaled an intention to continue to exclude Africans from meaningful political participation, was eventually too much to swallow. Few Africans lamented its passing. "The federation crumbled because racial partnership was a sham and every African in every village knew it."[9]

For their part, Europeans who had chosen fictitious partnership as a defining label proved to have been too clever by half. By 1960, the CAF was moribund, the government in London no longer willing or able to sustain it. The Monckton Report published that year permitted secession and, though it proffered no definite alternative vision for the region, it reserved for Britain the role of final arbiter. "Most white Rhodesians saw in it a passport to doom."[10] Some expressed their uncomprehending dismay as outrage. Roy Welensky was furious. "The British Government have ratted on us. . . . They have been guilty of an act of treachery. . . . I say that Britain has lost the will to govern in Africa and that Britain is utterly reckless of the fate of the inhabitants of the present Federation, including those of our own kith and kin."[11] As the crippled superstructure neared its collapse, Whites in Southern Rhodesia had to decide what path to take if, as expected, Britain was reluctant to grant independence to the Whites without guarantees that Black majority rule would shortly follow. The settlers' decision would mark either the ending or the continuation of White minority rule in the colony. Given the prevailing global discourse on race, as well as empire, it would be a decision laden with moral significance.

Only desegregation of social life, along with an increased awareness of African realities in the reserves and in the towns, could have created the conditions for a sincere partnership between peoples who knew and understood one another. As in South Africa at that time, there was no shared consensus as to what, or even who, was "real." Trevor Huddleston noted that "the *real* life of the African—his home, his family, his interests—are as unknown to the European in Johannesburg as they are to the European in Paris."[12] Albert Luthuli observed that "we Africans are de-personalised. . . . We are 'boys,' 'girls,' 'kaffirs,' 'good natives' and 'bad natives'; but we are not to them *really* quite people."[13] Both might have been describing African lives in neighboring Southern Rhodesia.

A Growing African Political Consciousness

In the wake of World War II, it became increasingly difficult to justify colonialism morally. A letter to the press from a former serving African soldier illustrates this point. Upon hearing that the provisions of the Atlantic Charter of 1941 would not apply to peoples in Europe's African colonies, Lance Corporal Masiye wrote: "The African has served his rulers with admirable devotedness. What is he to receive for this? A continual exclusion from human rights? If so, our rulers must be quite shameless."[14]

After 1945 there was an embryonic militancy among the educated African elite, some of whom were no longer content to ask, in vain, to be invited into the settlers' system. At the same time there was a radicalization of African workers. For a while there was something of an alliance between these two groups across the social divide. After all, "urban" Africans of all classes had to reside in the same low-grade townships. Their joint cry continued to be for inclusion. But this was nonetheless a phase of transition, as illustrated by the resignation of the moderate Methodist Church minister Thompson Samkange from the presidency of a still infant congress (an organization that lacked not only funds but also significant support outside Bulawayo). For two decades, this mission-educated African had appealed to Whites and organized Blacks in the cause of humanity and justice, his political views arising from his Christian beliefs and a Christian morality. But by the mid-1940s even Samkange was disillusioned.

Nevertheless, he remained cautious. Regarding territorial politics, Samkange was conformist and conservative. In a remarkable 1947 presidential address, he declared: "No sensible African would wish that the Africans take over the government of this colony from Europeans, even after a hundred years or even a thousand."[15] Though postwar Southern Rhodesia saw increased racial discrimination and repression in the towns, and increased government intervention in the countryside, he urged restraint for his fellow Africans. To young men in the towns, he said that "we as leaders strongly condemn the growing tendency to hooliganism, lack of moral restraint, indiscipline, insolence, vulgar language. . . . We urge them to behave themselves as members of our race, to be sober, honest, reliable, truthful, punctual and stable at their work." And "to our people in the rural areas, we urge them to employ scientific methods in tilling the land and caring [sic] their herds. . . . It is our duty to educate our people to follow the good work being done by all types of demonstrators provided by the government."[16] These somewhat schoolmasterly strictures, however, now fell on stony ground. Sensing that his role had been played out, Samkange decided to withdraw from the congress leadership, and by the end of 1948 a new generation of young, educated Africans, more critical of the colonial rule that they endured and more radical in their political response, was taking his place.

The African rural areas were much disturbed in the years after World War II. White owners of "investment estates" who had until this time allowed squatters to remain in return for rent now evicted these African farmers in order to sell or lease large plots to White settlers who wished to participate in the first boom that White farming in the colony had enjoyed. Spurning the alternative of entering into labor agreements with new White owners, Africans were moved into the reserves—already overpopulated—only to experience further coercion there. A distinctive African opposition built up in Matabeleland, where there was lasting resentment that their historic lands had been taken from them, despite the promise of Cecil Rhodes himself during the negotiations that ended the 1890s revolt that they could return to them. In the words of one embittered Ndebele chief, reported years earlier, Ndebele "wanted to remain in the district where they had lived all their lives; but they were always being cleared off farms and had no place to which they could go."[17] It was increasingly hard to find space for people and cattle. By 1946 there was growing opposition to destocking; cattle were an insurance against poverty, and forced destocking interfered with *lobola*, the time-honoured custom of bride-price paid with cattle. The native commissioner for Matopo noted that "there is a spirit of nationalism among these [Ndebele] people," adding that the situation called for careful handling.[18] Indeed, in Matabeleland links were formed between protesters in the rural areas and the urban-based Matabele National Home Society.

To a great extent, these were the delayed repercussions of the legislation passed in 1930. As the Gwanda, Matabeleland, Annual Report put it in 1948, recognizing the link between grievance and political radicalization: "It is true . . . that large scale population removals brought about directly because of the Land Apportionment Act serve well the cause of these malcontents."[19]

Evictions took place across the territory. In 1942, the European Native Commissioner (NC) in Inyanga identified the impending crisis in uncompromising terms. "If the natives are to be given adequate land and if the land for each kraal is to be properly allocated it is a very big thing indeed . . . especially in this district where the arable land is very, very difficult to find. . . . To carry out the terms of the Land Apportionment Act in this district I must double the population in the reserves and that is *absolutely impossible.*"[20] In the same year, another Mashonaland NC, deeply concerned by overcrowding in the reserves, asked "Have we an economic dictum that a man can maintain himself and his family on 4 to 6 acres?" and added, by way of answer, "Unfortunate political trends are certain to develop."[21] A particular grievance associated with this overpopulation was the requirement—urgent, in view of the need for more intensive farming while conserving the soil—to carry out contour ridging to trap rainfall. This was hard work and time-consuming, subject to close supervision by government employees known as African Demonstrators. Terence Ranger observes that by the early 1950s, these officials formerly valued by entrepreneurs among African farmers "came to be seen as hated agents of unjust and arbitrary authority."[22]

Rural and urban grievances introduced a new era of protest by innumerable Africans impatient with compromise. While top-down White government initiatives alienated Africans in the reserves, urban protest took its own form. The 1945 Bulawayo-based railway strike involved thousands of African workers with no history of trade union organization. Members of the African elite raised money to support the strikers, and they brought into being the African Workers' Trade Union of Bulawayo. Concessions were won. But the subsequent 1948 general strike exposed the limits of this African alliance. The first general walk-out in the history of Southern Rhodesia spread from Bulawayo to Salisbury and then to all urban and mining areas. But it was a failure. It had arisen spontaneously, in the absence of sound organization and leadership. The African middle class would not condone a strike that threatened to undermine the capitalist economy in which they had a stake. When workers in Bulawayo walked out on April 14, 1948, they did so against the advice of major African organizations, including congress (still under Samkange). And the railway workers who had successfully struck for extra pay in 1945 did not participate.

This 1948 episode had a three-fold significance. First, the only concession gained by the strikers was the promise by the government of a commission of inquiry into their grievances. Strikes were somewhat discredited by this modest outcome, and they came to be replaced as a tool of African activists by boycotts. This change of tactic was in part necessitated by a second outcome: seeing sinister political ambition where there was none, the settler government passed a Subversive Activities Control Act in 1950. This authorized the White regime to prohibit strikes and trade union activity at will. It owed much to a morbidly exaggerated fear of communism. Thus Joshua Nkomo, already a prominent trade union leader, was prosecuted under its terms for bringing back into Southern Rhodesia published materials he had picked up overseas from a meeting of the World Federation of Trade Unions. He was found guilty but let off with a reprimand. Third, it led the African elite to shed their identification with trade union activity and hopefully to test instead the potential of the CAF.

As we have seen, however, by the later 1950s most Africans were sadly acknowledging the CAF's real purpose and concluded that "partnership" was mere rhetoric. Their aspirations dashed, a disillusioned elite was alienated, as were Southern Rhodesia's Africans in general. The elite came to identify more closely again not only with urban radicals but also with the disaffected of the countryside. This fresh alliance took political shape in 1957 in the refounding of the ANC. Soon afterward, gradually but inexorably, Africans abandoned faith in the common roll and, inspired by what was taking place elsewhere in Britain's African empire, sought majority rule instead. In June 1953, Robert Mugabe—at that time a young teacher, radical though not yet engaging in political activity—had written: "Sir Godfrey Huggins has made it abundantly clear that it [the CAF] is primarily aimed at nipping African nationalism in the bud."[23] But the White advocates of the CAF brought into being the very thing it had been designed to forestall.

Postwar White Immigration

The CAF strategy was well served by the high rate of postwar White immigration into the region, especially into Southern Rhodesia. It was thus a much-enlarged White community that would face before the end of the 1950s (and the imminent demise of the CAF) a historic choice for the future of the settler colony. It was the dilemma facing any conqueror: After conquest, do you dominate, or do you share? As Philip Mason put it in 1958, with no knowledge of the choice they would soon decisively make, White Rhodesians' thinking and government policy thus far could be summarized as dominate now, share later. Up to a point, the dilemma presented a choice between the two White visions of local provenance: that of Livingstone and that of Rhodes. Representatives of more progressive Whites were in government for a while during that decade. They sensed that it was both right and necessary to share sooner rather than later. But they would struggle to persuade the community as a whole that to dominate was no longer desirable or even possible.

Who were the Whites of Southern Rhodesia at this critical time? How did this much-enlarged caste see themselves—in particular, what did they think about the British Empire, their place in it, and their ongoing relationship with the Africans whose land this once was and who so heavily outnumbered them?

In an age of "identity politics," we might pause to consider the most appropriate label for this expanding race of rulers. The postwar ruling minority tended to regard the appellation "Whites" as unacceptably crude. They preferred "Europeans," often presenting themselves as guardians of European "civilization." They did not care for "settlers" because this labeled them as *arrivistes*, ex-immigrants. "Colonists" would have been honest but was anathema to critics abroad. "Rhodesian" was acceptable up to a point and sustained by the fact that White Southern Rhodesians had produced an accent of their own. This was "a phonetic amalgam compounded of Afrikaans, Scottish and Cockney elements," and it was significant. "The [Southern] Rhodesian school child picks up the new speech which . . . evens out older class and national divisions and marks off the 'Ridgebacks' as a recognisable group apart."[24] But "Rhodesians" as a label would only draw attention to countless Black Africans who, if they had wanted to (and increasingly they did not), could have described themselves as Rhodesians too. Many regarded themselves as White Africans. But how could they call themselves "Africans," asked Robert Tredgold, himself from one of the longest and most liberal Rhodesian lineages, when they institutionalized separation from the ordinary people of Africa and condemned themselves and their descendants "to be for all time aliens in the continent in which they live"?[25]

"British" was a questionable alternative for two reasons: provenance and loyalty. The provenance of postwar immigrants, who more than doubled the number of Whites in the colony, is striking and significant.

Of the more than 91,000 total immigrants who arrived between 1951 and 1957, the 36,000 from Britain were outnumbered by the 44,000 who came from South Africa. Indeed, during the 1950s, the British were outnumbered by the aggregate of Afrikaners and other Europeans. Greeks and Italians, for example, were encouraged to settle in the colony as the settlers' preferred alternative to training Africans as skilled workers. Among the largely rural Afrikaner community, there was no loyalty toward Britain; the Boer War was still a painful memory for many.

British-born Southern Rhodesians were in turn ambivalent toward those of a South African background. They were alienated by the wartime prominence in South Africa of the anti-British Broederbond, the racist Afrikaner secret society dedicated to the consolidation of White supremacy, and they found the ideological tone and pseudoscience of apartheid distasteful. Doris Lessing noted that, on the whole, White Rhodesians preferred "to think of themselves as 'British,' meaning good, kind, decent, civilised; and not 'Afrikaans,' which meant crude, backward, bad."[26] Though the structures and legislative framework of segregation in Southern Rhodesia differed little from those of South Africa, Whites of a British background in the colony believed that they knew better how to behave toward Africans. Even so, a degree of racial solidarity was unshakeable, and from 1945 the British-born increasingly recognized South Africans as valuable allies against international communism in the Cold War. Anthony Vermeer's nice conclusion is that, whatever they chose to call themselves, between 1923 and the middle 1950s Southern Rhodesia's Whites succeeded in being "British by precept, Boer by practice."[27]

Not all of the White Southern Rhodesians with British backgrounds in the postwar period were bound by a sense of loyalty to Britain. To be sure, following a global war in which a disproportionally high number had served in the armed forces, many Whites did describe themselves as British. Ties of kith and kin and language help to explain this. But the identification was qualified. There was a general repudiation of British government policy, especially that of the Labour Party, which was in power from 1945. The view was widely held, moreover, that the British *in Britain* were now decadent: Britons no longer resembled great forebears such as Cecil Rhodes and Joseph Chamberlain. So Ian Smith could describe the many White Rhodesians who volunteered, as he had, to serve in World War II as "people who were more British than the British."[28] It was "the Crown" to which White Rhodesians of British background felt loyalty. And it was outside interference by political leaders of a distant former homeland whom they regarded as ignorant and wrong-headed that Southern Rhodesia's British-born Whites came to resent most. Meanwhile, the White community's lifestyle was perhaps more American than British. A sizeable proportion dwelt in the suburbs of Salisbury and Bulawayo, reliant on car ownership and measuring one another largely in terms of income and material standard of living.

In the end, "Whites" is the least exceptionable term for those we otherwise refer to, for convenience, as Europeans. Moreover, at a time when issues of color and race loomed largest, this label is appropriate. Political consciousness was racial consciousness, for second-generation White Rhodesians and new immigrants alike. It is no more an oversimplification in discussing the politics of the 1950s to refer to the "Europeans" as White than to refer to Africans as Black. It is important, nonetheless, for this decade especially to avoid easy assumptions about how all Whites saw their future with the Africans. To use the aforementioned categories introduced above, broadly speaking, a gap opened up among the Whites between "sharers" and "dominators." This can best be explained not by provenance but by two other distinguishing features: occupation and length of time in the colony.

Several contemporaries judged that on questions of race and race relations, the minority of Whites with a more liberal outlook tended to be "old" Rhodesians rather than newcomers. Robert Tredgold believed that new settlers reacted directly to their own experience with Africans. "Very often," he observed, "white people who come from outside the country, without any conscious feeling, and possibly with a somewhat sentimental attitude toward the African, suffer a revulsion of feeling, after a time, and become the most intolerant of all."[29] Similarly, on her return to Southern Rhodesia in 1956, Doris Lessing was told repeatedly: "If you want to see the natives badly treated, then you should see the people just out from Britain: they are worse than anyone, much worse than the old Rhodesians."[30] Richard Grey, another informed contemporary, concluded that "the worst and most damaging tensions occurred in the households of newly-arrived immigrants."[31] Years later, Judith Todd stressed that "some of the most fanatical supporters of the Rhodesian Front are undoubtedly the post-war immigrants who vigorously oppose any threats to their new-found riches."[32] Nathan Shamuyarira held a similar view. He observed that "Rhodesia-born liberals are years ahead of immigrants from Britain, who may have voted Labour there but somersault as soon as they land here and start defending white privilege."[33]

Although the newcomers shared an "open-air ethos and an enduring faith in the white man's mission in Africa . . . they had come out to do good for themselves, not for anyone else."[34] Many English immigrants of the postwar wave who were of average ability could enjoy an above-average standard of living and status unattainable back home. Apart from a sense of adventure in an exotic and sunny location, it was the aforementioned tripod that attracted them and tended to determine their political priorities. Along with the severely restricted franchise, each tripod leg underpinned the advantageous position of the European population as it more than doubled. There were individual exceptions of course. No postwar White immigrant was more committed to multiracialism in theory and in practice than Guy Clutton-Brock, who arrived from England in 1949 and established a nonracial community at St. Faith's mission, to the east of Salibury. However, it seems reasonable to accept Clutton-Brock's judgment that, among Whites in the 1950s, those like him who were more liberal in thought tended to be from settled Rhodesians of the prewar vintage.

We should note that a prevailing conservatism regarding race relations survived from the prewar period and was diligently propagated by older Whites among the new. Assumptions of racial superiority remained for the most part unshakeable. Commenting on the doubling of the White population in the seven years after 1947, Joshua Nkomo, who met a wide range of Whites, concluded that "Europeans tended to keep their liberal views for a few years after arriving in Africa, only to abandon them once they became absorbed in the settler community."[35] Similarly, Hardwicke Holderness, a Rhodesian-born liberal, regretted that immigrants tended to conform to traditional settler attitudes rather than stick their necks out.

The more conservative of the longer-established settlers did what they could to educate new arrivals in how to behave toward Africans. The code was one of contrived civility. Social etiquette can be seen in part as the Whites' response to insecurity. Historically, where the power to coerce has been limited (or distasteful), alternative forms of social control have been adopted. Thus, the reign of Louis XIV in France has aptly been termed "government by spectacle." In Southern Rhodesia, there was, up to a point, "government by etiquette." As historian Allison Shutt has observed, "manners were part of a coercive structure of racial authority."[36] But whatever their origin and purpose, it should be stressed that these interrace relations were far removed from those of master and slave. Most Whites aspired to behave toward Africans with unwavering patrician courtesy, fairness, and even kindness. This was partly because these were regarded as the characteristics worthy of a ruling class, but partly because such behavior would reduce friction and so avoid resistance that might have to be dealt with by other means.

The White administration in Southern Rhodesia instructed postwar newcomers on what to think and what racial etiquette to adopt. A 1946 pamphlet, "Southern Rhodesia for the Townsman: Facts and Figures to Help the Immigrant," warned that life in the territory was far from easy. Rather, it added somewhat curiously, "continual effort is necessary if the whites are to justify their standard of living and maintain their intellectual and physical superiority. The European," it went on, "if he is to keep ahead, cannot afford to slacken"—a somewhat ironic statement in a society and economy where most physical, unskilled, and menial work was undertaken by Africans.[37] Meanwhile the pamphlet assured newcomers that Whites were not racists but pragmatists. A comparable 1950 pamphlet for European housewives was entitled "Your Servant and You." Though certainly patronizing, it was not in itself singularly offensive—though "the African" was, as always, the *singular* term adopted to describe diverse peoples who by then numbered over a million and a half. "The African has dignity," it observed; "the African is modest." It urged new arrivals to "adopt the right attitude towards the African." This was because "he naturally looks for courtesy and justice."[38] Arguably well-intentioned, the pamphlet nevertheless relentlessly repeated the message of White superiority and described the behavior by which Whites could sustain it. In 1955, another guide was published for immigrant women that gave precise instructions for dealing with servants (who, it advised, routinely stole and lied), including everything from how to give orders to how much bedding to provide. The message remained the same. Whites must show dignity, fairness, and restraint in their dealings with Africans.

This barrage of advice for new settlers helped to ensure, above all, that the latter kept their distance from Africans. Social segregation was secure. It was all but universally believed, moreover, that physical contact was dangerous and so to be avoided. At the end of the relatively liberal decade of the 1950s, most Whites continued to regard even shaking hands with Africans as bad for race relations. For the most part, propaganda throughout this period was pushing at an open door. For many Whites, maintaining correct manners was something of an obsession. But it was an unhealthy one in the long run. This evolving etiquette of a ruling caste was an inadequate substitute for the spontaneous social interaction that would have been the norm in a relaxed, unlayered, and multiracial society, and which would have informed Whites about the realities of African hopes and fears. Since the races were, until the 1950s, generally segregated, the etiquette applied primarily to those daily interactions where they were not: in the Whites' own homes, in particular, and in shared public places such as shops, parks, and pavements (where Africans were expected to step aside to let Europeans pass). Such distancing was the manifest dimension of a far deeper color bar. In short, etiquette was no substitute for desegregation. The code of behavior was laden with indignities for the African, to which most of the Whites were insensitive, and so in time it engendered not deference but insubordination.

However, the most fruitful way to differentiate between the more and less progressive Whites is not by their ancestry or date of arrival but by their respective place in the economy and society. According to the 1951 census, the economically active European population comprised: 7,582 employers (over 4,000 farmers, 1,000 traders, 700 in construction, and 500 in manufacturing); 547 self-employed; 8,780 central government employees; and 43,858 other employees (3,000 on farms, 2,400 in mines, 9,000 in manufacturing, 5,700 in construction, 10,000 in commerce, and 400 in transport). We note in passing that the twenty-six successful URP candidates in the 1954 election represented an illustrative cross section of these Whites: ten businessmen, seven farmers, five lawyers, and a single mining expert, doctor, former newspaperman, and housewife.

As pressure grew from Africans to participate more fully in the society and politics of the territory, fissures within White society began to be disclosed. For most, class and class interest defined their political viewpoint. "Even today," wrote Philip Mason in 1958, "the barrister and the doctor do not fear African competition: they are a trained aristocracy of the intellect used to sharp competition, and from any quarter; not so the manual worker who knows African muscles are no weaker than his and that his own skill can be learnt."[39] After the War, around 10,000 new immigrants a year settled in the growing towns and suburbs of Southern Rhodesia. They belonged largely to the artisan class. They were not inclined to be liberal in their attitude toward the Africans. As Clutton-Brock put it: "Over half the colonists are ordinary people, who have gone to Rhodesia since the last war and are gaining a standard of affluent living far higher than they could achieve anywhere else in the world, simply by virtue of being White. If they came into direct competition with Africans, they would go down and they know it."[40] "Ordinary people," indeed, but soon having to face choices of extraordinary significance.

Doris Lessing returned to Southern Rhodesia, where she had been born, in 1956. She was struck by what she found among the colony's poor Whites. In general, she wrote, White people "live within a slowly narrowing and suffocating cage, like so many little white mice on a treadmill." But life for some was more miserable; there was the insecurity of poverty, even during the CAF boom years. Lessing quoted a White woman talking to her husband at breakfast: "You can't have bacon *and* eggs—not on what you earn." Another woman told her: "Some of us white people have hard lives. Things aren't easy for some of us." And Lessing notes that the core of the committed segregationists was the White working class, who were afraid that skilled Africans would take over their jobs.[41]

Patrick Keatley offered his reflections on White society a few years later: "Rhodesia's little band of liberal reformers consists of people who are almost always highly educated and above the intellectual average—doctors, lawyers, students, professors, clergymen—people who feel the prick of conscience, who are self-confident and secure, who are not afraid to be different from their neighbours, who read books, who will make the effort after working hours to go out and meet African neighbours."[42] For his part, Lewis Gann, who favored White settlement, observed that "a good deal of money is spent on sports and entertainments; Rhodesia after all possesses a splendid climate" but, he added, "few libraries."[43] Only a few were reading the new and disturbingly persuasive insights of fellow White writers such as Alan Paton and Trevor Huddleston on life for Africans in South Africa. As before, there was a minority of Southern Rhodesia's Whites, secure and confident, who were more openminded, interested in other people's lives, and flexible in their views—especially of the future. But few were so reflective or, perhaps, could afford to be.

The relative security of some Whites compared to others was used by some to explain differences in behavior toward Africans. A nice observation on this (which serves as a metaphor, too, for general White dependency on Blacks) comes from Vambe. If a White man's car got stuck in the muddy road by his village (Chishawasha, near Salisbury), embarrassed White occupants were dependent on the assistance of African villagers. Such African rescuers judged Europeans by their responses to the help. The wealthier and more educated Europeans, Vambe wrote, said "Thank You." The poorer Whites, however, "were hard, coarse and foul-mouthed."[44]

At the end of the decade, the African campaign against the color bar threatened poorer Whites more than the well-off. Rich Europeans did not have to use the segregated buses, so they were less inconvenienced, or outraged, in 1961 by African "freedom sitters" who broke the existing code. Similarly, the possibility of municipal swimming pools being opened to all races did not directly affect prosperous Whites, who had their own pools. To be sure, the African nationalist priority by 1961 was to secure the vote, not to desegregate public spaces. As Joshua Nkomo told the White community in general, "It isn't enough now for us to swim in the baths with you. We say it is time to swim with you equally in Parliament too."[45] But most Whites were fearful, alleging that Blacks bore contagious diseases and that Black men would ogle and intimidate White women and girls. "You must never leave your daughter with an African male," as the instruction leaflet "Your Servant and You" put it.[46] Prime Minister Edgar Whitehead suggested that the city council simply raise prices for admission; the council in turn considered limiting access to people who were taxpayers and voters (though either of these tactics might have excluded some Whites). Regardless, the liberalization of access went ahead, but not before it had sent shudders through the White community and undermined the authority of the governing party.

Outside observers of White Rhodesians noted the fear. Reginald Reynolds called the 1955 record of his remarkable overland journey from Cairo to the Cape "Beware of Africans" after a notice he had seen in Northern Rhodesia. His summary of the general outlook of the region's White settlers was sharp:

> What was it that made the Rhodesias so much more sinister than Kenya, with all its brutality and lawlessness? Not even the more rigid colour bar but, surely, a feeling that all but a very few Europeans preserved *an alert defensiveness* against any good word on behalf of Africans. "They defend," I had written earlier, "before they are attacked, as though they all had bad consciences." An exaggeration, of course . . . but hatred and fear were in the air. That included fear of ideas, even of the pale pink Fabianism which has long been so eminently respectable in England. "The word Fabian," a friend had explained to me when I once showed bewilderment, "is pretty high in the Rhodesian hierarchy of abuse."[47]

Denis Hills reflected toward the end of the liberation war that "in Rhodesia there must always have been fear—the insecurity felt by a minority now outnumbered 24 to 1 by black citizens—and, based on this fear of the multitude, a determination to uphold white authority through the rule of privilege and non-miscegenation."[48] They shared a belief that their long-term survival, as well as their future prosperity, would depend on ever higher levels of White immigration. Insofar as most could only envisage the perpetuation of White supremacy, such a belief was, of course, rational though incapable of realization.

A prominent African had earlier detected the fear. In 1948, Samkange had seen exactly what was changing in the wake of World War II. "Africans are awakening. . . . Everywhere in the world today, the greed of money is separating those who have it from those who have not, filling the latter with angry plans of revolution . . . and the former with *the nervousness of power*."[49] At the heart of the color bar was apprehension, detected in myriad ways. Some caused derision; in 1947, after seeing an advertisement for "European" teachers for African schools, one exasperated African wrote, "If I were a European, I would sink my head in shame were I to know that my highest and most decisive qualification for a post, or my right to earn a comfortable wage, was based on the pigmentation of my skin."[50] There were individual exceptions, but a pervading "nervousness of power" had long been discernible among the White settlers. Godfrey Huggins had risen to prominence in 1933. His uncompromising party program for that year's election was designed to appeal to White supremacists. His manifesto set the tone for all subsequent political competition: the tactic of most parties in opposition from 1945 was to criticize the government for going soft on the Africans and for failing to stand up for the settlers' rights. Policies had to appease fearful artisans, small farmers, and others among the European electorate—especially the Afrikaner. As the elections of 1958 and 1962 illustrated, if European supremacy appeared threatened, the effective rallying point for an opposition party was fear of African economic advance and political competition.

In summary, during and after the end of the 1940s, the Whites, "old" and "new" alike, appeared largely homogeneous in their attitudes toward and relations with Africans. However, there were differences of outlook not far below the surface. A near-universal prewar consensus shaped by isolation from the rest of the world, as well as isolation from the Black majority within the colony through self-segregation, collapsed when it was challenged, and alternatives had to be considered. Whites responded in various ways. By the end of the decade, moderates, liberals, and radicals emerged in sufficient numbers to articulate an alternative, progressive, nonracial path for the colony. But it was difficult to dissuade the majority from carrying on as before.

Segregation continued to ensure that nearly all Whites not only lived separately from Blacks but adopted a formula for interacting with them that fell far short of facilitating mutual knowledge and understanding. Few newcomers objected. Clutton-Brock described his fellow postwar arrivals in the late 1940s as "not rats, but no great bearers of the best of Western civilisation either. Fleeing the Labour Government's high taxes, theirs was the quest for easy money and warm sun." Not only did they not have deep roots in their new homeland, but "beguiled by the cash and the climate, most are ignorant of the situation into which they have blundered, are blind to their limitations and convinced of their righteousness."[51] What were they doing there? Robert Blake's summary is characteristically dry: "The whites were there because they liked the climate, hoped to make money, enjoyed a way of life that was a pleasant mixture of the English and the un-English" while "the blacks were there . . . because they were there."[52] Southern Rhodesia's Africans remained generally quiescent for the time being; but if the Whites were to choose a reactionary path, their future relations with an exclusively White government would inevitably become confrontational.

Huggins's Legacy

The emergence of a more assertive African labor movement, along with an increase in overall numbers that created pressures in both urban and rural areas, led to two significant legislative changes in 1951. In apparent defiance of progressive opinion articulated overseas at the United Nations and elsewhere, each was introduced by the government to bolster the interests of the White minority. As Huggins himself observed two years beforehand, "The old days when the native did exactly what he was told have passed."[53]

The first significant change followed a review of the right to vote for members of the legislative assembly. In order to protect Whites from African political advance, it was decided to raise the common roll qualifications. When South Africa abolished the common roll in the Cape in 1936 (which had been from the outset the model for Southern Rhodesia), Prime Minister Huggins had considered following suit in Southern Rhodesia. With the figures as they stood (there were only 258 Africans on the register, contrasted with 47,000 White Rhodesians), such action hardly seemed necessary. In fact, nothing changed at that point. But after the war, African restlessness raised the question of the franchise again. In September 1948, Huggins went into the general election promising to close the common roll to the Blacks "for the foreseeable future." Having thus appealed to White supremacists, he won. Yet he did not proceed with that dramatic policy change, in part because the British government applied pressure that had to be respected while Huggins sought British approval for a federation. In the event, his 1951 Franchise Act retained the nonracial, common voters' roll, but the tests were tightened. Qualification was raised to £240 income per annum (up from £100) or property worth £500 (up from £150).

In more than doubling the income bar, Huggins raised it to a level that, even a dozen years later, was three times the average for African wage-earners. And the only reason for the qualifications not being raised even further at this time was anxiety that they might disenfranchise some Whites. Though retaining the common roll, the 1951 franchise adjustments illustrated continuing White commitment to the exclusion of Blacks and keeping African participation in the political process to a minimum. The many Africans who sought at this time not to overthrow the government, but to exercise some "self-determination" by having a share in electing it, were thwarted.

The second legislative change had even greater significance. In part a response to unintended consequences of the Land Apportionment Act of 1930, the Native Land Husbandry Act of 1951 was intended to promote better farming methods, though critics suggested that its main purpose was to tighten control over Africans and maintain a flow of cheap labor for Europeans elsewhere. It was also an initiative to tackle overcrowding in the reserves. Overall, however, it was a clear case of "seeing like a state"—that is, arguably well-intentioned and rational, narrowmindedly proceeding with its task, but in ignorance of the implications. This most ambitious policy was blithely undertaken without talks with Africans themselves about the problems or about solutions that might have served both government and people. Though it was intended to be, this was not "good government." Because officials had not listened to voices among the tens of thousands of Africans who would be affected by its radical agenda, neither its negative reception nor its harmful consequences could be anticipated.

The plan was to divide up communal native reserve lands and to allocate roughly equal plots to every African family with rights there. In due course, these small holdings might be consolidated into larger ones. Grazing rights were included in this partitioning, but only for as much stock as the Native Commissioners (NCs) judged it possible for the land to maintain. This reform was intended in part to produce a class of peasant farmers who would be conservative and so easier to govern. As Doris Lessing dryly observed while the policy was being implemented, "Competitive individualism is much more effective than policing."[54] The act would not, however, bring into being an independent entrepreneurial peasantry. Rather, individual property owners would be required to cooperate in land use measures (to maintain fertility, for example) according to the requirements of a higher authority. Chiefs and headmen were involved as intermediaries, but the real power would continue to lie with European NCs, not African NCs.

A liberal White critic wrote that NCs "tended to feel that what was needed in the reserves was more of the stick and less of the carrot." They were "like little kings, and their wives like queens, and the natives were expected to make obeisance to them."[55] Africans were still required to show, or be taught, deference. They could be punished for arriving late to a meeting; for complaining about waiting; for arguing with the NC; for wearing a hat; or for sitting in a chair rather than on the ground. But White insistence on such self-humblings served not to normalize but to aggravate race relations. It alienated and radicalized Africans.

The Native Land Husbandry Act did bring benefits to some, though. Years later, in 1957, Prime Minister Garfield Todd could claim that it had allowed 300,000 African peasant farmers the freedom to cultivate as they pleased. Individual tenure had greatly raised productivity per acre and at the same time given those farmers dignity. Nonetheless, implementation of this scheme led in the following years to the enforced removal of thousands of African families from the lands they had been occupying. The act limited an African family to, on average, six acres of land, though some plots were as little as one acre and a half. At this time, by contrast, the minimum estate allocated to any White immigrant was 750 acres. Bitterness intensified: the White regime made many oppressive demands of African farmers in their overcrowded reserves, but there were no matching demands of White farmers despite swaths of their estates remaining unutilized.

There was more to the significance of the Native Land Husbandry Act than reinforcing racial inequality. It ignored fundamental customary land rights. The principle of common ownership of the land had formerly cemented African tribal bonds and loyalties. But after 1951, a new African generation would grow up cut off forever from the possibility of owning land in reserves that had been for long regarded, realistically or not, as a potential sanctuary. The act undermined the structure of tribal life, and the measures were widely criticized, not only by African farmers directly affected on the ground, but also by educated urbanized Africans who saw them as restructuring White domination over African lives.

Once enforced with vigor, there was widespread opposition from the mid-1950s onward. African proprietors in the reserves challenged soil conservation measures and destocking. Nathan Shamuyarira observed that, "to the simple villager, cattle were his wealth, his means of livelihood, his bank account and his insurance for old age."[56] Many

Africans who lost the right to occupy land in a reserve had no security in the White towns either, whether in land ownership or employment rights. And now their number was being increased by the arrival in the towns of many who chose to, or were forced to, leave the reserves. In short, both rural and urban grievances intensified.

For all its professed good intentions, the Native Land Husbandry Act of 1951 did as much to disadvantage and alienate innumerable Africans as the tripod legislation of 1930, 1934, and 1946 did. Introduced in the same year as the raising of qualifications for voting, it showed Africans that the White regime was intent on tightening its control over their livelihoods while barring any means of contesting such legislation constitutionally. Meanwhile, the primary underlying reality was the growing size of the African population. Managing the rapidly increasing numbers would have been a sizeable social and economic problem for any administration, but they amounted to a most unwelcome predicament for an exclusively White government. The settler regime could redouble its efforts to counter growing numbers of native Africans by attracting more immigrant Europeans. But in founding a political economy on racial discrimination, at the heart of which were inequitable land allocation and an industrial color bar, it had tied its own hands. Tensions arose within the heart of government: from the 1930s, for example, conflict developed between the lands department, which wanted African squatters cleared off alienated land, and the native department, which insisted that there was no land onto which it could move them. In such a context, it was likely to be impossible for a minority White community, committed to the perpetuation of racial privilege, to manage frustrations experienced in every section, at every level, of African society. Clearly, difficult choices lay ahead. Rising African discontent and resentment only raised the stakes of the decisionmaking that Whites would have to exercise before the end of the decade.

Notes

1. Clutton-Brock, *Cold Comfort*, 74.
2. Quoted in Woodhouse, *Garfield Todd*, 156.
3. Vambe, *An Ill-Fated People*, 241.
4. From *The Rhodesian Herald*, May 19, 1956, in Lessing, *Going Home*, 188. Italics added.
5. Nkomo, *My Life*, 36, 37.
6. Quoted in Verrier, *The Road to Zimbabwe*, 77.
7. Nkomo, *My Life*, 64.
8. Tredgold, *My Life*, 205.

9. Clutton-Brock, *Cold Comfort*, 106.
10. Cleary, *The Life of Winston Joseph Field*, 73.
11. December 1962. Quoted in Bowman, *Politics*, 28.
12. Huddleston, *Naught for your Comfort*, 38.
13. Luthuli, *Let My People Go*, 138.
14. Quoted in A. Mlambo, *A History of Zimbabwe*, 138.
15. Quoted in West, *The Rise of an African Middle Class*, 168.
16. Quoted in Ranger, *Are We Not Also Men?* 122.
17. Quoted in Ranger, *Peasant Consciousness*, 112.
18. Quoted in Ranger, *Peasant Consciousness*, 120.
19. Quoted in Ranger, *Peasant Consciousness*, 121.
20. Quoted in Ranger, *Peasant Consciousness*, 105. Italics added.
21. Quoted in Ranger, *Peasant Consciousness*, 146.
22. Ranger, *Peasant Consciousness*, 154.
23. *Bantu Mirror*, June 27, 1953, in West, *The Rise of an African Middle Class*, 190.
24. Gann, *White Settlers*, 75.
25. Tredgold, *My Life*, 151.
26. Lessing, *Going Home*, 239.
27. Verrier, *The Road to Zimbabwe*, 6.
28. Smith, *Betrayal*, 9.
29. Tredgold, *My Life*, 55.
30. Lessing, *Going Home*, 88.
31. Gray, *The Two Nations*, 231.
32. Todd, *Rhodesia*, 147.
33. Shamuyarira, *Crisis*, 18.
34. Blake, *A History*, 282.
35. Nkomo, *My Life*, 42.
36. Shutt, *Manners*, 7.
37. Quoted in Shutt, *Manners*, 22, 81.
38. Quoted in Gunther, *Inside Africa*, 622, 623.
39. Mason, *The Birth of a Dilemma*, 316.
40. Clutton-Brock, *Cold Comfort*, 75, 76.
41. Lessing, *Going Home*, 14, 63, 84–85.
42. Keatley, *The Politics of Partition*, 243.
43. Gann, *White Settlers*, 74.
44. Vambe, *An Ill-Fated People*, 210.
45. Quoted in Keatley, *The Politics of Partnership*, 320.
46. *Your Servant and You*, in Gunther, *Inside Africa*, 623.
47. Reynolds, *Beware of Africans*, 258. Italics added.
48. Hills, *Rebel People*, 182.
49. Quoted in Ranger, *Are We Not Also Men?* 119. Italics added.
50. *Bantu Mirror*, June 14, 1947, in West, *The Making of an African Middle Class*, 161.
51. Clutton-Brock, *Cold Comfort*, 48, 112.
52. Blake, *A History*, 230.
53. Quoted in Ranger, *Peasant Consciousness*, 129.
54. Lessing, *Going Home*, 136.
55. Holderness, *Lost Chance*, 56.
56. Shamuyarira, *Crisis*, 37.

5

Liberal Dawn?

FOR THE TIME BEING, THERE APPEARED TO BE ONLY BREEZES, rather than winds, of change. The American journalist and travel writer John Gunther produced a striking composite picture of Southern Rhodesian society in the first years of the 1950s. He dwelt on the unequal, segregated lives of the Africans in the colony. On the railways, the train crews were all White, except the African coalman on the tender; though he did most of the hard work, his wage was just one-fifth of the White man's wages. There was no dignity to be found in the daily experience of the color bar. Africans could not enter a White hotel or, in metropolitan areas, go out after curfew without a pass. There was no meeting hall for Africans in Salisbury, and they were not allowed in the European theaters. Africans were permitted to travel second class on the trains, but in segregated compartments, and there were no African waiting rooms or restaurants in the stations. Africans were not allowed to use the lifts in office buildings, and the schools were rigidly segregated. Gunther's most depressing experience came when he went on an escorted visit to a native purchase area near Salisbury, during which his party went to a school. "The poverty, the pitiable lack of equipment, the sheer inhuman primitiveness, were bad enough. But what really hurt was that our White escort, a senior government official, refused ostentatiously to shake hands with the perfectly decent, perfectly respectable, and perfectly humble black school master."[1]

Severe segregation also applied to Indians. By the time of Gunther's visit, Indians were no longer allowed to settle in the territory on the most curious grounds that they lowered economic standards (especially strange, given their central place as artisans and retailers in the colonial economies of British East Africa). But segregation patterns were perhaps most heartless regarding the Chinese. When a former cabinet minister of the nationalist government of China (an ally during World War II just ended) visited Salisbury, he had to sleep in a laundry, as no hotel or resthouse would take him in. In such ways, White racism was wide-ranging and brooked no exceptions. As for most of the African majority, before 1953 their lives had not, in key respects, changed for the better. They were denied dignity, and "everywhere—on the farms, in the mining compounds, in the townships, on the reserves, in the White suburbs—the African was exploited, dominated and kept apart."[2]

Todd in Power

In 1953, Garfield Todd succeeded Godfrey Huggins as prime minister. A New Zealander of considerable charm, he had spent many years as a missionary among the territory's Africans. He could sound patronizing. For example, in a 1956 speech he said: "One of the pleasant things in Africa is the people themselves. . . . With their singing and their patience and good humour, they are a pleasant people."[3] Yet these were positive observations—not all Whites found Africans "pleasant"—and he had experience of the native peoples that very few could match. He had moved into politics by chance. During the general election campaign of 1946, Huggins addressed a meeting in Shabani (between Bulawayo and Fort Victoria). Todd turned up to listen, as the meeting was within reach of the Dadaya mission where he lived and worked. When Huggins traduced New Zealand and its Labour Party's program, Todd interrupted him with an impromptu speech in defense of both. Huggins, to his credit, later sought out his heckler and invited Todd to join his United Party and stand for election. Todd was attracted by the chance to be an unofficial advocate of African rights in a parliament that excluded Africans. He accepted Huggins's invitation and was elected.

Belief, experience, and a sympathetic imagination prompted him to seek a cautiously progressive policy path that incorporated the improvement of African conditions and prospects during his premiership. His outlook on race relations was unconventional. He had perceived that "intelligent, thinking Africans do not wish to see the European standard of living lowered; their wish is to see African standards raised."

In February 1951, he had expressed his radical yet defining belief that accident of birth (and so of racial identity) should not be relevant regarding the right to vote: that it was "fundamentally unsound to demand, as a qualification for the vote, a state which cannot be obtained but (which one) must be born into."[4] This was honest, though not likely to reassure those who took pride in their (White) race and felt that it was all they had to legitimize their social and political preeminence.

Todd came to power despite his more liberal views, not because of them. His ability and manifest sincerity, as well as the frank way he handled even the most controversial issues, initially allayed the doubts of detractors. In several respects, Todd was a conservative during the first part of his premiership, emerging as more progressive as he became increasingly aware of both the desire and need for reform. He may have been complacent at first, but when no longer so, he found that the coalition of groups represented in his United Rhodesia Party (URP) cabinet rendered him anything but a free agent. He was initially acceptable to the coalition that was his party. He was more than a missionary. He was a farmer, too, with at one time a 90,000-acre property. And he was a no-nonsense pragmatist. Here was a White leader whose decisive response to an industrial dispute early in his premiership in 1954 confirmed his authority among Whites who could not at this time dismiss him as being "soft" on Africans.

Within a year of his accession to the premiership, Todd was faced by a strike by over 9,000 workers at the Wankie Colliery in the west of the colony. Coal from these mines was the sole source of power for the Central African Federation (CAF): the railway system depended on it. Todd called out the army. He insisted that he did so "not to break the strike but to keep the peace."[5] Law and order were his priorities. Perhaps he feared clashes between Black miners and the Whites who went underground to keep the mine in operation. In any event, no lives were lost. It was typical of Todd that, after learning about them, he was horrified by the working conditions that had led to the strike, and less than two weeks afterward he set up the Wankie Native Labour Board to ensure improvements. For the time being, though, he had reassured White reactionaries. Even Ian Smith grudgingly conceded that Todd "had dealt surprisingly firmly with black agitation, which was beginning to rear its ugly head."[6]

Above all else, he was a dynamic and natural leader. His oratory had impressed the *Sunday Mail* from the start. Reporting on the 1946 Legislative Assembly, it wrote: "Of the new speakers, Mr R. S. G. Todd takes the palm. He has a sure, broad, well-informed humanitarian outlook and his way of address is attractive."[7] Many years later, when Todd addressed the United Nations (UN) in 1962, it was said that "his oratory was devastating. . . . He spoke like one possessed."[8] Even so, perhaps his most uncommon—and most controversial—characteristic was that he not only talked but listened.

Todd's enlightened views crystallized as his premiership progressed. They blended principle with pragmatism. In an article for the *Rhodesia Herald* in March 1956, Todd succinctly stated his political credo: "What is demanded of us together," he wrote, "is to co-operate courageously and generously with the inevitable."[9] This was a mature political position. Todd was not idly speculating on what would be pleasant, but recognizing that, if trouble in the future was to be avoided, Whites must recognize the aspirations of the African majority. Such a course was ethical; it was also the only one that was rational and realistic.

But pursuing this course required generosity of spirit and courage. In 1954, after returning from Kenya during the Mau Mau insurgency, Todd had told his MPs, in broader terms: "I believe that only if we move reasonably with the times and only if we are prepared to let common sense and decency have its way, and meet our problems one by one without leaving too big a time-lag, will we be able to carry on and build up the good feeling which today exists between the races here."[10] The fact that, shortly after his fall, Todd wrote a foreword in April 1959 for Ndabaningi Sithole's *African Nationalism* is remarkable, suggesting that his personal liberalism had gained momentum since the decade's early years. In February 1959, Todd's successor as prime minister had declared a state of emergency, so the sympathetic tone of what Todd wrote was striking. Commending Sithole, he wrote of "the handicaps and indignities which his own people face in the country of their birth."[11] He knew the possible consequences of blithely carrying on as before and failing to recognize the extent of African alienation.

Meanwhile, as prime minister, would there be enough "generous," "reasonable," and "decent" Whites to join Todd in gradual, piecemeal problem-solving, and so avoid an emergency comparable with Kenya's? Politically his fellow Europeans tended to be neither courageous nor generous. Todd himself began with no grand program for African advancement. In these changing times, much of what Todd said and did (or attempted) was reactive. He was sufficiently conservative and politically aware not to promote any sudden transformation in relation to land, or votes, or the color bar. He posed no threat to the Land Apportionment Act. Political progress for Africans, by a widening of the franchise, was not high on Todd's initial agenda. It did not seem as urgent as it was to appear, say, three years later. In fact, Todd's most substantial initiative was at first sight unthreatening to Whites: to promote African education (getting Africans to fund it by doubling their poll tax). Overall, Todd appeared content in the mid-1950s with a government for the people rather than by the people.

At this time, as a humane individual with evidently liberal leanings, he was not alone. The mid-1950s were for a while something of a heyday for Whites committed to multiracialism. They were paternalistic, perhaps, in taking for granted the superiority of Western culture, but they did advocate the piecemeal integration of Africans fully into White society as steps toward a future state of nonracial meritocracy. They were sympathetic with what growing numbers of middle-class Africans wanted; aware, too, of the cost of frustrating them. As a congress spokesman put it in 1954, "Today, the African people—particularly the educated and civilised among them . . . demand a place in the sun. And he who thwarts their legitimate aspirations will do so at his own peril."[12]

Two organizations were prominent as expressions of White liberalism: the Inter-racial Association (IA), led by White professionals and businessmen from 1953; and the Capricorn Africa Society (CAS), from late 1952, created by a distinguished former colonel in the British army. Each welcomed participation by Africans. The IA was a pressure group for legislative reform. It focused on Southern Rhodesia and explored ways in which society and politics might change, with the races in partnership rather than at loggerheads. The issues discussed included land and votes, of course, and the (social and industrial) color bar. Seeking progress through practical measures, the IA sent influential deputations and memoranda to government. The CAS had a wider, more visionary, scope. It envisaged a multiracial union of six territories—British East Africa as well as British Central Africa—and at its peak in 1958 could claim 2,500 members, 65 percent of whom were African. Members of the IA have been depicted as "instinctive Fabians," and members of the latter as "misplaced Tories."[13] But membership overlapped. Both found Southern Rhodesia parochial, in urgent need of reform. There were no differences of substance: each organization positioned itself as equally averse to apartheid on the one hand and militant African nationalism on the other. And they had a brief window of opportunity.

Men and women—not numerous, but influential—met across the racial divide and talked to, and listened to, one another. Both White liberals and prominent educated Africans were for a while associated with the IA. Charles Mzingeli was a former activist in the Industrial and Commercial Workers' Union (ICU) and a member of the South Rhodesian Labour Party when it opened its doors to Africans; he deplored intra-African tribalism and sought a multiracial future for the country. James Chikerema was an activist from the City Youth League, subsequently co-founder of the revived African National Congress (ANC), and later still a colleague of Bishop Muzorewa. George Nyandoro's grandfather had fought against the British South Africa Company (BSAC), his father had been deposed as a chief, and he himself became secretary-general of the ANC in 1957. He too was later an associate of Muzorewa. Leopold Takawira, teacher and headmaster, became an executive officer in the CAS. His arrest, among others, sparked the July 1960 riots. He died in a Rhodesian Front (RF) prison in 1970. None of these people associated with liberal Whites for long; they became disillusioned and radicalized by the evolving situation in the country. The point, however, is that for a short time in the later 1950s, such figures, with standing among their fellow Africans, were exploring, with moderate Whites, various ways in which Africans might find a deserved place within the system the Whites had built for themselves.

Moreover, there was some African participation in national political processes. In June 1956, African branches were energetically represented at a congress of Todd's URP. At this time, "for Africans in Southern Rhodesia the possibility of achieving progress in co-operation with whites was still credible."[14] At other levels, too, there was some productive contact between the races. One outstanding example was in the east, toward the Mozambique border, where Guy and Molly Clutton-Brock were running a cooperative farm at St. Faith's amid a village life of racial partnership.

In such ways, social and political space was found for interracial dialogue. Moreover, the (re-)birth of the ANC in September 1957, while alarming to some Whites (though not to Todd) was to some extent a confirmation, not a denial, of this political reality. Clutton-Brock played a large part in drawing up its constitution; that document called not for the immediate overthrow of settler colonial rule, but for measured, nonviolent reform toward multiracialism and power-sharing. But multiracial initiatives of mid-decade bore little fruit. Ironically, just when a point had been reached when Africans could believe that a White government was taking account of them, in early 1958 members of Todd's own government rose against what they saw as his excessive liberalism by ejecting him from office. Whatever hopes there may have been of Blacks and Whites moving forward together in a true partnership were destroyed by that single act—an act which marked diehard Whites' initial response to the political and moral challenge posed by moderate Africans and liberal Europeans in mid-decade.

Thoughtful, moderate Whites argued for an approach, such as Todd's, that seemed both ethical and realistic. Perceptive observers had realized its merits many years earlier. Even before World War I, a farsighted researcher, Wilson Fox, had advised Southern Rhodesia's BSAC rulers that a policy of White supremacy was neither moral nor intelligent. "Can a system possibly be *right* or *successful* that bases itself upon the principle of complete segregation? On the contrary, every European and every native should be jointly engaged in making the most of this country's resources."[15] It was inhumane to keep Africans apart, subjugated, in less favorable conditions; and the young country would need all the (skilled) manpower it could muster if it was to reach its potential. Half a century later, Robert Tredgold offered his own somber reflection regarding ongoing social segregation. He, like Fox, perceived two parallel flaws: segregation prevented healthy interracial relationships, and it strangled economic progress. "At best it is a policy of escapism, of the postponement of the settlement of problems that sooner or later will have to be squarely faced and squarely solved."[16] He added that "the European is still thinking in terms of the days when the African did nothing but unskilled work. . . . Under the conditions of a modern, industrialised society all this, apart from its moral aspect, is economic lunacy."[17] But the voices of Fox and Tredgold went largely unheard.

* * *

From the start, Todd was not a free agent. The passing of the Franchise Act and Land Husbandry Act just before he took office illustrated the mountain he had to climb if he were to steer all the peoples of his country along a path of parallel development and interracial cooperation. Even modest liberalizing steps on the franchise that Todd might envisage would require a turn in the mood of White politics. Meanwhile, the accumulating effects of the top-down 1951 measures to transform African agriculture were unlikely once instituted to encourage Blacks to join a White-dominated regime evidently disinclined to listen to their mounting grievances, let alone include them.

Nonetheless, in due course Todd committed himself to a gradual reform of the franchise. He was determined to retain the single voters' roll in Southern Rhodesia. Heir to both Livingstone and Rhodes, he was personally convinced "that an inevitable result of two rolls was that those on the lower roll would see themselves as second-class citizens."[18] In Todd's own words, "Much better that men, irrespective of their colour, should become voters because they qualify in the normal fashion, not because they are black or white."[19] Conceding that the future of the country depended on "the maintenance of what we term European standards," he nevertheless stressed that "opportunity must be provided for Africans to advance to those standards."[20] In this context, the central preoccupation of the commission that Todd set up under the CAF's chief justice (Tredgold) was, in the shadow of 1951, a review of qualifications for the common roll. There was scope for amendment. When the Tredgold commission began its work in December 1956, there were 52,184 voters on the electoral roll, of whom 646 were Indian, 593 colored, and 560 African (in an African population of around two million). The commission's findings were discussed the following year and, after amendments, passed into law as the Franchise Act in October 1957.

Tredgold was a prominent, enlightened figure in the White community. He stood within the Livingstonian tradition in the colony; of eminent ancestry, he was related by blood to the Moffats, Robert and John, and by marriage to the greatest missionary of them all, Livingstone himself. He represented the educated, humane, principled, and liberal minority among Whites of his own day. Of his 1968 memoir, written after compromise had been jettisoned, Todd told his former colleague that "in your book you mark out clearly areas of truth." When Tredgold died in 1977, the New Zealand–born Todd wrote of him and his ancestry: "Being the fifth generation since the Livingstones, and his father having been Attorney-General in an earlier government, he was of the essence of the true Rhodesia: but they were the great exceptions, above the calibre of most Rhodesians."[21] Tredgold explained that he proposed piecemeal reform—modest enough, he hoped, to avoid alarming fearful Whites, yet substantial enough to win over aspirational Africans (and also be in line with contemporary British government preferences). His were the proposals of a cautious liberal reformer at a potentially decisive turning point in the colony's history. They were well informed and reasonable. But they were blown away by a wave of White reaction that would later lead to his own resignation.

A simple one-man, one-vote system was ruled out. An untrammeled universal franchise can function only under certain conditions, Tredgold argued in his report. "It requires a homogeneous electorate, at a fairly high standard of civilisation and divided by *political* divisions, based on the policies and record of the government and opposition, and not confused by differences, such as *race* or colour, that tend to create artificial divisions cutting across the real issues."[22] The chief justice was trying to produce qualifications for voting that were appropriate for his society's stage of development. From his own experience of the Rhodesias, he believed it was both necessary and right to tread warily. He was happy with his commission's terms of reference, which required his team to ensure that government remained "in the hands of civilised and responsible people." He was required to confine the franchise "to those who are capable of exercising it with reason, judgment and public spirit."[23]

His core recommendations in March 1957 were clever but, much like contemporary federal franchise thinking, very complicated. They are spelled out here in order to emphasize just how much rested on the question of qualifications at this moment of potential transition. The terms and conditions of the franchise were designed to reassure Whites who, after all, were the people with the authority to pass them into law. They were largely unintelligible to many Africans who enjoyed no such authority. It was tragic that what might reassure Whites would either baffle or simply frustrate the Black majority.

There would continue to be a common roll, the report insisted. But on it there would now be registered two categories of elector, ordinary and special. Qualification for ordinary voters was high (relating to income, property, and education). Considerably lower was the qualification for special voters: income of £180 per annum plus literacy. In an election, votes of ordinary electors and special electors would all be cast in the same constituencies. Why, then, the distinction? In practice (and as before), qualification for ordinary votes would be met by most if not all Whites, but by few Blacks. Special voters would be overwhelmingly Black. In this distinction lay the core of the proposal: ordinary votes would carry more weight than special votes. Or rather, as Tredgold explained, "Their votes would count equally, but the total 'special' vote in any constituency would never be allowed to count more than a third of the total vote in that constituency." This limitation, he added, "would give the white electorate reassurance against swamping"; it was "a safety device in the electoral machine."[24]

Todd welcomed the proposals, but though cautious and self-limiting, they went too far for many among the White electorate. Todd saw qualifications through the lens of Africans gaining access to them by educational and material advance. His right-wing political rivals, however, valued them as an ever-rising barrier to African political participation. Todd's ambition was to include, theirs to exclude. All questions relating to the place of the Africans in the political life of the country exposed fault lines within the White community. Broadly speaking, a contest for the future direction of the country was to be waged between those of a more liberal persuasion, their leadership to be found among insiders of the relatively secure "establishment," and outsiders of increasingly conservative, racialist conviction who feared, and became inflexibly antagonistic toward, even the partial admission of Africans into politics and government. In 1956, between 1 and 2 percent of Africans qualified to vote, and that is how an increasing number of implacable Whites wanted it to stay.

In July 1957, addressing a gathering of the IA, Todd had to threaten to resign unless his reforms were accepted in full by his own skeptical party. In the end, he had to accept significant amendments. The party and legislative assembly insisted on a further devaluing of special votes; but the headline amendment was that qualifications for special voters were tightened. The simple qualification of £180 per annum was dropped. Now, special votes would be awarded to anyone with basic literacy plus £240 per annum or to anyone with two years of secondary education and, thereafter, two years of continuous employment with an income of £120 per annum. In short, Todd was proposing that the number of Africans on the common voters' roll should be increased beyond 2 percent. His own party, including some of his own cabinet, considered this heresy.

The predominant Black response was dismissive not of mere detail but of the whole franchise-doctoring enterprise. The White minority government did not appear to be opening its arms to inclusion. Ndabaningi Sithole, a moderate nationalist at this time, was scathing in his opinion. "And so the European finds himself engaging in a faith-shaking occupation of manufacturing countless ingenious definitions of 'civilised' so that he can exclude ... Africans from the political process."[25] The late amendments made the whole package still more suspect. "A sop thrown out to keep hungry people quiet never becomes a satisfying meal," wrote Doris Lessing.[26]

Only around 6,000 more Africans qualified as potential electors under this reform, and they proved slow to register. Todd's successor as prime minister, Edgar Whitehead, attributed such sloth to "apathy." But why should Africans have been enthusiastic about voting in such an inequitable system? In any case, there were obstacles to registering. One prosperous African businessman, among the few in his district qualified to vote, went to register at his district office and to claim this rare right. "What: give you the vote, my boy? Not me. Get out," was the reply. The law was easily subverted by local officials, and any appeal was costly and tortuous.[27] Enthusiasm to register in the White man's system waned. Most of those eligible to register declined to do so.

Tredgold and Todd wanted to take steps toward eventual multiracial representative government. And a positive aspect of this reform was that no candidate could base his appeal to the ordinary (White) electorate on racial grounds without alienating special (Black) constituents and thus jeopardizing his chances. However, because they had to take with them the bulk of the White community, Tredgold had produced overall a damp squib of a reform in the eyes of even moderate African nationalists. His complex scheme enfranchized very few Africans. "The whole aim of this set-up," concluded Sithole, "is to maintain the ascendancy of Europeans over Africans . . . to ensure the domination of the African majority by a White minority."[28] To an African eye, Tredgold's proposals resembled those of the CAF. There was no disguising the fact that tests were to disqualify Africans.

Moreover, Sithole continued, the wider socioeconomic context in the colony remained hostile to African progress. "While there is a qualified franchise in Southern Rhodesia, the economic structure of the country is so arranged that the African finds it very difficult to qualify economically."[29] No leg of the tripod of separation and discrimination had yet been removed. White governments continued to be capable of limiting economic African opportunity for rising property and income, as well as of restricting educational provision. Colin Leys disparagingly noted, among Whites at the time, a "desire to extend the vote to Africans *without running any risk* that they might use it to change the foundations on which the existing system rested."[30]

The Tredgold report was an honest attempt to find a temporary practical compromise between current African aspirations and European fears. It failed because, by the late 1950s, even the very cautious liberalism that it embodied was enough to alarm and alienate most Whites. The proposed franchise change was slight indeed: the vote was not being granted to every farm laborer, domestic servant, or unemployed worker in the African townships, but only to Africans who met the criteria of "civilized," which the Whites had propounded repeatedly. But the giant constitutional conundrum remained: any apparent further underpinning of White power would fail to win African support, while any apparent concession to African demands would alienate the Whites. "The franchise was really the common focal point of African aspirations and white fear of change."[31]

Meanwhile, the increasingly bold prime minister found himself out of step with party colleagues on several issues other than the franchise—some substantial, others symbolic. In 1954, Todd made minor amendments to the Land Apportionment Act to make it possible for hotels, clubs, and restaurants to be multiracial if they wished (though most did not) and possible, too, for African professionals to occupy offices (though not to dwell) in the Europeans' towns. There was a further loosening of the act later to allow for the establishment of a multiracial university college in Salisbury. This initiative revealed the growing divergence of opinions among Whites. It was welcomed by those genuinely committed to a "civilizing" mission. Thus, Hardwicke Holderness spoke in 1954 on behalf of educated Africans:

> There is no other way for these people to go than the European way . . . what they want to do is be accepted on their merits. There is in Southern Rhodesia a whole section of African people who are *knocking on the door of Western civilisation.* . . . At this moment, and I do not know how long it will last . . . the leadership of these people is firmly in the hands of people who want racial cooperation, and people who will come in 100%, as liberals, cooperating in our Western way if the door is not closed on them.[32]

But when a bill came before parliament to amend the Land Apportionment Act to enable this to happen, a settler newspaper, the *Umtali Post,* saw only "an attack on the safeguards the European enjoys." Nevertheless, this was a modest innovation. At its outset, University College of Rhodesia and Nyasaland in Salisbury—the colony's first higher education institution, funded first by the CAF and then by Britain—had just eight African tertiary level students out of seventy-one. Doris Lessing observed: "People in Britain are shocked because the new university will be segregated. But even more shocking is that, unique among the universities of the world, there is provision that the government of the day, through the Minister of the Interior, can dismiss any African at any time without giving reasons for doing so."[33]

There were other worrying initiatives. Todd's attempt to dismantle the institutionally conservative Native Affairs Department for having outlived its usefulness appeared to presage further changes. He did not reassure Whites in general by proposing higher wages for the lowest paid (that is, African) workers. A seemingly trivial decision in November 1956 that Africans should henceforth be called "Mr." by officialdom, rather than be referred to as "Native" or "African Male," was unsettling for some. Todd gave African schooling a huge impetus and sought to abolish racially defined trade unions. He was also personally dismissive of attempts by conservatives to extend legislation to prevent "immoral" sexual relations, naively going so far as to celebrate the territory's colored community. But it was his commitment to African political progress, albeit gradually, even ultracautiously, that lay at the heart of the reactionary Whites' case against him. In a desperate attempt to convince his critics, he argued that his path was that of Cecil Rhodes: one who had abhorred race antagonism, had faith in the common roll, and had famously advocated "equal rights for civilised men regardless of color." But this was not enough to save Todd.

At this time, there were some revealing parallels in the worlds of politics and religion. Strains among White Christians may be glimpsed in the experience of Guy Clutton-Brock. In the late 1950s, there was tension between his St. Faith's cooperative and the diocesan standing committee. A leading diocesan official was damning. "I totally disagree with this co-operative. It will mean that the natives will get control, and where will the missionaries be then?"[34] In this local struggle, reactionaries in the Anglican Church triumphed: the state of emergency saw six leading Africans of the community arrested. Church authorities took over the village farm and its funds and sold the bulk of the land to the government for a native reserve. Here, church and state were working together, but not as Christians dedicated to the well-being of Africans. Nathan Shamuyarira wrote in the 1960s about the more recent immigrant missionaries. "When they arrived from England, they were all smiles. . . . But after a year or two you could not recognise the same person. They had become reserved and stand-offish." These younger missionaries, he concluded, "quickly became more reactionary than the older tried hands."[35]

Insofar as one may generalize, African attitudes toward Christianity itself were changing. They could distinguish between individual missionaries and their schools, which could inspire generations of African Christians, on the one hand, and an institutionalized church whose commitment to African advancement was questionable, on the other hand. "The great work of the pioneer missionaries had created a deep fund of loyalty and gratitude among Africans, but the days when the missionary often stood out as a unique champion of African rights had passed."[36] Africans could see that in the White man's church, European clergy lived at a far higher standard of living than they did. They saw, too, that most Europeans were not churchgoers. Those who were churchgoers belonged to a bewildering number of denominations: fourteen in Bulawayo alone. Some Africans reacted by joining separatist churches, others by returning to spirit mediums and belief in the religion of their ancestors.

During Todd's premiership, Africans who talked to Whites opened themselves up to criticism for doing so, as did Whites who talked to

Africans. It was no easier for prominent Blacks than for the more enlightened Whites to meet and proceed together. In the run-up to the CAF, Joshua Nkomo and Jasper Savanhu had been criticized by some fellow Africans for accepting an invitation to attend talks in London. Later, leaders of the radical City Youth League (CYL), founded in Salisbury in 1955, were critical of Charles Mzingeli, moderate leader of the Reformed Industrial and Commercial Workers' Union (RICU). He had challenged the authorities frequently and organized small-scale boycotts; he believed in communicating with the administration, in arguing with them. But the radicals of the CYL argued that even talking with the Salisbury city council was to be avoided, as it would be a recognition of the White officials' superior position.

Todd Falls

To effect change, Todd had to stay in power. But the actions he took, the statements he made, and the image he projected all counted against him in the increasingly feverish world of White politics, where old conservative certainties were challenged by open-ended alternatives. Unfortunately for Todd, the gestures he made and the steps he took did little to deliver substantial African progress, and yet in aggregate they provided nervous internal critics with a case for his removal from office. Todd was politically weakened, moreover, by the merger of his URP with the United Federal Party, in which he had fewer sympathizers. But there were divisions even within his own cabinet, to which he had had to appoint ministers of differing views. These divisions became more obvious and deeper, as in society at large, when options for the future assumed momentous significance. Robert Tredgold's modest franchise reforms, introduced in late 1957, dispelled doubts. The White political class as a whole represented an electorate whose main concern was to preserve its privileges. Todd may have been "trying to help the whites to save themselves in time."[37] But, conditioned to be suspicious and fearful, few Whites could see that his understanding of Africans and his relations with them were a strength rather than a weakness.

In February 1958, Todd was ousted as prime minister. The key player in his fall was a right-wing colleague, Patrick Fletcher, whom Todd had appointed minister of native affairs. Described by Shamuyarira as "a tired and cantankerous man whose thinking had been set since the old days," Fletcher led the attack on the prime minister, claiming that Todd "has stirred up the natives to want more than they can be given."[38] Concerned that Todd seemed more interested in African advancement than in White apprehensions, Fletcher had told him in November 1957 that defeat at the next election to the insurgent right-wing and racist Dominion Party was likely. Shortly afterward, Fletcher stood against Todd for the leadership, albeit unsuccessfully. He did not shine in the leadership debate at the party congress on February 8, 1958. When asked to substantiate a charge he had brought against Todd for misleading his colleagues, Fletcher replied "The Prime Minister said . . . he said . . . he said. . . . Well, I can't remember just what he said, but I know it wasn't true."[39] Opponents struggled for words, but Todd had become so toxic that after he had been thrown overboard to protect the URP's chances in the forthcoming election, even his offer to remain in the cabinet was not accepted.

By this time, educated Africans could see that, during his premiership, Todd had recognized their interests. This prime minister enjoyed widespread confidence among politically conscious Africans. Tredgold recalled that by 1958, "it became apparent that something approaching veneration for him was growing amongst the Africans."[40] While "nit-picking and hair-splitting" distinctions regarding the CAF played a part in the feverish White politics of Todd's fall, "he was removed because he offended the *amour propre* of some federal politicians," as one observer claimed—it was essentially his standing among Africans that made a critical handful of Todd's colleagues lose confidence in him.[41] The real significance of the CAF lay elsewhere. Supporters of the CAF boasted of "partnership" when most in the White community did not believe in it and their leaders were clearly not going to implement it. The CAF's claims to be progressive in its approach to race relations were dishonest and recognized to be, including by Africans in Southern Rhodesia who might in their absence have been drawn more enthusiastically into a real partnership with Todd. "These moderate men . . . who supposedly were to inherit a portion of the white man's earth, were put in the intolerable position of resisting Federation because of the absolute hypocrisy of its proclaimed ideals."[42]

In retrospect, Todd was eloquent as to what had happened to him. He recalled in 1963 that "I was unable to persuade the white electorate which had given me power that we had no option but to come quickly to an understanding with our fellow citizens and to share government with them."[43] Looking back later still, in 1970, while confined to his mission station during the Unilateral Declaration of Independence (UDI) period of RF ascendency, Todd spoke to Robert Blake. "How can one expect the Europeans to give up all this when they haven't got to?

Living as we do, all of us here are guilty, but I sometimes think that it is asking for a generation of white saints to hope that they will voluntarily abandon what they hold." As for his rebellious colleagues in 1958: "They were convinced that I would lose them the next election, and they were probably right, you know. I expect we would have lost."[44]

Defiant when confronted by a liberal alternative, Europeans who favored the continuation of White minority rule became ever more intransigent. Their interests, culture, and attitudes resisted interracial cooperation. Most Europeans were set against any meaningful dialogue with Africans—even, ironically, with those Africans who, under their tutelage, had attained "civilized standards" and were still prepared to talk to them. In short, Todd was condemned by his own party for the direction in which he wanted to take them—toward African advancement.

The Cost of Segregation

Bernard Chidzero, an economist who would later serve as finance minister in the government of Zimbabwe, observed in 1960 that "the almost complete lack of intercourse between racial groups remained as it had always been a most serious obstacle to mutual understanding and confidence."[45] This habit of White self-separation, hardened by self-justification over time, arose and persisted from a combination of arrogance, apprehension, and short-sightedness. After World War II, the Southern Rhodesia Federation of Women's Institutes complained that newcomers were in "danger of overfamiliarity" with the Africans.[46] The "danger" was unspecified. Meanwhile, for the most part there was no "familiarity" at all—and that was where the danger lay.

Governments did not make social mixing obstacle free. In 1956, when Doris Lessing tried to visit an old African friend of her youth who now lived in Harari, the African township near Salisbury, she had to apply to the Native Affairs Department for permission. The official told her, "We do not encourage visiting between white and black. . . . Social visits are discouraged, they lead to all sorts of complications."[47] As for the Africans with whom she talked, their conduct did not pass unnoticed, though when they were routinely interviewed, police detectives were evidently more suspicious of the Whites with whom they had been talking than of the Blacks themselves.

The original scale of the disparity of cultures diminished over the years as successive generations of Africans benefited from European schooling and from participation in the colonial economy. But continuing differences were enough to deter incidental familiarity between peoples and, for many Whites, to justify social segregation. The political supremacy of the Whites despite their limited population compared to Blacks may have seemed to be evidence of moral superiority. Even so, the tripod of discriminatory legislation, plus the restricted franchise, were needed to fortify their privileged status and to give their supremacy teeth. A sense of insecurity persisted, evident in the constant search for more and more White immigrants; it was reinforced no doubt by a grudging awareness that White dominance in society and the economy was almost entirely dependent on the labor and continued acquiescence of Africans. Meanwhile, alongside the economic structures and legal framework, the social etiquette was both a consequence and cause of social distancing. In the 1950s, "there were still many whites who found it really offensive to see a fellow white associating, on other than master-and-servant terms, with a black man—a defiance of the proper order of things, irresponsible, dangerous."[48] Even educated Africans of the emerging middle class received neither political nor social acceptance.

The perpetuation of segregation had damaging results. One, arguably, was the fall of Garfield Todd. It was his readiness to talk and listen to African leaders that did much to bring him down. A number of his own ministers strongly believed that European leaders must remain apart to sustain their authority. They objected to the prospect of congress leaders "coming to the government," even to say that they would conform to democratic requirements, in case the prime minister might have a direct discussion with them. For those ministers, Holderness noted, "a personal interview between a member of the Government and any of the 'naughty boys' on the African side of the fence is quite abhorrent."[49] And yet Todd did meet African leaders. One senior colleague, Jack Quinton, by no means a right-wing diehard, complained that Todd "had visited the offices of the African National Congress in Bulawayo regularly."[50] Such critics, it should be stressed, were not Todd's implacable political rivals in, say, the Dominion Party, but colleagues within his own party.

Yet the most damaging outcome of segregation in all its forms was that Whites failed to detect or acknowledge the mood of those they had long ago vanquished. In particular, they did not sense the reality of African resentment. Because they knew and understood so little, it was easy for Whites to label African critics dismissively as half-baked socialists or committed communists—in either case, tools of outside forces—when in fact their complaints arose from daily life within a society that discriminated against them and in innumerable ways denied them dignity. With characteristic earnestness and humanity, Tredgold could write: "I firmly believe that if the average decent white Rhodesian could be made aware of a tithe of the misery and distress these policies cause he would himself reject them peremptorily."[51] Patrick Keatley perceived that "the average white Rhodesian cannot get inside the skin of his black neighbours to feel just how deeply all the indignities penetrate, from second-class taxis and second class prices for their maize, to second class votes in the polling booth (if they have any vote at all)."[52]

The denial of dignity became insufferable. Doris Lessing describes a visit to a vegetable shop in 1956. She stood in line behind two African men. "The woman behind the counter eyed the Africans coldly, and then in a cool curt voice I know so well said 'Can't you see the white missus, boy? Get to the back." Lessing continues: "And for the thousandth time I tried to put myself in the place of people who are subjected to this treatment every day of their lives. But I can't imagine it: the isolated incident, yes; but not the cumulative effect, year after year, every time an African meets a white person, the special tone of voice, the gesture of impatience, the contempt."[53]

There were numerous individual exceptions. As we have seen, some well-intentioned White liberals did talk to Africans and sought to end discrimination and their exclusion from political life gradually. They challenged the prevailing consensus in Southern Rhodesia on race relations and political relationships. Social life in Bulawayo and Salisbury being on the scale it was, in the 1950s such men had an influence on government thinking. Indeed, Todd was among their number. But their experiences and views, and their imagining of a different future, had nothing in common with most of the thousands of White immigrants pouring into the country at that time or indeed with most of the prominent men in positions of power. The absence of normal social contact and hence of genuine dialogue proved damaging at every level in Southern Rhodesia, from housewife to cabinet minister. Without knowledge and understanding of how Africans lived, or what they thought and hoped for, Europeans fostered false fear—and false hope too. For the most part it was fear of people conventionally regarded as unreliable and uncivilized. But alongside the proliferation of negative images there could also be a blithe assumption that most Africans were fully contented and that Black critics of the White regime were mere agitators who did not voice the grievances and resentments of the common man of town or country.

African National Congress Reborn

The definitive revival of Southern Rhodesia's ANC in 1957 came from a merger of Salisbury's CYL with the Bulawayo branch of the preexisting ANC. Members of the CYL tended to dismiss individuals among the African educated elite who were associated with the IA and the CAS as "tea-drinkers." They despaired of any progress through the qualified common roll and sought instead a universal franchise. In August 1956, the CYL made an impact by organizing a bus boycott in Salisbury against the raising of bus fares that, after three days of empty buses, succeeded in getting them reduced. The Bulawayo ANC had only forty members (including Joshua Nkomo). But from this embryonic coalition a new congress was able to bring together under one umbrella aggrieved and frustrated Africans of all classes and backgrounds, and to provide for them new purpose and belief. Nothing better signified the shedding of former deference than their choosing to announce their renaissance on September 12: Occupation Day, belatedly renamed Pioneer Day, a day on which the settlers continued to honor the White invaders of 1890.

Though this timing might have appeared provocative, and the new organization itself somehow a threat to White society, both its president, Joshua Nkomo, and its program were moderate. This tone partly arose from the need of the CYL's radicals, such as James Chikerema, to win over and incorporate the elite. Here the leadership of Nkomo was critical, since he was a seasoned nationalist of moderate temperament and a man whose own education enabled him to establish himself among some of his fellow African graduates. The ANC's stated goal was a multiracial society of equals and, although the CAF was failing to live up to its own rhetoric, a future political system genuinely committed to inclusion of the African majority. The ANC manifesto was not racialist or anti-White or inflammatory. It was gradualist. It did not insist on overnight transformation, but it did envision a society in which the races became increasingly integrated. Teasingly echoing the language of the CAF, it claimed that peaceful progress in the country was possible only through "partnership between people of all races." The real danger to future stability in Southern Rhodesia, it argued, was in denying most of its people the vote, not in extending the franchise.

Guy Clutton-Brock, who had helped draft the manifesto, stressed that it contained no hint of socialism, let alone communism. Rather, its demand was "to share justly in the capitalism which prevailed." Despite the other standard criticism by the colony's Whites (many of whom could not accept that the society they had built could alienate the African majority), it owed nothing at all to outside influences. This was Southern Rhodesia's own "movement of the unprivileged and unenfranchised," and it was led mainly by Christians educated in mission schools. Clutton-Brock added mischievously that at this stage congress had no need to be violent, for "when the houseboys walk back to their land, leaving the colonists' breakfast uncooked and their pants unwashed, the revolution will have come overnight."[54] It seems likely, meanwhile, that at this point a commitment to nonviolence reflected a continuing hope that Britain would intervene on behalf of the Africans in their struggle.

After half a century, the social ingredients for a mass movement of national opposition to White rule were coming together: landless youth, workers, peasant farmers, and rural traders, along with disillusioned and frustrated professionals and businessmen. Educated Africans had been typically accommodating in their political stance initially, but they were pushed toward more radical positions first by the indifference and later by the open hostility of the bulk of the governing White caste. The rural masses helped to propel the nationalist movement at this time. Far beyond the towns, bulldozers moved in to evict at least 100,000 Africans from "European" land between 1945 and 1955 to make space for new White immigrants. These unfortunate farmers were transported into the reserves, where implementation of the Land Husbandry Act was provoking widespread opposition, or into inhospitable and tsetse-ridden unassigned areas. Moreover, by the end of the 1950s women, who had so far played little part in the narrative of African protest, were beginning to be more active in support of the nationalist movement. By the early 1960s, women would be participating in sit-ins and courting arrest by defying discriminatory laws.

The reemergence of the ANC marked not merely another stage in the development of African opposition but a qualitative change in coherence and support. Within a year Nkomo would claim 170,000 members: possibly an exaggeration, but there was no doubting the groundswell. At its heart lay the two abiding issues of land and votes. Capitalizing on the ongoing implementation of the Land Husbandry Act, congress gained many supporters in the reserves. Although Africans came into ownership of property in the reserves, only land owned in their native purchase areas enabled Africans to qualify for the vote. George Nyandoro, the general secretary for Southern Rhodesia's ANC, called the Land Husbandry Act "the best recruiter" that congress ever had.[55]

Yet, as the ANC's manifesto put it, "the franchise laws intended to bar Africans from participating in government are the chief cause of our suffering." In this same year (1957), the Tredgold reforms brought only an additional few thousand onto the common roll. The fall of Todd shortly afterward was a blessing in disguise for congress. The panicky internal party coup that toppled Todd was unmistakeable evidence of the direction the Whites were choosing to take. The inflammatory language adopted by White reactionaries opposed to Todd, "the alpha-champions of white Rhodesia, always a loquacious assemblage with a penchant for hyperbole," only seemed to confirm that multiracial compromise was an illusion, and so strengthened the cause of radical African nationalists.[56]

Even so, in these critical years not all Black Southern Rhodesians became committed to the African nationalist movement. Not all were politically conscious, let alone politically active. Personal security could be regarded as more important than political freedom. Many who had some stake in the system preferred a form of "good government" to the uncertainties of self-government. Todd probably identified some of these when he proudly observed, in 1957, that there were 60,000 Africans employed in secondary industry.[57] For the individual and his family, the current security of a job in business or a post in the civil service, albeit under a White minority regime, was acceptable and not intolerable. Moreover, the long-established institutionalization of White power was more than enough to sustain the status quo among the more cautious. Furthermore, no doubt some Africans hoped, still, that the qualified liberalism that Todd's successor, Edgar Whitehead, seemed to favor might steer the country toward a meaningful future partnership. There was, in short, potential African endorsement of a conciliatory, reforming White administration. For the time being, though, Africans were united in wanting an end to the color bar and to be treated with respect. In 1957, congress placed "the attainment of human dignity" first on its list of objectives. Nothing was more corrosive of relations between White and Black than nonacceptance by the former of the latter as human beings of equal worth. Nkomo reports that even in the 1950s, Africans "were treated as children and expected to behave like children."[58]

The system could appear ridiculous as well as degrading. When in 1954, Herbert Chitepo, a Black mission-educated Southern Rhodesian who had studied law in South Africa, wished to work as a barrister in Salisbury, an amendment had to be grafted on to the Land Apportionment Act to allow him to live and work in the White man's capital.

Eight years later, still the sole Black barrister practicing in the country, he chose exile and became director of public prosecutions in independent Tanganyika. He later explained his departure. "Partnership" had failed, he wrote, not only in parliament and in industry "but in the shops, on the staircases, and at office counters where someone denied to the African his essential dignity as a person and violated his sense of justice and self-respect." Chitepo himself had been so humiliated: he had been required in office buildings in Salisbury not to use the lift or the stairs but the fire escape, the proper place for "boys."[59] Even at work he had been humbled: on one occasion he was required by a Native Commissioner (NC) to conduct his defense of an African accused of breaking the Land Husbandry Act while sitting cross-legged on the floor.

And here was nothing new. In 1942, Samkange had turned on a senior, paternalist White Methodist with the words: "It is time that you should regard some of us as grown up people."[60] For Samkange, this was a moral issue, and within a decade the values he stood for, nourished by the Christianity he had acquired from the White man, were helping to define the moral challenge to the continuation of the White man's privilege and power. Deep resentment lay below the perennial etiquette of courtesy: resentment enough in due course to fuel a war of liberation in the 1970s after Ian Smith and the RF chose reaction over progress and to consolidate White supremacy.

Hardening Attitudes

During the 1950s, most Whites resented and resisted the many winds of change: the circulation of new ideas since World War II; the global push toward decolonization; the articulation by White liberals of a different approach to race relations; the growing number of Africans and, in spite of new immigration, a shift in the ratio of races in the territory; the evidence of African dissent in towns and country and the emergence of African nationalism as a political force; the CAF's failure to answer any of the questions facing the peoples of Southern Rhodesia; and the need to consider an alternative politics with which to seek independence from Britain. Meanwhile, they noted the decisive shift to an intensifying apartheid in South Africa. For many Southern Rhodesian Whites, South Africa's consolidation of White racial supremacy was preferable to taking untested steps toward desegregation and nonracial meritocracy.

There were major questions to be settled by White settlers who, for the most part, were not inclined to dwell on great matters of state or morality but simply wanted to continue to enjoy their "Rhodesian way of life."

There was a keen sense among Whites that the emergence of the ANC in 1957 marked a disagreeably crucial moment. Most, including some senior government ministers, saw the congress as deplorable and labeled Clutton-Brock an agitator. The police followed the ANC's every move. It was soon banned under the state of emergency in February 1959. But if the ban was intended to stem African political activity, it failed. Congress was reborn on January 1, 1960, rechristened as the National Democratic Party (NDP). Attracting increasing numbers of educated Africans, the NDP gave organizational shape to, and articulated, African demands for all but two years. These demands encapsulated a new ambition. The NDP interim president (before Nkomo succeeded him) was Leopold Takawira, secondary school headmaster, who had no record of extremism. Yet it was he who succinctly stated the position at last adopted by politically conscious Africans across the territory: "We are no longer asking Europeans to rule us well. We want to rule ourselves."[61]

How were Whites to respond? Changing social attitudes in the rest of the world, as well as within the colony, were generally dismissed as both misguided and irrelevant. For the majority of Whites in Southern Rhodesia, challenges to their accustomed certainties served to harden outlooks, not to change them. Theirs was a life of privilege and power which they (or their parents) had quite deliberately chosen. Sustaining it became a commitment, at least for the foreseeable future. Loss of status from the advancement of uncivilized African masses was to be resisted; voluntary relinquishment was not to be countenanced.

In retrospect, the most fascinating individual Whites were not the diehard racists or even the committed White liberals, but rather those more complicated—albeit unexceptional—men and woman who defy simple categorization. John Gunther was a perceptive observer of this generation of Whites. "One should not think that Rhodesia is populated by monsters," he advised his readers in 1955. His comments conveyed remarkable understanding, even leniency. "There are, no doubt, honest English people," he wrote, "who have a sentimental attachment to Rhodesia, and for that matter honest Rhodesians who have no basis of comparison with other countries and who are blind to what is happening under their noses—ignorant of the fact that racial discriminations in Rhodesia are among the most barbarous, shameful and disgusting in the world."

Gunther seizes on the heart of the matter with "no basis of comparison with other countries" and "ignorant." The minds of many Whites were closed to any reconsideration of what they had so long taken for granted.[62] Nor, despite his disparate views, was Tredgold entirely unsympathetic toward them. "The majority of Europeans accepted the fact that African advancement had to come," he wrote. "At the back of their minds they knew what was the right thing to do, but they could not bring themselves to face the risks involved." This being the case, "the European electorate insisted on playing for safety, or at least their political leaders thought they insisted, and shaped their courses accordingly."[63]

But how do we explain Major H. G. Mundy? Hardwicke Holderness, a central figure in the newly formed IA, wrote in his 1954 election manifesto: "We have a wonderful combination of resources in this country, but I believe that abundance and harmony can only be achieved if individual people who are capable of taking an interest in national affairs work together, irrespective of race, to examine the problems and find solutions for them." After reading this, Holderness tells us, Major Mundy, an "impeccable senior civil servant living with his severe wife in a gloomy, immaculate residence not far from Government House," wrote to him. "If you are to win the seat, your statements of policy must be more explicit and less equivocal," Mundy advised. "I suggest you declare yourself in favour of the purity of the white race in Southern Rhodesia and opposed to inter-marriage between Whites and Coloureds or Africans, and equally of course against illicit intercourse between Whites and the darker races." Holderness's response was to ask the question: "How could it be that, within ten years of Hitler and Goebbels still emitting their poison about racial purity, someone like Mundy—*who was really a nice man and very kind* to me in the end—could bring himself to talk about the maintenance of the purity of the White race?" Mundy was clearly not what Gunther would have termed a "monster": rather, here was someone who was both "a nice man" and a diehard racist.[64]

Perhaps Southern Rhodesia was doomed by its origins—conquest and land alienation, discrimination, and subjection—and irreversibly damaged by the near total authority acquired in 1923, which the White minority as a whole could not contemplate giving up. Nor did they feel a need to, as long as new settlers arrived. As noted above, the size of the White community doubled in the late 1940s and the 1950. Newcomers were attracted by the promise of a privileged lifestyle that depended on the continued subjection of the Black African majority. That is what they sought to preserve through the ballot box, as did older generations. Immigrants knew what they wanted, and for most it was not to be bit players in a political experiment that threatened their economic and social prospects or their political power . . . especially when concessions to African nationalists elsewhere on the continent were having alarming consequences.

Successive White governments depended on the votes of a spectrum of White opinions, from liberal to diehard; but by the late 1950s the latter strongly outweighed the former. The Dominion Party stood further to the right, poised to sweep up the votes of any electors alarmed by the pace and direction of Todd-inspired change. On November 30, 1957, St. Andrew's Day, Todd had addressed his party and, under growing political pressure, adopted a position critical of the African nationalists (in a speech he later regretted); but that was not enough to reassure his colleagues, let alone the bulk of the White electorate. Indeed, how could any European politician retain the confidence of both Whites and Blacks in such a society? The Whites were determined to veer right. Todd, regarded by his supporters and by his critics as the only man who had any chance at all to steer the Whites and Blacks of Southern Rhodesia toward a multiracial polity, demonstrated through his personal fate the somber reality that, without an improbable shift of White hearts and minds, it could not have been otherwise.

Whites in the colony were fully aware of historic events occurring in South Africa at this time. Their longer established and most powerful neighbor was comparable in key respects. Its influence on Southern Rhodesia's settlers, many of whom had origins in South Africa, was enormous. Even before the birth of the CAF in 1953, and Todd succeeding Huggins as Southern Rhodesia's premier, South Africa's Whites had made their strategic political choice. The victory of D. F. Malan, his National Party, and the ideology of apartheid occurred in May 1948. This movement could not have been more out of step with the global postwar re-enlightenment that led to the UN Universal Declaration on Human Rights six months later. In defiance of that liberal agenda, a cascade of discriminatory legislation followed in South Africa. In 1950 alone arose the Group Areas Act, which crystallized urban segregation, and the "hideously cruel" Population Registration Act, which required every individual to be bureaucratically differentiated on racial lines.[65]

In the first year of Todd's premiership, 1953, the Bantu Education Act prescribed a vocational syllabus for Black children in South Africa and led to the segregation of university education, a move with which the imminent founding of the University College in Salisbury would be very much out of step. This was not the only divergence: Todd's very tentative steps to widen the franchise in Southern Rhodesia took place in the wake of colored people being removed from the Cape Province common roll and so deprived of the franchise. Nonetheless, there were Whites in South Africa who opposed the new racist orthodoxy. In 1955, they joined men and women of all races at a congress of the people, no doubt inspiring liberals to the north, across the Limpopo. This produced the Freedom Charter, which insisted that South Africa belonged to all its peoples, irrespective of color.

There was no shaking the governing party, however, and the enduring commitment of White South Africa to racist intransigence was marked in the general election of April 1958. The National Party won again, this time under the uncompromising White supremacist J. G. Strijdom, who had succeeded Malan. This emphatic confirmation of the direction South Africa was taking (and would take for the next three decades) preceded the election in Southern Rhodesia by just two months, which saw the far-right Dominion Party secure more first-preference votes than the party that Todd had, until recently, led. Chief Albert Luthuli described that time in South Africa as having witnessed "further cleavage between South Africans who stood for two opposed ways of life." He might have been describing the Whites in Southern Rhodesia; and he was echoing Black opinion in the colony when he went on to write (in 1962): "Perhaps foolishly we have never quite abandoned hope for the whites. But I think that very little *reasoned* hope survived the year 1957."[66]

There is more to the South Africa dimension than parallels and influences. The moral debate there—or rather the clash of values that persisted through the 1950s, after the Whites had collectively nailed their colors—was not only starker than in Southern Rhodesia but also more widely publicized. There can have been few observers in the West, at least, who were not aware of it and, recognizing its global significance, taking sides. In turn, the Whites of Southern Rhodesia could not eventually have become more aware, given the context of developments in their great southern neighbor, that they were themselves at a comparable point where historic choices had to be made. As would be the case with the newly emergent African states, South Africa stood either as a warning or as an inspiration. Notwithstanding some misgivings, for most White settlers in the self-governing colony, policies of the regime to the south were considered to be on the right lines.

* * *

In the late 1950s, the prejudices and privileges of the more reactionary Whites in Southern Rhodesia were openly challenged. They were subjected to reasoned criticism from liberals, within the colony and beyond, who had an alternative, progressive vision of the future. However, the diehards did not yield to the moral force of objections raised against them; they consolidated their power, and it was they who determined the colony's future course. By contrast, liberals were guided by the emerging new global consensus. At the end of a pivotal decade and in response to the emergence of African nationalism, the White settler government would pass a Law and Order (Maintenance) Act. Tredgold, chief Jjstice of the CAF, reacted strongly against it and resigned. He agreed with those who labeled it vicious and hysterical and himself termed it "an anthology of horrors." "It almost appeared," he later recalled, "as though someone had sat down with the Declaration of Human Rights and deliberately scrubbed out each in turn."[67]

The modest franchise reform introduced in 1957 serviced only one election, held under a new prime minister, Edgar Whitehead. His United Federal Party (UFP) narrowly saw off the Dominion Party and retained power in June 1958. For this election, Todd led a small alternative party, its slogan "Forward without Fear." Though its third place "represented the high-water mark in Rhodesian-style liberal politics," it won no more than 12 percent of first preference votes cast.[68] But there was nothing conclusive about Whitehead's victory. By the end of the decade, it was becoming clear that a major strategic choice still lay ahead, should the CAF collapse. If Northern Rhodesia and Nyasaland were to be allowed to leave in giant steps toward their independence, the Whites of Southern Rhodesia, believing that they had earned it over many years, would expect to be granted full independence too.

But on what constitutional basis might independence be conceded by London, reflecting what kind of partnership between the races? As the CAF floundered, there was no avoiding a further review of the Southern Rhodesian constitution and franchise. The outcome would be presented to Britain as the basis for recognizing Rhodesia's independence. But the old dilemma would not go away. A revised constitution would have to give the colony's Whites the assurances they needed; but, to persuade London to let go, it would also have to offer Africans greater political participation and the prospect, albeit distant, of power. As we see in the next chapter, arguments about this next constitution of 1961 would expose widening differences between the races. But more significant would be continuing differences among the Whites, and in this arena the defiant hardening of attitudes proved irreversible. In retrospect, there was something prophetic in what Todd had said in 1957, that "we were in danger of becoming a race of fear-ridden neurotics."[69]

Notes

1. Gunther, *Inside Africa*, 620–621.
2. Hancock, *White Liberals*, 17.
3. Quoted in Bowman, *Politics*, 32.
4. Quoted in Gray, *The Two Nations*, 310.
5. Quoted in Woodhouse, *Garfield Todd*, 111.
6. Smith, *Betrayal*, 35.
7. Quoted in Casey, *The Rhetoric*, 3.
8. Joshua Nkomo, quoted in Casey, *The Rhetoric*, 93.
9. Quoted in Woodhouse, *Garfield Todd*, 322.
10. Quoted in Woodhouse, *Garfield Todd*, 118–119.
11. Quoted in N. Sithole, *African Nationalism*, v.
12. Quoted in West, *The Making of an African Middle Class*, 193.
13. Hancock, *White Liberals*, 50.
14. Holderness, *Lost Chance*, 167.
15. Quoted in Keatley, *The Politics of Partnership*, 293. Italics added.
16. Tredgold, *My Life*, 150.
17. Tredgold, *My Life*, 159.
18. Quoted in Woodhouse, *Garfield Todd*, 204.
19. Quoted in Woodhouse, *Garfield Todd*, 150.
20. Quoted in Woodhouse, *Garfield Todd*, 208.
21. Quoted in Woodhouse, *Garfield Todd*, 364, 415.
22. Tredgold, *My Life*, 213. Italics added.
23. From the Report, in Tredgold, *My Life*, 216.
24. Tredgold, *My Life*, 218.
25. N. Sithole, *African Nationalism*, 126.
26. Lessing, *Going Home*, 188.
27. Quoted in Clutton-Brock, *Cold Comfort*, 74.
28. N. Sithole, *African Nationalism*, 128.
29. N. Sithole, *African Nationalism*, 100.
30. Leys, *European Politics*, 220. Italics added.
31. Holderness, *Lost Chance*, 176.
32. Quoted in Woodhouse, *Garfield Todd*, 118. Italics added.
33. Lessing, *Going Home*, 92, 93.
34. Quoted in Clutton-Brock, *Cold Comfort*, 96.
35. Shamuyarira, *Crisis*, 119.
36. Gray, *The Two Nations*, 274.
37. Clutton-Brock, *Cold Comfort*, 81.
38. Quoted in Shamuyarira, *Crisis*, 24.
39. Quoted in Blake, *A History of Rhodesia*, 310.
40. Tredgold, *My Life*, 226.
41. Bowman, *Politics*, 32.
42. Verrier, *The Road to Zimbabwe*, 90.
43. Quoted in Woodhouse, *Garfield Todd*, 278.
44. Quoted in Blake, *A History of Rhodesia*, 317–318.
45. Chidzero, *Good Government*, 174.
46. Quoted in Shutt, *Manners*, 89.
47. Quoted in Lessing, *Going Home*, 78.
48. Holderness, *Lost Chance*, 117.

49. Quoted in Blake, *A History of Rhodesia*, 316.
50. Quoted in Woodhouse, *Garfield Todd*, 245.
51. Tredgold, *My Life*, 159.
52. Keatley, *The Politics of Partnership*, 380.
53. Lessing, *Going Home*, 52.
54. Clutton-Brock, *Cold Comfort*, 80, 112.
55. Quoted in West, *The Making of an African Middle Class*, 215.
56. West, *The Making of an African Middle Class*, 212.
57. Holderness, *Lost Chance*, 196.
58. Nkomo, *My Life*, 46.
59. Keatley, *The Politics of Partnership*, 380.
60. Quoted in Ranger, *Are We Not Also Men*? 9.
61. Quoted in Shamuyarira, *Crisis*, 59.
62. Gunther, *Inside Africa*, 622.
63. Tredgold, *My Life*, 225.
64. Holderness, *Lost Chance*, 128–130. Italics added.
65. Wilson, "Southern Africa" in *Cambridge History of Africa*, 289.
66. Luthuli, *Let My People Go*, 161. Italics in original.
67. Tredgold, *My Life*, 229.
68. Bowman, *Politics*, 31.
69. Quoted in Holderness, *Lost Chance*, 196.

6

Turn to the Right

SUCCEEDING GARFIELD TODD, EDGAR WHITEHEAD CAME TO power in February 1958 by chance and convenience, not charisma. On Southern Rhodesia's White political spectrum, he was a pragmatic moderate. Judith Todd, whose father knew what it was like to be nominally in charge of the course of events, wrote: "Sir Edgar himself quite obviously wished to establish a non-racial state, in his own good time." But there was too little time. He would lose power in 1962. What decided his fate was not his lack of political skill or personal charm, though he had nothing of Todd's rapport with African nationalist leaders. Nor was he in touch with the anxieties of the majority of the White electorate. Whitehead tried to satisfy a spectrum of European and African opinions but, by the start of the 1960s, the gulf between White and Black political expectations could not be bridged. Todd wrote sympathetically that Whitehead "found himself in the impossible position of any white politician in Rhodesia who has to cherish white votes while attempting to make it possible for Africans to take their rightful place in society."[1] Moreover, he had achieved the premiership in debt to the more reactionary elements of his party.

Whitehead's leadership began with an embarrassing and significant setback, which demonstrated how the liberalism he valued was threatened. Having relinquished a post in Washington, DC, he needed a seat in the assembly after his return to Southern Rhodesia to replace Todd as party leader and prime minister. When he stood in a by-election to get one, he lost to a candidate of the Dominion Party, the White nationalists deeply critical of Garfield Todd and of the country's liberal drift. This outcome confirmed "the inner law" of European politics in Southern Rhodesia: that the electoral strategy of any opposition party was to appeal to racial fear, and that the irreversible bias in White politics was to the right.[2] This setback led Whitehead to call the general election of June 1958. He won it, and indeed acquired a seat for himself, this time in a different area of Salisbury.

But the Dominion Party came a very close second overall, signifying that the political weight of White reaction was by now formidable. And supporting the Dominion Party in this election were members of the further-right Confederate Party. The judgment of Eshmael Mlambo is persuasive. A Christian-educated former teacher, graduate of University College Salisbury, one-time political detainee, and from 1971 the African National Congress's (ANC's) representative in Europe, Mlambo identified this election as the one which drew a dividing line between the races. Following the fall of Todd, which a few months earlier had dismayed them, Africans "discovered to their utter horror that the White population was squarely behind the White supremacist leaders. . . . Racial fear, suspicion, tension, hate and unrest increased after the victory of Sir Edgar Whitehead." It was this election, adds Mlambo, that "created a watershed in the relations between black and white" in Southern Rhodesia.[3]

Only by looking outside Southern Rhodesia can we understand the apprehensions that gripped White politics in the territory. Since 1945 great developments in the wider world had had their impact; now momentous changes were taking place in Africa, north of the Rhodesias, which could not be ignored. Indeed, they were not ignored but, rather, adopted by one racial community or another in the territory as illustrations to justify their domestic position. For example, Ghana's achievement of independence in 1957 inspired Black Southern Rhodesians; but as Kwame Nkrumah's regime became more and more dictatorial, it was used as evidence by Whites that Africans were not fit for self-government. Around the same time, Whites were alarmed by the dashing of settler aspirations for the future of Kenya. Still more shocking, the Belgian Congo's abrupt transition to independence led to racial violence and the arrival in Rhodesia of traumatized White refugees. With President Charles De Gaulle at the same time hastening French decolonization across the continent, anxious White Rhodesians saw European powers abandoning their kith and kin to the wayward forces of African nationalism.

Within the Central African Federation (CAF) even closer to home, the Africans of Nyasaland and Northern Rhodesia agitated for secession as a step toward independence. They had opposed this unstable superstructure from the start, and the franchise proposals published at around the same time as Todd's for Southern Rhodesia only alienated them more. By July 1960 there was already an African majority in Nyasaland's legislative council. And October 1960 saw the publication of the Monckton Report in London. This had been established by Harold Macmillan's British government to seek ways of preserving the CAF, but its nuanced report was interpreted by African critics as permission to secede from it. There was no evading the question now: On what grounds might Southern Rhodesia, too, achieve full independence from Britain?

Whitehead's dilemma—how to reassure both Whites and Blacks that his government was serving their interests and in tune with their hopes—throws some light on the contradictory policy initiatives of his period of office up to, including, and after the publication of a new constitution in 1961. Whitehead's government, while in some respects more liberalizing than Todd's, also introduced repressive legislation of unprecedented severity. The strategy appears to have been to appease White opinion by trying to crush African political activity while implementing sufficient reforms to placate Africans and, more urgently, to persuade the British government that the regime could be trusted to make (as an independent state, following the break-up of the CAF) sure progress toward one day fully enfranchising the African majority.

The dominant theme of Whitehead's early years was a further shift to the right. Just twelve months after Todd's fall, on February 26, 1959, Whitehead took the dramatic step of declaring a state of emergency. Was there an emergency? To be sure, Whites were discomfited by the 1957 rebirth of congress, and there was unrest among the African masses in the townships and in some rural areas. Nonetheless, Whitehead himself admitted that he was anticipating trouble rather than responding to any immediate crisis. He acknowledged that "it is a very ancient tradition of the British people that governments should defer action against subversive movements until actual rioting or bloodshed has occurred. My government does not subscribe to that tradition."[4]

Whitehead's approach—that "he would see to it that trouble did not arise"—brought scathing criticism from White liberals. For Robert Tredgold, it was a "dangerous doctrine [which] strikes at the heart of the rule of law."[5] Guy Clutton-Brock judged that "clearly panic prevailed in colonist circles," and "the white man's rule of law was proving a sham."[6] Moreover, before and after he took this step, Whitehead eschewed dialogue with Africans when it was offered. He refused to receive a two-man delegation, George Nyandoro and Robert Chikerema, from the ANC, who were "ready to state their grievances and to outline the views of their followers *and to do so in a civilised way around the table.*" Whitehead declined, explaining that "he was sure he knew already what they would tell him . . . and he believed they were extremists and not really representative of African opinion."[7] Ironically, his drastic and unwarranted initiative did not prevent trouble, it caused it. Under the terms of the state of emergency, congress was banned; but this was the action of an unconfident government, an inept response to African grievances. African nationalism as a movement could not be withstood by such measures. For example, in Tanda, a tribal trust locality in Mashonaland, there had been only 150 fully paid-up members of the ANC; ongoing rural grievances ensured that membership of the National Democratic Party (NDP), which succeeded it, rose to 1,700.

On July 19, 1960, three leading Africans in the NDP were arrested at dawn. When two other NDP leaders led a protest march to a local police station in Salisbury, they asked to be connected by phone to the prime minister, but Whitehead declined to talk. By the time they had marched another eight miles to see him in person, Whitehead was so angered by strikes and demonstrations of African workers that, instead of talking to these spokesmen, he called in the army. This action, following the arrests and presumptions of guilt, sparked the worst riot of the century. Mass protests in Salisbury and Bulawayo led to eleven deaths and scores of arrests. Nyandoro and Chikerema were among the 495 individuals taken from their homes before dawn and imprisoned without charge or trial. A line was crossed in July 1960 with the first instance of direct confrontation and bloodshed in the colony since the revolt of the late 1890s.

These events were laden with tragic irony. They occurred after the state of emergency and in defiance of it. Ultimately, the three arrested NDP leaders were freed. Under the Unlawful Organisations Act, which presumed the accused belonged to an unlawful organization unless they could prove the contrary (the ANC, in this case), the court found that they had no case to answer. Whitehead's aversion to talking with Africans had made the situation worse. He "would not show that he was in any way impressed by the fact that the NDP leaders had kept a crowd, now numbering about 40,000, under strict control for a full day"; rather, he acted on the old rule that a government elected by Whites was expected to be tough with "cheeky natives."[8]

This episode proved to be a public relations disaster on a global scale. On October 11, 1960, Joshua Nkomo, the most prominent and popular African nationalist leader, a moderate who continued to seek a political compromise with the White community, addressed the United Nations in New York. Speaking of the July riots in Salisbury and Bulawayo, he compared the police's use of force against them with the mass shootings by South African security forces earlier that year at Sharpeville. Conscious of the UN's involvement in Central Africa at that time because of the Congo crisis, Nkomo requested the UN to force Britain to intervene in its own colony of Southern Rhodesia and to arrange a constitutional conference which would lead toward power for his people. If they did not, he predicted, there would be race war. Nkomo's initiative was much resented by Whitehead's government and all supporters of the continuation of White minority rule. The Whites in Southern Rhodesia hated the scrutiny of the world beyond its borders. But Nkomo was proved right.

In response to these unprecedented disturbances, Whitehead's government introduced the Law and Order (Maintenance) Act. This had much to do with the pursuit of order and little to do with the rule of law. And it was too much for Tredgold. He resigned as chief justice of the CAF, decrying his country's transformation into a "police state." This act, he later explained, was "not intended as emergency legislation to be invoked in times of national peril. It was to become part of the ordinary law of the land." The act and accompanying legislation were "vicious" and "hysterical."[9] While the act shocked White liberals, it also further alienated Africans: the more so, perhaps, for having been introduced by a government that continued to profess a degree of liberalism. More, not less, violence followed.

An element of ambiguity in Whitehead's administration is captured by its revision of the Industrial Conciliation Act. Introduced in 1934 as part of the tripod of White supremacy, it now took on a liberal, nonracial appearance. For the first time it covered all employees, African as well as European, and allowed for Whites to negotiate terms and conditions with Black workers. But regarding multiracial unions, the minister of labor conceded: "It could be argued that to provide for these associations is nothing more than a control measure and, let me be perfectly frank, it is."[10] The Europeans of Southern Rhodesia needed an acquiescent and biddable African work force. By this measure, Black workers would be absorbed into relatively stable, established unions in which procedures (mirroring political arrangements in the colony) guaranteed continuing European control.

Increasing numbers of White Southern Rhodesians remained uneasy. They had reacted against the liberal inclinations of Todd; following his fall, they were alarmed by some even bolder aspirations of Whitehead's administration. Todd had set up a commission to examine the effects of the Land Apportionment Act on urban Africans. Its report was radical; it recommended, for example, freehold tenure for urban Africans, African representation on some key municipal committees, and the abolition of the pass system. The timing of its publication—February 1958, the month of Todd's fall—torpedoed it.

But it was followed up by a sensational report that had been commissioned by Whitehead himself and was published in 1960. The Quinton Report recommended no less than total repeal of the Land Apportionment Act. It proposed, moreover, that the native reserves should be opened up. The report's author, Jack Quinton, owned and ran four farms, but he could see no future for exclusive White ownership. His report argued that "land in general, whether urban or agricultural, should be purchasable by anyone, anywhere, irrespective of race or colour."[11] This was no mere whim of an unrepresentative radical White minority. These were the unanimous conclusions of a committee comprising not only three cautious members of the governing party, the United Federal Party (UFP), but also two members of the more extreme Dominion Party, who began by being strongly opposed to any such scheme. The Quinton Report "was an unusual example of conversion by weight of evidence."[12]

It was surely an illustration, too, that if far more Whites had the chance to study seriously the prevailing conditions and to reflect without prejudice on the options facing them, they would have come to the same conclusion. In the case of the committee members, knowledge had led to understanding and so to progressive thinking. It seemed very different to most Whites, however. Though in the long term the report's radical strategy could have been to their advantage, it would first have destroyed the status quo. The tripod was being emasculated. One enraged Dominion Party critic expressed the fears of others when he traduced this report as "a sledgehammer blow at European settlement."[13]

Whitehead did indeed propose to amend the act. He released 10 million acres of unoccupied land for African acquisition hitherto reserved exclusively for Europeans. This may be seen, however, less as a liberal gesture than as a pragmatic response to the increasingly pressing land question and to the multiplying grievances it caused. So too was the parallel soft-pedaling on implementation of the Land Husbandry Act. Perhaps all the liberal gestures of Whitehead's administration were trivial—mere gestures that "combined minor modification of long-standing patterns of racial control with public relations efforts to convince Britain of the government's concern for Africans."[14] But for worried Whites, it looked as though the very foundations of their supremacy were being undermined and that the tripod itself could fall. Ian Smith (soon to be prime minister as leader of the Rhodesian Front

[RF]) defended the Land Apportionment Act as essentially a protector of African interests and, with some additional intellectual dexterity, argued that its repeal "would be absolutely catastrophic for our African people."[15] But in the long run, White refusal to allow African farming on European land would prove damaging to their own interests.

The 1961 Constitution and the Death of Compromise

This perpetuation into the new decade of intra-White arguments over the future of White-Black relations was the strangely contradictory, and unsustainable, political background to the promulgation of the 1961 Southern Rhodesia constitution. Here was a government that had not only introduced a state of emergency that alienated Africans but also had shaken confidence among growing numbers of Whites that their long-established political domination was secure. Whitehead could not continue his balancing act for much longer. As prime minister while the CAF was breaking up, he naturally sought independence from Britain, such as was being offered to Nyasaland and Northern Rhodesia. But this could only be achieved legally if the British believed that his government, currently all-White, was committed to making concrete, irreversible steps toward multiracialism and, eventually, majority African rule.

Franchise clauses of the February 1961 constitution would therefore be subject to special scrutiny. Introduced, as it was, by a regime still manned entirely by members of the White minority, its terms, though deliberately open to a range of interpretation, indicated a continuation of White rule, at least (to repeat that phrase much favored by White politicians at the time) for "the foreseeable future." The franchise remained convoluted, but it contained one central feature that distinguished it from its predecessor and signaled a reactionary turn. Two separate electoral rolls replaced the common roll.

The White framers of the constitution did not see it as their business to deprive themselves of power. This was a constitution designed by Whites to maintain White minority rule. To be sure, it could be and was claimed that it would lead to Africans in government "over time," even an African government. But this distant prospect of democracy was shrouded. It would have been odd indeed if the new constitution had ushered in any meaningful partnership or extended the franchise to significantly bring forward the prospect of majority rule. It was a reaction against White liberalism (by now a waning influence), but it was primarily a barricade against rising Black aspirations.

In recognition of Southern Rhodesia's growing population, both White and Black, the national assembly expanded to sixty-five seats (replacing just thirty). Fifty of these would be constituency seats, for which members would be returned by a predominantly White electorate. The remaining fifteen would be district seats, for which members would be returned by an overwhelmingly African electorate. Qualifications resembled those for "ordinary" and "special" voters, now on A and B rolls, from the Todd/Tredgold franchise. The territory was thus divided into two different sets of overlapping voting areas: a number of districts superimposed on a large number of constituencies. Each voter had two votes, one for his constituency and one for his district. In counting the votes, a system of "reciprocal devaluation" operated, which essentially devalued B-roll votes if they exceeded a quarter of A votes cast in a constituency, and vice-versa in the districts. The extension of the franchise was modest: somewhere between 40,000 and 70,000 Africans now qualified—around 4 percent of the adult African population.

This bafflingly complex system was beyond the comprehension of the man in the street, or on the farm, whatever his race. Yet there was enough in the constitution to draw some qualified approval. Fair-minded as ever, Tredgold saw the benefit of predominantly African districts producing fifteen members of parliament (MPs) who were African, but he found no prospect here of African majority rule. Nor did Guy Clutton-Brock, who dismissed a constitution that only "provided for a meritocracy into which a handful of well-fledged Africans could creep."[16] Many years later, David Coltart, a lawyer who believed in justice and who would assume a high political profile as a White liberal during the late Robert Mugabe years, seemed to endorse the 1961 constitution. In his memoir he wrote: "It is ironic that majority rule was only achieved through armed struggle, years after it might have been achieved in terms of the 1961 franchise proposals"; the 1961 constitution "offered a peaceful evolution towards majority rule."[17] But Coltart's interpretation presupposed: first, that the sanguine forecasts of majority rule in "twelve to fifteen years" (made by Whitehead; readily accepted by Britain) were well-founded; second, that increasingly politicized Africans would acquiesce in this possible mirage; and, third, that White hard-liners would not use (or misuse) the amendment clauses in order to tighten their grip on power once the constitution was in place.

The British government approved. In doing so, it acquiesced in the elimination of most, though not quite all, of its reserve powers. It did so in light of not only the modest extension of the franchise but also two novelties: a declaration of rights and a constitutional council. The former would be "ultimately justiciable" by the privy council of the Crown; the latter would have the authority to report discriminatory bills that came before the Southern Rhodesian parliament. But how robust were these measures for safeguarding the interests of the African majority? Judith Todd's verdict was acerbic. In her view, the "pigmentocracy" was being deceitfully perpetuated: the declaration of rights "proved a complete farce," while the constitutional council lacked serious weight through having no power to alter any law already on the statute books (and even its powers regarding new legislation were severely limited).[18]

Among the most critical clauses of any constitution are those which relate to amendment: who has the authority to change it, and by what process? In this respect, too, 1961 was complicated. While in general a two-thirds majority of the whole legislative assembly was all that was needed for a constitutional amendment, there were certain issues, relating to questions such as race relations, that required something in addition: a majority vote in favor by referenda held separately by all four racial groups, as well as the approval of the British government.

Though it remained unclear as to what it betokened, two referenda were held on this new constitution. These highlighted the deepening racial division in the colony. On July 26, 1961, the government held a referendum which, in part because it was boycotted by almost all qualified Africans, produced a conclusive "Yes" vote for Whitehead. For the time being, Whites were reassured. There was a very different result, however, when the NDP held its own unofficial referendum. The reputation of the NDP had wobbled when its leaders, including Nkomo, attended a conference in London on the proposed constitution and, encouraged by some of its terms, shelved the party's commitment to one-man, one-vote. But support was renewed when the NDP elite finally moved away from the pursuit of racial partnership (via the non-racial qualified franchise) to a firm commitment to a universal franchise. Inspired by the civil rights movement in the United States, it now favored direct action such as "freedom sitting" to defy the color bar in the White towns and "freedom farming" in defiance of the Land Husbandry Act in the countryside. In this referendum, just 471 voted "Yes," while 372,546 voted "No."

However, the NDP was not allowed to relish its prominence or this powerful statement for long. A meeting on December 3, 1961, was attended by 15,000–20,000 followers. Their leaders chose this occasion to shed European clothing (shoes, ties, jackets) in a symbolic exercise promoted by Robert Mugabe, publicity secretary of the NDP and head of its activist youth wing. Mugabe had returned to Southern Rhodesia only the previous year, after spending much time abroad, to become active in a nationalist movement that had been radicalized since the proscription of the ANC. But this gathering turned out to be the NDP's last. Six days later, on December 9, the party was banned, despite it being (or perhaps due to it being) a political organization enjoying unparalleled African support. Coincidentally, that was the day of Tanganyika's independence. Congress, the NDP's predecessor, had been banned in the year of Ghana's independence. The achievements of African nationalism elsewhere on the continent had encouraged the movement in Southern Rhodesia; but as these instances illustrated, it was easier for Africans elsewhere to free themselves from direct British metropolitan authority than it was to wrest power in Southern Rhodesia from an entrenched and determined White settler regime.

African opposition was becoming the movement it was earlier unfairly accused of being. As described by one who was present in 1957, the first meeting of the ANC in Salisbury had been "full of humour and optimism as well as condemnation of injustices." The police in attendance witnessed "no grim-faced demagogues or tight-lipped terrorists pouring forth racial hatred." Rather, at that time, "there was the confident though naïve belief that meetings of thousands would impress the colonists with the need for reform."[19] But neither optimism nor naivete could survive a state of emergency and whole-hearted repression. Congress became more confrontational toward the White regime, and at the same time more authoritarian and ruthless in dealing with internal opposition from dissenting Blacks. In this fully equipped police state, it may have had no alternative. Its successor, the NDP, in turn grew increasingly intolerant of Blacks who continued to seek political compromise or who were tamely identifying with the regime on the White man's terms. Demanding obedience and loyalty, it turned to violence against perceived opponents, as the ANC had briefly done, which in turn contributed to its proscription.

Against this background, opportunist White authorities chose to explain the apparent growing support for African nationalism in terms of intimidation. This caused resentment. "No person who came to the nationalist meetings was believed to have come of his own accord," even though the NDP could claim a membership of a quarter of a million; "intimidation" was a flexible term, covering canvassing, distributing leaflets, and "even reminding a neighbour about a meeting."[20] Not all campaigning was so innocent, of course: acts of violence increased, predominantly intra-African. But no race had a monopoly on violence. Police excesses provoked riots in the towns and, less widely reported, in the countryside. Young White thugs adopted their own intimidatory tactics, too.

Just ten days after the NDP was banned, another party of African nationalism came into being, the Zimbabwe African People's Union (ZAPU), with Nkomo as president (albeit initially in his absence, as he was abroad) and Sithole as chairman. This was really congress and the NDP under a new name, but the new name chosen was doubly historic: it proudly recalled the greatest cultural achievement of the region's past, and in doing so it unceremoniously buried "Rhodesia." Cecil Rhodes's grave was secure in the Matopo Hills, but sixty years after his death only White diehards wished to retain his name for the territory he founded.

This African nationalist party was prepared to consider any means of resisting the continuation of White supremacy. In October 1961, shortly before it was proscribed, the NDP had announced a significant new policy: the party declared itself ready "at the appropriate time" to turn to methods of violence. Campaigns that merely targeted the color bar were marginalized. As an African correspondent to the *African Daily News* put it, "Let's forget about this hotel business and get down to the job of getting back our land."[21] To take on this "job," a Zimbabwean Liberation Army (a mere 100 or so men) came into being in September of 1962. For some young African radicals, "the appropriate time" for violence had already arrived. There followed reports to the police of numerous, albeit small-scale cases of looting and arson, the blocking of roads and railways, the cutting of telephone wires, and the bombing of European homes and supermarkets. In addition, by way of resistance to the government's imposition of unpopular farming methods via the Land Husbandry Act, cattle dipping tanks were destroyed. There were attacks on persons, too, mainly the police. Nkomo, who had previously foresworn violence, by this time regarded his people as being under attack. He called these first attempts at the violent overthrow of the White regime "amateurish." But they were enough to worry White farmers into joining the police reserve, as well as to persuade Whitehead's government in late September to ban ZAPU, as it had earlier banned the ANC and then the NDP. This did not save Whitehead's premiership. Meanwhile, those Europeans and educated Africans who had sought interracial political cooperation and compromise were further marginalized.

Southern Rhodesian politics—that is, political exchanges among the White minority that chose every government and determined every policy against a background of growing African discontent—remained distant from the wider world and impervious to its promptings. Even so, the situation in Britain and the personnel of its government throw some extra light on how things turned out in the colony. For the most part, the British government was advocating a transition to majority rule in Southern Rhodesia sooner rather than later. The British prime minister, Harold Macmillan, clearly sympathized with Garfield Todd, who continued to be politically active after his loss of power, telling him in January 1960: "Keep up the good work. You're right, you know."[22] Political realities guided Macmillan too, not least pressure from the UN and from the Commonwealth of Nations . . . all within a Cold War context, wherein sustaining colonial rule would be a self-inflicted public relations wound. But as the British prime minister, Macmillan had little power or authority. Britain had effectively handed over power to the settlers in 1923, and recognized that its reserved powers were theoretical, not real.

The Whites in the colony were determinedly choosing a fork in the road down which there would be no reversing. In 1962 came a punitive tightening of the Law and Order (Maintenance) Act, adding to the already drastic curbs on freedom of speech, movement, and assembly. This prompted the symbolic, headline-grabbing resignation of Jasper Savanhu. A Southern Rhodesian African who had achieved prominence in the CAF administration, Savanhu was regarded with some suspicion by more ardent nationalists. Having been the first president of the Bulawayo African Workers' Trade Union, he became one of two specially elected African members of the first federal parliament in 1953, representing Mashonaland. Some years later, he was appointed the first Black African parliamentary secretary in the federal government. He was thus actively participating in an institution that was dominated by Whites and dedicated to the preservation of White political control. He even accepted humiliation arising from the question of where to house him: the Land Apportionment Act did not allow Savanhu to live in a minister's house in the White Salisbury suburbs, so an expensive house had to be built specially for him in an African township.

By 1962, however, Savanhu had had enough. He decided he could no longer retain his position in the CAF. He resigned. In his letter to Roy Welensky, federal prime minister, he wrote: "Your government, in spite of strong representations from the African party members and other quarters, has failed or has no intention of implementing a policy of partnership." He added, at a subsequent press conference, that "Europeans are quite incapable of treating other races fairly. . . . Southern Rhodesia is on the verge of exploding. I wish to identify myself with the African people."[23] Savanhu did not speak for all Africans, but his individual decision revealed a disturbing wider truth. The 1961 constitution was disguised as a sensible compromise, but it failed to convince even Savanhu, just as it was dismissed by nationalist African leaders who were barred from open political activity. Challenged by progressive forces elsewhere and liberal criticism at home, the Whites of Southern Rhodesia were choosing to move toward defiant isolation.

The December 1962 Election: The Rhodesian Front

The banning of the NDP provoked more country-wide violence and so, by further alarming Whites, contributed to the success of the Rhodesian Front (RF) in the December 1962 election. If Whitehead's negotiating position with the British was difficult, by 1962 his domestic position had become impossible. Taking Whitehead's gestures at face value, Whites were fearful that the tripod on which their supremacy was erected was facing complete dismantlement, and that their minority rule and historic defence of "civilization" was ending. And when, along with others, Whitehead had sat down with Nkomo during an early 1961 constitutional conference in Salisbury, White diehards were shocked. The recently formed Southern Rhodesia Association (soon to combine with the Dominion Party to form the RF) could not countenance a White prime minister trying to resolve differences with African leaders through discussion and negotiation. Whitehead, like his predecessor Todd, may have been persuaded by experience, context, and reason to become more openly progressive during his tenure of office. During the general election campaign at the end of 1962, he wooed African voters with the by now wholly improbable slogan "Build a Nation." But to no avail. The campaign "was a shambles from beginning to end."[24] Though Whitehead predicted that 50,000 Africans would register to vote, just over 10,000 did. Africans were more than skeptical of any concessions reluctantly handed down by a police state; they wanted the substance of political liberation immediately, not in a distant, uncertain future.

When the December 1962 election was held, the overwhelmingly White electorate in Southern Rhodesia sensed that they faced a choice at least as significant as that facing their predecessors forty years earlier at the close of company rule. The result was historic. It came as a surprise and a shock for Whitehead. He lost. The RF won thirty-five seats, and Whitehead's UFP won twenty-nine (including fourteen by their candidates in the "districts"). In fact, the result was remarkably close and, somewhat ironically, was in part a consequence of the low African turnout. It was estimated later that if just 5,000 more B-roll Africans had turned out for Whitehead's party, he would have won and remained in office. Up to a point, it should be noted, his UFP was a multiracial party, embodying partnership. At their November party congress, a third of the delegates were Black. But by this time both the Whites and the Blacks in the UFP had ceased to represent the majority opinion of their respective races. Robert Mugabe's verdict was telling. "Europeans have decided to stand in one camp as our political enemies. We accept the challenge."[25] This was a welcome for confrontation, in that an RF government would hasten the coming of majority rule.

The primary reason for the UFP's defeat was White rejection of its professed promotion of African advancement. Despite the state of emergency and general repression of African political activity, Whitehead's government had proceeded with some reforms and, as we have seen, was toying with the legislative foundations of the tripod. Growing numbers of White voters were thus driven into the arms of the diehards. For their part, the RF, led by Winston Field, campaigned on a program that was not extreme, and there was no public hint that some of its leaders were contemplating a unilateral declaration of independence from Britain. But they did promise a reversal of the direction in which Todd and then Whitehead had been taking the country. In particular, the RF campaigned to retain the Land Apportionment Act of 1930 in full and to stop imposing social integration. It rightly sensed that the core of White opinion was coalescing into a single political goal: to avert any danger of Europeans being ruled by Africans who were "not yet civilized."

Whitehead had underestimated the darkness of the mood of his fellow Whites. RF policies were a populist articulation of the hopes and fears of "ordinary" White Rhodesians from the White working class and a stratum of farmers, rather than members of the Salisbury and Bulawayo Clubs. Pre-election African activity served the RF well: not only calls from African nationalists to boycott the election, but also evidence of an increasing resort to violence (albeit inter-Black, in some townships) as a means of achieving political ends. Robert Blake put the 1962 result into context. After World War II, he wrote, about a third of the European electorate was deemed relatively progressive and a third (including the Afrikaners) reactionary—leaving another third of "floaters." For these, "in 1953 and in 1961 [the referendum on the new constitution] it seemed safe to float on the tide of progress. In 1962, that tide had suddenly begun to ebb."[26] At the very least, reacting against what they regarded as the smugness and complacency of the UFP, White Rhodesians wanted to put the brakes on a rate of African advancement which they deemed far too rapid. As the independent MP Ahrn Palley observed, in Southern Rhodesia's politics, "liberal has come to mean something frightfully fluffy and indecisive."[27]

The new prime minister, Winston Field, had risen to prominence because he stood out. As his admiring biographer put it, "In a small population of around 230,000, men of ability were soon noticed."[28] Robert Blake was unsympathetic to Field and his like, asserting that they led the life "as nearly as it could be led a century later, of the planter aristocracy in Virginia and Kentucky."[29] But this was no aristocrat. Sent to Southern Rhodesia in 1921 at the age of sixteen when his formal education ended, Field had to work hard to learn farming, to acquire his own farm, and to become president of the Rhodesia Tobacco Association. After distinguished service in Europe during World War II, he returned to Southern Rhodesia. He did not enjoy town life or seek political power. But in 1952 he joined the Rhodesia Party, which was opposed to the CAF for not prioritizing European interests; and, later in the decade, he joined the White-supremacist Dominion Party. His independent-mindedness, personal integrity, and sense of duty won him respect and support among numerous fellow Whites fearful for the future. His forthright views were in accord with many, founded on his interwar experience within the inescapably racist context of a settler colony. "Certainly, there is a duty to Central Africa's more primitive inhabitants," he once told the federal parliament. "But there is also a debt to the more developed and better equipped and more enterprising minority who also made their homes in a wilderness, but who changed that wilderness into a productive society."[30] In short, "he sought the preservation of the future of the White man in Rhodesia."[31]

The RF was a new party, an amalgamation of a group that had coalesced around Ian Smith, plus members of the Dominion Party, including Winston Field, which had run Edgar Whitehead so close in 1958. Two clauses of the Dominion Party program at that time are particularly striking. First, it proposed an amended franchise for Africans who wanted a vote on the common roll that was astonishingly complex and demanding, even in this territory with its history of political racial exclusiveness. It entailed testimonials, referees, and interviews. The process resembled that of applying for a job. Conversely, all Europeans would be assumed to be "liberal, tolerant, fair-minded and reasonable," and thus would qualify automatically. Second, it stressed "the absolute necessity for large-scale immigration, which shall be confined to Europeans." Boldly (if somewhat unrealistically) it looked to a total population for Southern Rhodesia, by the year 2000, of forty to sixty million, a full half of whom would be European. Dominion Party thinking lived on in the RF.

There was a case to be made for increasing White immigration, and it was put most coherently by the academic Lewis Gann at this time. He unapologetically praised the contributions that White settlers had made in Central Africa: transforming the territories they colonized and transforming the opportunities of Africans among whom they lived. He took up the argument the imperial government had made since World War II, that considerable further economic development and class formation was a prerequisite for handing political power to the Africans in such a way as to ensure both economic and political viability. Until now, he emphasized, Europeans supplied "all the plans, the skill, and the capital." The mines, the railways, and the tobacco barns were not "things which the White man stole away from the Africans." Moreover, the European "imports his skill and training as permanent assets for which his homeland has paid. . . . The settler, in other words, acts as a social yeast in regions in which development has been held back by disease, malnutrition, poverty and tribalism."[32] It was entirely reasonable to encourage more immigration, he insisted; and this would not happen, he added, unless the colony remained congenial, offering the incoming Whites a high standard of living and political security.

But such a reasoned economic argument ignored political reality and especially racial sensibility. By the time Gann was writing in 1962, racial attitudes, not economic projections, were determining the outcome. Social distancing from their own African people at home, along with alarm bells rung by political developments elsewhere in the continent, steered the majority of Whites toward more segregation and racial dominance, not less. The colony's Africans in turn resented ever more strongly the daily indignities of racial discrimination that appeared to harden with every influx of Whites.

In Rhodesia, the RF case was at heart racist, especially regarding social integration. Their political advertising for the previous year's election had included posters, some showing the legs of schoolgirls, both Black and White, mingling; others asked, "Do you want a mutt as your neighbour?" The September 1963 party congress revealed its nature. There were many expressions of hostility toward the (more liberal) White media, and the (multiracial) University College was condemned as a center of subversion. RF delegates self-righteously equated criticism of their program with treachery to the country. Clutton-Brock's informed and withering contemporary view of the RF is worth quoting at length:

> A tough and cynical minority forms the hard core of the Rhodesia Front. . . . Determined to retain control of the country and exploit its people and resources, they spread the philosophy of the master race and promote the practice of racism. Behind this perverted handful, most ordinary colonists fall in, not because they wish to emulate them

but . . . for want of seeing a better alternative. Moved by the fear of losing their substantial gains, they huddle together as Whites in self-defence. Looking ever inwards, they remain unconscious of surrounding Africa and the world, following thoughtlessly the Rhodesia Front lead. African people are seen as a threat to be denigrated to justify suppression. . . . The Rhodesia Front colonist sees himself as one of a gallant band of cultured puritans, holding high the standard of western Christian civilization in a perverted and permissive world. . . . Otherwise normal people become neurotic and hypersensitive, unable to meet the inevitable demand for majority rule with constructive thought or action.[33]

In reaction to opinions such as Clutton-Brock's, the RF newspaper, *Newsfront,* asserted in May 1964 that "our main enemy is reeking run-to-seed liberalism." Government minister P. K. van der Byl proclaimed: "We are in a war as much as in 1939–1945, a much more dangerous war because it is directed against us." Shortly afterward, the government imposed complete censorship on every newspaper in the country.[34]

This authoritarian act was typically myopic. If White Southern Rhodesians, of whatever status, had been curious about what Africans were actually thinking, up to this point they could have read the *African Daily News.* But they chose not to. The story of this newspaper in the early 1960s is most instructive. It was a respected publication, acquired in 1962 by the Canadian magnate Lord Thomson of Fleet. Previously a paper that had played it safe—ready to condemn African nationalist leaders as "extremist," for example—it changed its editorial tune during the state of emergency years. In early 1964 it threw its full weight behind Joshua Nkomo and his party of African nationalism. By the time it was banned in August 1964, its circulation among educated, English-speaking Africans was around 15,000. To justify the ban, the RF government accused the paper of inciting subversion. But "the real reason was that it had become the voice of the voiceless masses, which the government did not want to hear."[35] This paper had some claim to represent African opinion. While it was bitterly critical of the RF government, it steadfastly and outspokenly set its face against any forms of subversion, violence, or any other unlawful activity. "I believe," wrote Tredgold, "that any fair-minded person who read through the files of this newspaper would be convinced that there was nothing in them justifying the ban, except that it expressed views that were contrary to those of the government."[36]

Fair-minded or otherwise, White people just would not buy the newspaper, even when its circulation manager positioned vendors at street corners in central (that is, White man's) Salisbury. Patrick Keatley, as a foreign correspondent, had no choice but to buy copies of this

African mouthpiece. "We *have* to know what the Africans are saying and thinking," he wrote. "The settler, up to now, has decided that *he* does not." The White minority did not want to know, Keatley despaired. "Blinding settler ignorance of the black world all around," he concluded, "is one of the most profound impressions awaiting a visitor to Central Africa."[37] As Trevor Huddleston had written of a comparable situation in South Africa: "The greatest tragedy of the present situation is the total ignorance of those in responsible positions of government of the way in which young Africa thinks, talks and lives."[38]

A tragicomic incident arose from this episode. Judith Todd recalled what happened when she and some other students, mainly African, were arrested and put on trial for protesting against the RF's banning of the *African Daily News:*

> An official was summoned to the witness stand.
> The magistrate asked him, "Why did you confiscate the placards?"
> WITNESS: "Because they were subversive, Your Worship."
> MAGISTRATE: "Did you see any of them before you seized them?"
> WITNESS: "Yes, I did."
> MAGISTRATE: "What made you think they were subversive?"
> WITNESS: "Because they had words like Freedom and Justice on them, Your Worship."
> The Court was called to order.[39]

When the RF was holding a rally, "civilized values" were mentioned but not always practiced. With several other students, Judith Todd attended a large meeting of the RF later that same year. "Mr. Smith's speech was the usual cottage pie of 'maintaining standards,' 'protecting our civilised heritage,' 'getting independence,' and so on."[40] The era of civilized control in Rhodesia would last for all time, he informed his audience, if they maintained their standards. But when Todd or another student tried to ask a question, they were shouted at and physically attacked. After the crowd had quieted down, Smith smiled and said of the students: "They just don't understand the meaning of civilised standards."[41] And we have more than Judith Todd's word for it. *The Chronicle* newspaper reported damningly on that incident and went on to question whether civilized standards were being maintained by "the lunatic fringe of the Rhodesian Front."[42] There was an uncrossable gap between what Whites professed and what they did.

Once in power, the party started to reverse some of Todd's policies. Changes in education were in the spirit of the Dominion Party's 1956 program, which had proposed that, for Africans, "training in honesty, loyalty, responsibility, hygiene, and vocational courses" should be of primary importance. The RF cut back spending on African schools at a time when White children throughout the CAF had £103 per head spent on them annually. Africans in Southern Rhodesia had only £8. And fees were introduced for the first time: too high for poor Black workers, so the number of Black children attending school declined. Commenting on this many years later, a one-time minister of education in independent Zimbabwe wrote that "no policy could have had a more deleterious effect on the way the Rhodesian Front was viewed by black people than this one."[43]

Toward Unilateral Declaration of Independence

The RF's priority was to bring about a relationship with Britain through which it could legitimately reverse the trend of recent developments and secure White domination for the indefinite future. It had won support from those Whites who, while having endorsed the draft constitution in a referendum in July 1961 (as bringing independence within reach), were shocked to find that the constitution formally approved in Britain in December of that year still reserved "full power and authority" for the Crown in matters concerning the judiciary and the franchise. Moreover, while many clauses of the 1961 constitution could be changed by a simple two-thirds majority vote of MPs, removal of these sensitive entrenched sections would also need confirmation in referenda for all races and the Crown's consent.

While Winston Field was negotiating with the British for full independence, his RF government sought to suppress increasingly assertive African political opposition, which was taking on new forms. In August 1963, African nationalism in Southern Rhodesia suffered an enduring split. Ndabaningi Sithole founded the Zimbabwe African National Union (ZANU) after being suspended by Nkomo from his leadership role within ZAPU. Others had been suspended, such as Leopold Takawira, who became ZANU's vice president, and Robert Mugabe, its secretary-general. A Christian former teacher, Sithole was not an extremist. His recently published *African Nationalism* had been a measured summary of how and why the movement had emerged across the continent. But like numerous other moderates, he was eventually driven by White intransigence into illegal opposition politics, and now into political factionalism.

At heart, this split was not primarily "tribal" but rather reflected "an elite split over leadership and unmet expectations."[44] Clutton-Brock, who had been closely involved with the congress, recognized at the outset a potential, rather than a present, danger when he wrote that "tribal differences were not significant, but a balance was maintained in the hierarchy." Eshmael Mlambo observed subsequently, in 1972, that "tribal differences are not a major factor among Rhodesian Africans," and that "the internecine rivalry" outburst between ZANU and ZAPU between 1963 and 1964 had been short-lived and largely confined to Salisbury townships.[45] Masipula Sithole, Ndabaningi's brother and an informed insider, who much later lamented that the 1970s liberation struggle had been "torn apart by tribalism and regionalism," makes no mention of ethnic rivalry in his detailed account of the early 1960s, even as a factor in those "horrible and murderous" events in Salisbury.[46] To be sure, ZANU had a predominantly Shona following—the Shona were by some distance the larger ethnic grouping in the territory—but ZAPU was not confined to Ndebele such as Nkomo, having two widely known Shona, George Nyandoro and James Chikerema, in central leadership roles.

Neither was there ideological disagreement. Indeed, there was little ideological content of any kind beyond a commitment to African majority rule. The division concerned, rather, personality and tactics. The most divisive single issue in Zimbabwean nationalism at this crucial time was Joshua Nkomo's leadership. For ten years Nkomo had been the most prominent African leader, but he was regarded by many as aloof and disengaged, and his record of challenging White minority rule was inconsistent. By 1963, his instinctive moderation was looking outdated and his continuing search for compromise doomed. He had attended the 1952 London talks on federation as what he himself later called a "token Black." He was subsequently a somewhat natural potential ally of Garfield Todd, though before Todd's fall the City Youth League (CYL) had already lost patience with Nkomo. Later still, Nkomo was attacked by his critics for not initially condemning the 1961 constitutional proposals (and for having placed too high a value on the bill of rights, which he and the NDP had negotiated). He was criticized more generally, too, for seeking to further the African nationalist cause by arguing its cause in foreign capitals ("we had to get outside support for our liberation struggle," he later insisted) rather than to stay in Southern Rhodesia and confront the White minority (and risk detention for doing so).[47] Sithole—not, of course, a disinterested party—accused Nkomo of cowardice, of deserting his people, and of deceiving his colleagues, while Sithole's younger brother focused on Nkomo's "innumerable witch hunts" along with his "indecision, vacillation, impulsive and irrational pronouncements and his fear to face the music."[48]

Nkomo in turn accused ZANU's Takawira of playing on Shona unease about the Ndebele (historically their effective masters in the years before the Pioneer Column) as a political device to justify the split. Although in later years ZANU did seem to be an agency for the Shona, and ZAPU for the Ndebele, in 1963 the party differences were essentially those of mood, intensity, and commitment. For the leaders of ZANU, the age of compromise—the age of Nkomo—was judged to be over. Even so, the rival parties continued to share much, not least their immediate political fate: in August 1964, Prime Minister Ian Smith banned both parties and jailed many of the leaders. Moreover, in those critical years, what ZAPU's Nkomo and ZANU's Sithole agreed upon was critical: in October 1965, when British prime minister Harold Wilson flew out to Rhodesia and spoke to both leaders, each in turn insisted on "no independence before majority rule."

Whites now reacted against the new radicalism among Africans, which they had done so much to bring about. The drift at the heart of Southern Rhodesia's variegated White community, from pragmatic moderation to dogmatic intransigence, was nearly complete. In this settler colony, as Colin Leys had earlier observed, "power tends to gravitate towards those who are least ready for change, having most to lose." He had sensed in 1959 that the system had already reached a point at which the "inherent trend towards illiberalism seemed likely to dominate." In a prescient passage that seemingly anticipated the arrival of the RF, Leys had argued that if the opposition party were to dislodge the government and establish itself firmly in office, it would stay in office because, at last, the most illiberally inclined sections of the electorate would be on the government side. This outcome would be "more logical, if less hopeful" than the one in which largely exogenous factors (the inclination to differentiate itself from South Africa or to appease opinion in Britain) had kept in office the party whose policies were more moderate.[49]

As we have seen, in December 1962, the Whites of Southern Rhodesia chose the illiberal option. But where would this lead them? Winston Field and his colleagues were not seasoned politicians. Not a single member of Field's government had held office in Southern Rhodesia before. Field was prime minister for just a year and a half. His primary aim was to secure independence for Southern Rhodesia as soon as the CAF was dissolved; but he was failing in this venture, and it was clear that he, unlike some others in the party, would not contemplate his country going it alone with an illegal, unilateral, declaration of independence. Moreover, more of a paternalist than a racist, he was less of a hard-liner on racial issues than most of his party's members. His followers no longer had time for moderation, and as a leader, Field was dispensable. His fall revealed the uncompromising aspirations of core RF supporters. He lost power in a ruthless internal coup.

He was replaced as leader of the RF and as prime minister by Ian Smith. "Obdurate and intransigent" as well as personally ambitious, he was "the epitome and symbol of the white Rhodesian ascendancy caste."[50] In September 1964, Southern Rhodesia's high commissioner in London described his own prime minister as "a stubborn old pig."[51] For Smith, negotiation was not a matter of finding a compromise but of wearing down an opponent until he conceded. He was contemptuous of his predecessor but one, Edgar Whitehead. Whitehead, he wrote, had been "a disaster" who had personified a "political world riddled with compromise, appeasement, indecision, all part and parcel of the deviousness which permeated our society."[52] Under Smith, the RF at once became more uncompromising toward African advancement and implacable in negotiations with Britain.

Rhodesia's own history provided Smith with his yardstick. In November 1963, he spoke about the Africans in the colony. "We have no apologies for our present policy," he said, "which of course is based on the fact that the mass of these people did not know what civilization was until about fifty years ago."[53] Smith's views on history and politics were nothing if not uncomplicated and might be summed up as follows: The 1890s had witnessed a clash between civilization and barbarism; White conquest and White rule were evidence of the superiority of Europeans; the latter had introduced primitive African society to the benefits of civilization, but Africans had much catching up to do and, in a still barbarous continent, civilization had to be safeguarded; since gaining independence from the late 1950s, African states elsewhere had resorted to "tribalism" and revealed the scale of danger that civilization faced, and it would be suicidal to civilization if Rhodesia's Africans were enfranchised for Black majority rule; barbarous Soviet and Chinese communism alarmingly sought impressionable adherents in developing nations; and, finally, the best way that the Whites could prepare Blacks for civilization was through giving them employment and the opportunity of material gains . . . so that Africans could care for European families in their homes and gardens and acquire discipline through unskilled physical labor. Otherwise, being still primitive, Africans must live apart.

Standard White assumptions such as these were self-serving distortions and short-sighted. It was one thing to claim to represent "civilized values"; it was another to embody them, and another, again, to recognize that a sizeable body of Africans had acquired them according to the

Whites' own criteria. Such an understanding was beyond Clifford Dupont, Ian Smith's deputy prime minister, a prime architect of the new party. In a passage that captures the mindset of a particular type of RF politician, Robert Blake wrote that Dupont was "the archetypical refugee from the bleakness and restrictions of post-war Britain," one of many "who developed more and more of an anti-British chip on their shoulders as the Empire began to crumble and the sunny world to which they had escaped to make their fortunes began to be menaced by alien shadows and incomprehensible forces."[54] Under the RF, with Dupont as minister of justice, the Whites' "rule of law" no longer resembled that of Britain or that of former Chief Justice Tredgold. Dupont proclaimed that "the laws are moral because they maintain order, and only with order can law-abiding citizens go about their business or go to church without fear for their safety or that of their children."[55] Harsh, discriminatory laws were to be maintained by force; there was no room here for the notion that order might best be maintained in partnership with justice.

In 1964 the RF sought opinions on the question of independence. This was no disinterested exercise in consultation: the public was not being put in charge of the country's future. This much was made clear by Frank Clements, a prominent Rhodesian politician, in the *Sunday Mail*, the paper with the largest circulation in Rhodesia at the time. "The truth is that ever since Mr. Winston Field was ousted, a determined, single-minded minority has been scheming to retain power at all costs. A break with Britain was an essential part of the plan. . . . All that the people can do now is to recognise what has happened to them and estimate what is still in store for them."[56]

Initially, Smith pursued an *agreed* break with Britain: he sought independence based on the 1961 constitution (which he had condemned at the time, but which he knew could be freely interpreted and, above all, amended); and he professed willingness to demonstrate that this is what the majority of all people in Southern Rhodesia wanted. But the British would not, or could not, let go. Harold Macmillan, conservative prime minister, posed the great question in his diary at the end of February 1963: "Southern Rhodesia is a government of several million Africans by 200,000 Whites. Are we to give this country, with this constitution and now under Field, formal independence?"[57] In the event, the answer to this question was "No."

No British government could yield to Smith's White regime in Southern Rhodesia. The UN was applying pressure; there were fears that the emergent post-imperial British commonwealth would break up; and at home an imminent general election discouraged the conservatives from risking the alienation of moderate, liberal British opinion. Moreover, Cold War sensibilities helped to shape every aspect of British international decisionmaking at this time. Britain could not concede full independence to a country with such a restrictive franchise and run the risk that an African people, prevented from running their own affairs, would turn to Russia or China for sympathy and support. The British government's position under both the conservatives up to October 16, 1964, and the Labour Party thereafter, boiled down to this: independence was indeed possible based on the 1961 constitution . . . but only if a majority of each race of Rhodesians accepted it, and if its application ensured "unimpeded progress to majority rule."

Personalities matter. It is significant that, at this time, Lord Home (formerly Sir Alex Douglas-Home) was a key figure in both Macmillan's and, later, Edward Heath's governments, but not Iain Macleod, Macmillan's colonial secretary from 1959 to 1961. Home was a remote paternalistic aristocrat, lacking in imagination, who believed Africans were hundreds of years behind on their journey to Western civilization. In contrast, Macleod was an energetic, bright, no-nonsense pragmatist who could sympathize with Africans and get along with them well personally. He was experienced in getting deals done. Out of office, he would criticize Home for being too ready to concede to Smith and merely offer economic assistance. "It cannot be stated too simply," he said, that "aid is no substitute for political freedom." He challenged the incoming RF government: "How long can this madness go on? How near must this boat go to the weir before a really determined attempt is made to stop it? Sooner or later men must get round a table and thrash out their differences."[58]

While Home was reluctant to put pressure on the White regime, Macleod would not have held back in forcing Rhodesia's White political leaders to talk to, and compromise with, African nationalists. But it must be acknowledged that even a leading conservative in Britain such as Macleod was anathema to White Rhodesian reactionaries. Doris Lessing discovered this. She lamented that "old-fashioned liberalism in this part of the world is indistinguishable in the minds of White voters from the extreme forms of sedition." By way of illustration, she quoted from a letter sent to her in the early 1960s, which was quite specific: "If you think that Reds like you and Macleod are going to ride roughshod over our rights . . ."[59]

* * *

To strengthen his case, on November 5, Ian Smith held a referendum open to all who qualified to vote according to the existing franchise.

Overwhelmingly White, they were asked if they supported his demand for independence based on the 1961 constitution (not, it should be stressed, if they would support a unilateral/illegal declaration of independence). The turnout of around 60 percent was lower than for the election of 1962 (76 percent), but 58,000 voted "Yes," with only 6,000 voting "No." However, bland statistics cannot reveal the motivation of individual electors. Take Denis Norman, for example. A postwar immigrant, he arrived in Southern Rhodesia in 1953, aged 22, and took up tobacco farming. In the November 5, 1964, referendum he voted for Ian Smith. But Norman was no racist diehard. He believed that the vote was for independence *to be negotiated* by Smith. He wrote later, "It was the first and only time I gave him my vote." He added that these issues divided not only communities but families. His own vote was canceled out by that of his wife, who did not trust Smith. This apparently typical White farmer in fact lamented the disappearance, in the preceding years, of "a middle-ground approach" to the colony's future. On the great political-moral question of the day he was, in effect, among the progressive challengers of the former conservative consensus. He went on to describe the Unilateral Declaration of Independence (UDI) as "ill-judged" and, with the arrival of majority rule in 1980, he became a minister in President Mugabe's first cabinet.[60]

How was Smith to show that Africans, too, supported his strategy? His very controversial answer was to hold an *indaba*, an assembly of 600 or so African chiefs and headmen. Meeting for a few days at the end of October (so before the White referendum), they, too, said "Yes." Unfortunately for Smith, this exercise was not taken seriously by others as an indication of the views of Southern Rhodesia's Africans. In 1898, Native Regulations had defined a chief as a "native" appointed to exercise control over a "tribe." Chiefs thereafter had to be cooperative and loyal; the independent-minded were mostly removed. In the early years of the century, chiefs might still have articulated the views of "the tribesmen," as Smith chose to refer to them, but by 1964 much had changed. European Native Commissioners (NCs), in place since before 1923, were expected to control Indigenous Africans through their chiefs and headmen, but in practice they themselves had come to usurp the chiefs' intermediary functions. The chiefs' authority was undermined. Meanwhile, over time, the administration of African affairs became more and more centralized. "As less and less was left to the Native Commissioner, he clung more closely to all he had and devolved less to the chiefs."[61] Implementation of the Land Husbandry Act of 1951 dealt a final blow to the chiefs' authority.

Sithole's comment is unambiguous. Before the Whites came, he wrote, chiefs were ultimately responsible to their people. But that changed with the onset of White rule. "The present African chiefs no longer represent the will of the people, but that of a foreign power."[62] The territory's involvement in World War II offered a nice illustration. When the NC of Gutu instructed tribal authorities in November 1940 to provide laborers for new aerodromes, popular opposition was vocal. The inadequacies of the system became clear and were noted in a subsequent intelligence report. "*So broken is the tribal system* that there is a regular chant that chiefs and headmen have no right to call upon anyone but their own sons to undertake these duties."[63]

By the 1960s, most chiefs were subservient players in the game of White politics. Whitehead's policy was to reduce their number and remaining powers; in contrast, after the RF's election victory in 1962, it set about to increase the numbers of chiefs and headmen, refusing to accept that anyone else could speak for the mass of Africans. As Terence Ranger put it at the time, Smith's cynical answer to the nationalist challenge "is to revive the power of the chiefs and indunas; to increase their salaries; to give them powers of arrest and trial; to give them representation in Parliament; and generally to treat them as the representatives of their people."[64] But by this time, chiefs and headmen, hired and fired by officials of the White minority government, were government-paid agents who mostly voiced the interests of few other than themselves. The chiefs were unenviably caught in circumstances not of their choosing. Their positions were dependent on the White regime, and would therefore be at risk in the event of one-man, one-vote African majority rule.

In this light, it is noteworthy that of the 800 or so chiefs invited by Smith to the *indaba* to discuss his independence strategy, in October 1964 around a quarter demonstrated an independence of mind by choosing not to attend. There is further evidence that, notwithstanding his claims, not all of Smith's chiefs were his avid supporters. By the 1960s, just five chiefs were entrusted by the RF to participate in "the propaganda work which claims that Africans are represented by chiefs for all political activities." When the chiefs as a whole wanted Joshua Nkomo to act as their spokesman during constitutional talks in 1961, though he was not among the five chosen by the government, "the White politicians . . . took no notice."[65]

Few outside the RF believed Smith's claims that his chiefs spoke for the mass of Africans. Neither conservative nor Labour administrations in Britain regarded Smith's *indaba* as a convincing exercise in testing African opinion. The conservatives declined to send an observer to the election; Labour rejected the result. Closer to home, Smith had sought advice from the department of African studies at the University College.

But he rejected it when they told him that "in African society . . . decisions are made by the processes which involve all adult members of the community. . . . In Southern Rhodesia, Africans are no longer organised solely based on the basis of a tribal system." The academics concluded: "We are utterly opposed to the idea that there is something peculiar to Africans which makes it impossible to test their opinions by normal procedures."[66]

Furthermore, Smith's precautions appear to betray his own lack of confidence in the chiefs and how they would behave. Before the *indaba*, government loudspeaker vans toured the townships with such messages as: "You must rally to your chiefs. Those who argue will be brushed aside." But when Judith Todd asked for government permission to visit a tribal trust area (native reserve), "the answer, in effect, was: 'No. *We are in the process of explaining to the chiefs what it's all about.* They have little contact with the outside world. Your presence might simply confuse them.'"[67] Indeed, the press was barred from the rural areas and also from the *indaba* itself—which was sealed off for five days by troops and police—until a select few journalists were able, on the final day, to interview a select few chiefs. It was observed a little later that "as chiefs they cannot be said to be political leaders. In fact the evidence is that *some of them and the majority of the people* regard their embroilment in modern national politics as a serious embarrassment."[68]

Tredgold's withering conclusion was that the RF's claims to have African support were "utterly and demonstrably untrue." He highlighted some pertinent facts: that "the regime finds it necessary to detain and restrict without trial hundreds of African leaders"; that it has "banned all political parties with widespread support among Africans"; and that "all African newspapers . . . expressing political views have been suppressed." These facts, he noted, "are hardly consistent with a genuine belief in a substantial measure of support amongst the Africans."[69] But Smith was unembarrassed by such criticisms. He continued to insist that "the chiefs represented the tribesmen, who constituted 90% of the population," and their decision "was one of unanimous support for independence on the 1961 constitution." As for urban Africans, they had had their opportunity to participate in the referendum: all Rhodesians, whatever their race, had equal access to the voters' roll. Years later, Smith still professed himself baffled. "What more did the British Government require?"[70] But the political reality was that the British did not accept that the RF had the backing of the majority of all the territory's peoples.

* * *

Why did Smith insist on independence, given the amount of power and authority the settlers already enjoyed? White Southern Rhodesians had had internal self-government in practice since 1923, if not before. Britain's reserved power was never formally used against them. As one contemporary critic put it, "Britain plugged its ears to any African voices for half a century, and let settlers trample African rights underfoot."[71] Specifically, why countenance an illegal break, and all the consequences: diplomatic isolation, economic sanctions, and the like? If the British Parliament had decided to resurrect its reserve powers and intervene to legislate for majority rule, a break might have made more sense. But it had not. Neither, successive British governments had made clear, was there any chance of military intervention to stop the RF proceeding with the constitutional coup it envisaged.

Smith claimed that there was a moral case. He was outraged by British hesitation. For him, Southern Rhodesia had a far stronger claim to independence than the other two territories of the CAF. It had exercised "responsible government" for forty years, during which "we had been a model of efficiency, correct constitutional behaviour and economic viability. . . . In all honesty, fairness and justice how could we be faulted on such a stand?"[72] Huggins, by contrast, though a fellow White supremacist, judged the UDI "a piece of madness, a sort of collective rush of blood to the head, which cannot be explained by rational means at all."[73] But if it was madness, the decision was not entirely without method. The RF wanted the White Rhodesian minority to have total, unrestricted authority to amend the constitution. Seeing as the 1961 version did not offer that sovereignty, and the British government was not going to abandon its reserve clauses unconditionally, a new constitution to accompany a severance of relations became a logical necessity.

Six months before the break occurred, Smith called a general election, confident that he would secure two-thirds of the seats for his RF—enough to undertake amendments of the 1961 constitution short of removing those reserve clauses. The White electorate did not let him down, and in May 1965 delivered him three-quarters of the seats. But with Britain, there remained a deadlock. Harold Wilson's government insisted on irreversible steps toward majority rule, but Smith demanded a constitution that would entitle the government of Rhodesia to make whatever amendments it chose. The commonwealth too remained adamant, and Smith did not attend its London conference in June. In October, Smith visited London, and Wilson visited Salisbury, but to no avail.

Smith insisted on not talking to African leaders, even though by now the stakes were higher than ever before. British government ministers thought differently. After the Labour election victory in Britain, the new colonial secretary, Arthur Bottomley, flew to Rhodesia. He turned down an invitation to attend Smith's *indaba* of chiefs and headmen and instead asked to talk to Nkomo and Sithole, leaders of ZAPU and ZANU, respectively, who were being held in detention. Smith turned down this request, categorizing them not as political leaders but as criminals (thereby seeking to justify not meeting them himself). Bottomley called off his visit.

On November 11, 1965, Smith unilaterally declared independence from Britain. The document was countersigned by the other eleven members of his cabinet. In doing this, Smith sought to convince the world that the interests of Rhodesia's three million or so Africans were best served by a government representing 224,000 Whites. Africans would attain majority rule, Smith declared, as soon as they demonstrated their fitness by qualifying for the vote in sufficient numbers. In his radio broadcast that day, Smith committed his government to "racial harmony." He insisted that the UDI was "a blow for the preservation of justice, civilisation and Christianity." This is not how everybody saw it. Smith's assertion was rendered less convincing by his follow-up claim: "The mantle of the pioneers has fallen on our shoulders." It would have been hard to demonstrate that many of the 200 adventurers who crossed the Limpopo in 1890 were wholly committed to all, or indeed any, of those three fine goals. And the link between the pioneers and the leaders of the RF was tenuous, in that three quarters of the latter had not been born in the colony. The declaration ended with the somewhat desperate rhetorical flourish of "God Save the Queen."

Smith declared that Rhodesia attaining independence without further delay represented justice "without question." But justice for whom? It referred repeatedly to "the people." These were presented either as a monolithic body—"the people of Rhodesia fully support the requests of their government for sovereign independence"—or, perhaps somewhat carelessly, as those who had "demonstrated their loyalty to the Crown *and to their kith and kin* in the United Kingdom and elsewhere through two world wars."[74] There is no mention here of the Africans who served in both wars. And yet 14,000 Africans had "put on khaki" during the second global conflict, including the 2,000 Africans in the Rhodesian African Rifles regiment who fought (and in 136 cases lost their lives) in Burma in 1944 and 1945. The RF's low estimation of the African majority is further detectable where Rhodesia is described as a primitive country. There was no recognition here, of course, that in the eyes of many contemporaries, kith and kin included, Smith had lost the moral argument.

A revised constitution was published on the same day. Though it resembled the 1961 constitution in many respects—the separate rolls, for example, and both the declaration of rights and the constitutional council—it abolished the whole concept of specially entrenched clauses (the final break with 1923) and opened any future constitutional amendment to the simple affirmation of two-thirds of MPs in the legislature (now renamed parliament). This amounted to a fundamental change that could never have been achieved under the status quo. As subsequent RF policies would illustrate, the purpose of the UDI and the new constitution was not so much to stop the clock as to turn it back—to open the way for Rhodesia's White minority to govern the Africans in ways Britain could not have countenanced.

As one of its fiercest White critics put it at the time, "This strange handful of recent immigrants, no more in number than the population of a British town, claimed the right to rule Rhodesia and its people for all time."[75] The UDI was a reckless act, and although not ultimately "disastrous" (as Blake provisionally described it in 1977 during the liberation war) it was highly damaging to the country and its peoples.[76] The RF appeared to believe that the grievances of Rhodesia's Africans were piffling (exaggerated by malign, alien forces), and could be ignored by denying them a meaningful vote. But an intensifying African discontent would have to be forcibly suppressed. Perhaps it was forebodings of such a future that led thousands of Whites not to commit themselves to the RF. Following substantial immigration from 1946 to 1959, the next five years, saw 63,000 Whites leave the country.

David Coltart was an eight-year-old boy at the time of the UDI. He recalls his father, a bank manager and a liberal among postwar White immigrants, turning to him and saying, "Oh, Davie boy—Mr. Smith has done a very silly thing."[77] Fellow White Rhodesian Peter Godwin, too, was eight at the time. His personal response to meeting the prime minister in the 1970s while a reluctant member of the Rhodesia security forces was comparably dismissive: "So this was the man—good ol' Smithy—followed blindly by White Rhodesians even though he had no bloody idea where to lead us." Godwin had detected, with some irony, that most Whites shared a characteristic: "Fiercely independent, the Rhodesians were easily led, and even more easily deceived."[78] Populist politicians proceeded to "lead"; a majority of Whites continued to deceive themselves. Godwin added, "Certainly no one said that Rhodesia would be isolated, that there would be economic sanctions against us and a war. That we would have to go into the army, that some of us would be killed, that we would be ambushed and attacked, that our farms would be burnt down and abandoned. No-one said that."[79]

* * *

The Southern Rhodesia fault-line had been segregation, and White isolation from African realities continued, damagingly, into the era of illegally independent "Rhodesia." As a rule, Europeans of all classes intentionally met with only one another and "encountered" Africans only at work and as domestic servants. Tredgold wrote in sadness, if not disbelief, that "great numbers of white people have never visited an ordinary African home, urban or rural, humble or more advanced. Even today," he added, three years after the UDI, "the vast majority of Europeans have never met an educated African on terms of real friendship."[80] Patrick Keatley had noted that "it is perfectly possible to live in a comfortable white suburb, drive to work by super highway to one's office in town, lunch in a white man's restaurant . . . and return home having scarcely exchanged words with a black man.'[81]

Richard West, a well-traveled English journalist, visited Rhodesia shortly before the UDI. "The dislike and fear of the blacks is aggravated by ignorance. . . . The whites and blacks in Salisbury scarcely mix at all. . . . The mass of the white population talk to no blacks except their servants." On one occasion, a White political leader asked West "in the tones of a stranger in town wanting to find the nearest brothel, 'Tell me, what are the Africans thinking?' I looked at him in astonishment, 'How should I know? I've only just arrived. This is your country.' Yet the same question was put to me over and over again during my stay in Southern Rhodesia, always by people who lived there and often by people who claimed loudly to 'understand the African.'" A Black taxi-driver offered West his explanation of the gulf that remained between the races. "The Rhodesians simply don't talk to us like you're talking to me, and we don't talk to them."[82]

Joshua Nkomo wrote of a conversation he had with a White Rhodesian in the most unpromising of circumstances. On April 16, 1964, he was arrested by RF security forces. The police "were perfectly polite." On the way to the place where he would begin ten years of detention, they stopped for a break at an air force base. "Was I going alone, I asked. Nobody knew, but they made me some coffee and we drank it together and waited in the officers' mess for three hours. It is strange how the separation of the races broke down at times like that."[83] It was surely more than strange—tragically ironic—that this chance contact between police and "terrorist" could so illuminate Southern Rhodesia's lost potential. More than ironic, too, that this detention should have been authorized by Clifford Dupont, the minister responsible for law and order. On the day of its occurrence, the *Rhodesia Herald* (a newspaper not always critical of the regime) portrayed the seizure of Nkomo as "an act of insanity" because it enhanced his status as a hero and further alienated his many thousands of supporters from the White settler regime.

If the choice of direction that White Southern Rhodesians made on either side of 1960 was not in itself "insane," it was nevertheless a palpable misjudgment. For much of the first half of the twentieth century, most Africans had acquiesced in White rule at a number of levels, many even finding opportunities for advancement within the colony. Lawrence Vambe describes how the young men of his Shona village, Chishashawa, were happy to become post office messengers, drivers, clerks, foremen, waiters, cooks, policemen, "and anything else . . . which gave them a sense of identification with the magic and prestige of the white man's civilisation." They "allowed themselves to be swept off their feet by this dream of personal identification with the white man's world," he goes on to explain, "because it promised them a freedom which tribal Chishawasha did not allow." But the wider constant reality of discrimination and segregation eventually took its toll. Vambe contrasts the mood of his community in the early years with that of the 1960s. In the 1920s, he writes, his native area was "throbbing with vitality." By the time of the UDI, however, much land had irrevocably passed into White hands, and Africans were insecure, fearing "the total erosion" of their right to occupy a piece of land that was once part of the kingdom of their forebears.[84] It was ongoing and worsening grievances arising from White domination—many relating to land and to the franchise as a mechanism for redress—that turned moderate Africans into radicals and a peaceful political movement to violence.

Smith and his diehard supporters had no idea of what they were failing to grasp through their lofty detachment from reality. In 1960, Bernard Chidzero stressed the force of "resentment among Africans today against paternalistic bureaucracy and haughty attitudes in white-controlled administrations."[85] When Patrick Keatley asked a former moderate in 1963 what had driven him to militancy, the African replied without hesitation: "The colour bar and separate lavatories."[86] "In hotels, public parks, on the railway and on the bus," wrote Sithole, "Africans—civilised or uncivilised, educated or uneducated—are discriminated against in a most humiliating manner."[87] Edgar Whitehead might describe such slights as "pinpricks." But this was an example of even a comparatively liberal White man's inability to sense the African mood—the extent to which African political consciousness had been shaped by the humiliating experience of the Whites' proudly exercised yet self-isolating etiquette. African nationalism arose as much from slights and humiliations as from barriers to advancement. Being patronized became insufferable. As Eshmael Mlambo put it, "paternalism expressed in terms like 'mature,' 'responsible,' 'civilised,' 'advanced'—which Africans must be before they can exercise power—only exasperates racial conflict."[88]

The multilayered alienation of Africans would prove to be White supremacy's undoing.

Notes

1. Todd, *Rhodesia*, 71.
2. Leys, *European Politics*, 292, 293.
3. E. Mlambo, *Struggle*, 126, 127, 135.
4. Quoted in Todd, *Rhodesia*, 67, 68.
5. Tredgold, *My Life*, 228.
6. Clutton-Brock, *Cold Comfort*, 89, 93.
7. Keatley, *The Politics of Partnership*, 305. Italics added.
8. Shamuyarira, *Crisis*, 64.
9. Tredgold, *My Life*, 229, 230.
10. Quoted in Brand, *Race and Politics*, 59.
11. Quoted in Blake, *A History*, 338.
12. Blake, *A History*, 339.
13. Quoted in Blake, *A History*, 338, 339.
14. Bowman, *Politics*, 38.
15. Smith, *Betrayal*, 92.
16. Clutton-Brock, *Cold Comfort*, 108.
17. Coltart, *The Struggle Continues*, 16.
18. Todd, *Rhodesia*, 65–67.
19. Clutton-Brock, *Cold Comfort*, 80.
20. E. Mlambo, *The Struggle*, 188, 189.
21. Quoted in Shutt, *Manners*, 160.
22. Quoted in Woodhouse, *Garfield Todd*, 295.
23. Quoted in Keatley, *The Politics of Partnership*, 348.
24. Bowman, *Politics*, 42.
25. Quoted in Cleary, *The Life of Winston Joseph Field*, 123.
26. Blake, *A History*, 343.
27. Quoted in Cleary, *The Life of Winston Joseph Field*, 151.
28. Cleary, *The Life of Winston Joseph Field*, 89.
29. Quoted in Cleary, *The Life of Winston Joseph Field*, 275.
30. Quoted in Cleary, *The Life of Winston Joseph Field*, 117.
31. Cleary, *The Life of Winston Joseph Field*, 89.
32. Gann, *White Settlers*, 114, 115.
33. Clutton-Brock, *Cold Comfort*, 112, 113.
34. Quoted in Todd, *Rhodesia*, 91, 92.
35. Shamuyarira, *Crisis*, 141.
36. Tredgold, *My Life*, 184.
37. Keatley, *The Politics of Partnership*, 303, 304. Italics in original.
38. Huddleston, *Naught for Your Comfort*, 17.
39. Quoted in Todd, *Rhodesia*, 119.
40. Quoted in Todd, *Rhodesia*, 107.
41. Quoted in Todd, *Rhodesia*, 108.

42. Quoted in Todd, *Rhodesia*, 109.
43. Coltart, *The Struggle Continues*, 23.
44. Dorman, *Understanding Zimbabwe*, 19.
45. E. Mlambo, *The Struggle*, 236.
46. M. Sithole, *Zimbabwe's Struggle*, 14, 45.
47. Nkomo, *My Life*, 80.
48. M. Sithole, *Zimbabwe's Struggle*, 50.
49. Leys, *European Politics*, 36, 174–177.
50. Blake, *A History*, 361.
51. National Archive, Kew, PREM 11/5039.
52. Smith, *Betrayal*, 45.
53. Quoted in Todd, *Rhodesia*, 129.
54. Blake, *A History*, 386.
55. Quoted in Cleary, *The Life of Winston Joseph Field*, 119.
56. Quoted in Todd, *Rhodesia*, 167.
57. Quoted in Blake, *A History*, 348.
58. Quoted in Shepherd, *Macleod*, 370–371.
59. Lessing, *Going Home*, 69, 241.
60. Norman, *The Odd Man In*, 31–33.
61. Mason, *The Birth of a Dilemma*, 279.
62. N. Sithole, *African Nationalism*, 99.
63. Quoted in Kenneth P. Vickery, "Wars and Rumours of Wars: Southern Rhodesian Africans and the Second World War," unpublished paper, North Carolina State University, 1984. Italics added.
64. Ranger, *Aspects*, 244.
65. E. Mlambo, *The Struggle*, 46, 47.
66. Quoted in Todd, *Rhodesia*, 139.
67. Quoted in Todd, *Rhodesia*, 137, 139. Italics added.
68. Report of the Pearce Commission on Rhodesian Opinion, 1972, Appendix 4. Italics added.
69. Tredgold, *My Life*, 244, 245.
70. Smith, *Betrayal*, 82, 90.
71. Shamuyarira, *Crisis*, 163.
72. Smith, *Betrayal*, 50.
73. Quoted in Blake, *A History*, 382.
74. From the Declaration, quoted in Smith, *Betrayal*, 104. Italics added.
75. Clutton-Brock, *Cold Comfort*, 113.
76. Blake, *A History*, 381.
77. Coltart, *The Struggle Continues*, 25.
78. Godwin and Hancock, *Rhodesians Never Die*, 9.
79. Godwin, *Mukiwa*, 72, 263.
80. Tredgold, *My Life*, 55, 223.
81. Keatley, *The Politics of Partnership*, 229.
82. R. West, *The White Tribes of Africa*, 75, 76.
83. Nkomo, *My Life*, 121.
84. Vambe, *An Ill-Fated People*, 196, 243.
85. Chidzero, *Good Government*, 179.
86. Keatley, *The Politics of Partnership*, 262.
87. N. Sithole, *African Nationalism*, 100.
88. E. Mlambo, *The Struggle*, vii, viii.

7

Cul-de-Sac

"FOR THE PRESERVATION OF JUSTICE, CIVILISATION, AND CHRIStianity." This defense of the Unilateral Declaration of Independence (UDI) is taken from Ian Smith's radio broadcast on the day of its announcement. The tone and content of that short speech suggest that his reactionary right wing had done more than see off the 1950s liberal challenge to White supremacy in Rhodesia: they imply that the right wing had won the moral argument, too. It was certainly bold of Rhodesia's prime minister to claim the moral high ground in these terms. A critical response should assume that Smith believed what he said; it would have been out of character for him cynically to adopt a convenient rhetoric to gain acceptance for his illegal act. But how credible was his government's stewardship of this cluster of the Western world's noblest aspirations?

It is likely that "justice" in this specific context applies not to relations between Whites and Africans in Rhodesia but to the regime's relations with Britain. As Smith saw it, and as he bitterly titled his political memoir, it was Britain that had committed "the great betrayal." The mother country had denied Southern Rhodesia independence (after the break-up of the Central African Federation [CAF]) but granted it to Northern Rhodesia and Nyasaland. Britain had ignored the Whites' proud record of de facto self-government since 1923 while recklessly empowering African majorities elsewhere. There was justice, therefore, seen through this lens, in the Whites holding on to power and authority in Rhodesia, where they had proved themselves more than worthy.

Nevertheless, White indifference to wrongs and grievances was persistent. In the year of the UDI, a White second-year student at the university in Salisbury was recorded saying: "I now realise the things I enjoy—a nice farm, a motor-car—and I'm going to fight for them. There's no moral basis for this. It's just that I like them."[1] A little later, it would have been hard to contradict Lawrence Vambe's understated observation, in 1972, that "the settlers' conduct was guided by material considerations rather than by impartial justice and moral values, especially where their interests clashed with those of Africans."[2]

What did justice entail? Since World War II, any country that chose to advertise itself as civilized, as Rhodesia did in 1965, opened itself to scrutiny of its values and behavior. The Universal Declaration of Human Rights adopted by the United Nations (UN) in 1948 leaves no room for doubt. "Recognition of the inherent dignity, and of the equal and inalienable rights of all members of the human family, is the foundation of freedom, justice and peace in the world." Rhodesia in 1965 was a land where the dignity of all was not recognized, and where there was no equal exercise of rights, irrespective of race.

Patrick Keatley was eloquent about how the Whites lived in Southern Rhodesia. "I marvel at the rhinoceros-hide skins that ordinary mortals develop—so quickly—in such circumstances, that enable them to enjoy their privileged delights, without the dilution that would come from a momentary backward glance to see how the other ninety-seven per cent are enjoying themselves."[3] And that was before the UDI. The settlers had brought order and prosperity, but not the fairness symbolized by the scales of justice. There was the rule of law, but, as it was argued by liberals at the time, this was the rule of unjust laws enacted to perpetuate privilege . . . and so injustice. The principled resignation of chief justice Robert Tredgold in 1960 was the clearest sign that justice and laws in Southern Rhodesia were not in alignment.

The best way to preserve "civilization" was to reinforce it through propagation. But this was not a preoccupation for most Whites. Roy Welensky observed in 1957 that "the Europeans came here to make homes for themselves and to bring civilisation to this area."[4] His order of priorities was honest. The daily lifestyle of Whites in both Rhodesias appeared to illustrate that homebuilding took precedence over civilizing, though its advocates would have denied any contradiction. Few resident Whites were disturbed by an all but unbridgeable prosperity gap, which for many somehow confirmed respective stages of civilization achieved. "We live side by side with an 'inferior people,'" Judith Todd wrote sardonically, "who threaten the security of our civilisation. Yet," she continued, "we direct these same people to cook our food, wash our clothes, make our beds, tend our children and generally minister to our welfare."[5] Numerous everyday occurrences belied White claims of a civilizing mission. "In the local white township, no African could enter a shop; he was served through a hatch at the back. White supremacy reigned unquestioned, in this British colony which was supposed to be spreading Christian civilisation."[6]

In 1952, Hardwicke Holderness, a prominent liberal, had drafted general principles in founding the Interracial Association of Southern Rhodesia. "We believe . . . that civilisation shall be available to all its inhabitants and for the good of mankind." "By civilisation," he continued, "we mean a state in which the fullness of life is possible, both spiritual and material."[7] But by the 1970s, "civilization" was little more than a banner for the Rhodesian Front (RF), as "partnership" had been for the CAF. The 1950s challenge and debate had turned it from an inspiring notion (which many Whites genuinely thought they represented) into little more than a rhetorical tool deployed by Whites who had lost that debate to justify their continued domination.

Some settlers evidently associated civilization with material success. Rhodesia-born company director Alex Maddocks was interviewed by the writer David Caute in 1976. "It's my country," he said. "Rhodesia means civilisation as we know it. It means well-repaired roads, telephones that work, it means sanitation, hygiene and medicine second to none in Africa." Going on to compare his country in the mid-1970s with newly independent African states, he stressed, at some length, freedom from corruption. "Rhodesia means to my mind banks run by men who won't scoop the till; a civil service based on merit, a police force uncorrupted by bribery and nepotism. It means due process of law before impartial judges, uninfluenced by intimidation."[8] According to the prevailing European definition of corruption, the contrast was indeed striking; but at this time it was unlikely to convince many Africans.

The White minority regime insisted repeatedly that it stood for Christian values, and so inadvertently invited keener scrutiny. While numerous Europeans there professed Christianity, increasing numbers of Africans perceived public life differently. Joshua Nkomo probably spoke for many when he said of Rhodesia: "As far as we are concerned, the whole thing is inhuman, uncivilised, uncultured, stupid, selfish and above all, unchristian."[9] Africans who grew up imbibing biblical teachings came to observe around them a White order—economic, social, and political—that fell short of Christian values. Inconsistency could be read as hypocrisy and served to frustrate and alienate. "By their fruits shall ye know them," Africans were taught. Although they were deeply impressed by individual European Christians who lived simply among them and championed them (men such as Arthur Shearly Cripps in the early days, or Guy Clutton-Brock in the 1950s), they were not persuaded that the policies of White governments, especially after the fall of Garfield Todd, were Christian in orientation. As one White Rhodesian wrote, "When Rhodesians used the term 'Christianity' they often did so to delineate or justify a *secular* world which was anti-communist, democratic and civilised (that is, white ruled); they showed little sign of being profoundly concerned with spiritual matters."[10] To this extent, Christianity represented a faultline in a White-dominated society that brought it and taught it but did not for the most part appear to practice it.

As early as the 1890s, the first bishop appointed to the diocese of Mashonaland had feared that the spread of Christianity in Southern Rhodesia would be undermined, rather than promoted, by the first White settlers. As we saw in Chapter 3, the vision of George Knight-Bruce did not coincide with that of Cecil Rhodes. He wanted missionaries to work in an African country in which settlers and the British South Africa Company (BSAC) played no part. As a prominent Christian, Knight-Bruce believed that "civilization" as represented by the pioneers would bring little good. Six decades later, after circumstances had changed, his (White) episcopal successors adopted a comparable perspective. In April 1964, sensing the drift of White politics toward an illegal break with Britain, Bishop Kenneth Skelton of Matabeleland issued a clear warning in a sermon in Bulawayo. "I think it would be true to say that the only circumstances in which the church could condone such an act would be if it were carried out at the will of the great majority of the people, as the only means of ridding them of a quite intolerable and tyrannical oppression. The idea that a unilateral declaration of independence could be so represented is so far from the truth that it would be laughable if it were not so tragic."[11] The RF went ahead. Just three days after the UDI, Bishop Cecil Alderson of Mashonaland gave his withering response in a sermon in Salisbury Cathedral: "I respect the integrity of my fellow citizens and Christians, but I suspect deeply the basic motives of a great part of the community as a whole which have led to this thing. I repudiate this illegal act."[12]

Over time, numerous Africans encountered Christianity in mission schools. Literacy and a grasp of English could lead to employment, income, and purchasing power. There was status to be gained, too. Ndabaningi Sithole, subsequently a minister in the Methodist church, wrote that, when he attended Garfield Todd's Dadaya Mission, "not to be baptised was a kind of social stigma." He went on to confess that "Christ to me meant no more and no less than a social badge."[13] This doubtless remained the case for others as well, Europeans included, but for critically inclined Africans it was difficult to see White Rhodesia as an embodiment of New Testament teachings. All men might be equal under God, but they were not equal under successive White prime ministers. Privilege and the color bar left little room for good neighborliness. It was easy to regard the church as the White man's church—one, moreover, in which the clergy were failing to promote practical Christianity among its White congregations.

Justice, civilization, and Christianity were the criteria by which Smith invited his rebellious Rhodesia to be judged in 1965. All three virtues properly entailed a growing inclusion of Africans in White society: respectively as equals, as deserving, and as God's creatures. But although Africans were attracted to justice, the White man's civilization, and the White man's religion, they generally found they were not welcomed by those other than the liberal White minority and were not included. Indeed, the UDI was a clear statement that there was no likelihood of their being included "in the foreseeable future." This may or may not have been Rhodes's legacy (he had been a complex figure), but it certainly was not the fulfillment of David Livingstone's vision.

And yet, after 1957, after 1962, and even after the UDI, there remained numerous Africans and a minority of Europeans in Rhodesia who longed for a harmonious transition toward majority rule. Progressive Whites understood that if they did not talk with Black representatives of moderation and liberalism while they were still secure, they would be in danger of losing everything once the odds were stacked against them. When the Zimbabwe African People's Union (ZAPU) and then the Zimbabwe African National Union (ZANU) came into being, and were for a while in conflict with each other, reactionary Whites could still congratulate themselves that they had been proven right. But African opinion as a whole was not extreme or radical. This was unmistakably demonstrated by the emergence in 1972 of Bishop Abel Muzorewa, hardly a frightening figure, as a popular nationalist leader who could speak on behalf of the mass of Africans (at a time when ZAPU and ZANU leaders were held pointlessly in detention). Here was the latter-day evidence of the much earlier potential (on the African side) for constructive interracial dialogue rejected by Smith. In the meantime, White liberals continued to dissent from RF orthodoxy by repeatedly voting against the government.

The First Decade of Illegal Independence

For some time, continuity and relative normality prevailed. While so many African political leaders were detained, there had been no spontaneous African groundswell against the UDI. It is striking that in Tsitsi Dangarembga's novel, set in this period, the year 1965 is singled out: not as marking a seismic shift in the White man's politics or in the experience of Africans, but as "the year of my uncle's return from England."[14] These were the "eleven wonderful years" or "twelve incredible years" of which Smith and his supporters would later speak, defiant if delusional. In these first years, Smith's regime consolidated itself, even prospered, largely untroubled by either internal resistance or international diplomatic pressure and interference. Smith repeatedly sought a settlement that would bring international recognition, albeit with a degree of nonchalance. However, nothing came of his meetings with Harold Wilson in 1966 (on HMS *Tiger*) and in 1968 (on HMS *Fearless*). Before his next talks with the British, his introduction of a new constitution and reactionary legislation on land ownership demonstrated just how confident he was that no concessions were needed on his part.

International economic sanctions had results opposite to those intended. Enterprise and self-sufficiency, import substitution, and diversification of agriculture transformed the Rhodesian economy. Buoyed by this remarkable success, White politics indulged in a further drift to the right. In 1969, the RF government introduced a new constitution. This was blatantly racist and, it was reported soon afterward, "no less a person than the Prime Minister, Mr. Ian Smith, has boasted that this is so."[15] The lower house of legislature would have sixty-six seats: fifty for Europeans (including those colored and Asian); and sixteen for Africans (eight for chiefs, eight elected). An upper house of legislature (senate) would be comprised of ten Europeans and ten chiefs (whom Smith still insisted were the true spokesmen of the Africans), as well as three additional members (two European) nominated by the head of state, who would be president. The link with the British Crown was finally severed in March 1970, when Rhodesia was declared a republic. Bishop Donal Lamont denounced the new constitution for its "moral violence, moral terrorism."[16] He was not the only critic. A White referendum on the constitution saw a notably large vote against it (20,000 against vs. 55,000 for)—in part through a continuing loyalty to the Crown or a longing for an end to total diplomatic isolation; but in the first general election held under its terms, the RF won all fifty seats. This was an election in which around 8,300 of the country's five million Africans voted.

An illustration of continuing diversity of opinion among Whites, as well as of a continuing liberal—albeit ineffectual—voice among them, lies in the story of the Centre Party. Formed in 1968 by young White professionals, it advocated nonracial meritocracy comprising representative democracy on a qualified franchise—an end to discrimination, African advancement, and the rule of law. In the April 1970 election, it won 24 percent of the vote in the sixteen White constituencies it contested, in some of them over 30 percent. It also won seven of the eight Black seats. But what looked like a reformulation of Toddism or Whiteheadism could only exist as a talking shop.

The RF had been formed to unite several smaller parties of the right: a "front," indeed. It thus brought together different strands of White opinion. From 1968 to 1970, there was a running battle between its two wings over White supremacy and segregation. Interestingly, nearly one fifth of all Whites recorded in the 1969 census had arrived as immigrants since the UDI and must have swelled the proportion of diehards. At this time, there was growing tension within the RF. Some, categorized as the hard-liners by Robert Blake were advocating White rule forever. Among these were two ministers of South African origin: P. K. van der Byl, "one of the hardest liners in the party," and Desmond Lardner-Burke, "an extreme hard-liner closely associated with the illiberal exercise of emergency powers."[17] Others preferred the notion of White rule for the foreseeable future; and we should note that Smith, voicing the latter, was regarded suspiciously as a "liberal" by proponents of the former.

Attitudes toward the University College of Rhodesia and Nyasaland in Salisbury illustrated that the RF was not of one mind. Influential RF politicians resented this conspicuous institution in the capital of the colony. It was multiracial, and it was also a center of dissidence. By 1970, a third of its students were Black, most of whom studied the humanities and social sciences. It employed outsiders and so could keep in touch with the world beyond Rhodesia (and that world's criticism of illegal White minority rule). It was known as "the little Kremlin" by RF backbenchers who wanted to increase political control over the curriculum as well as over students and staff. Radical staff were deported. But a pragmatic Ian Smith stepped in to defend the institution from extremist critics. "We inherited the thing, which was wrong," he conceded; but, he continued, excessive criticisms were damaging its reputation and encouraging White families to send their children to respectable alternatives abroad.[18] The university's distinctive qualities were needed, he argued, if only in a public relations demonstration that Rhodesia was a civilized society.

Sensing no need to appeal to either radicalized African opinion in Rhodesia or liberal European opinion at home or abroad, the RF replaced the Land Apportionment Act of 1930 with the Land Tenure Act of 1969. This divided land on a racial basis, and it imposed tighter restrictions on Africans. The former act could be altered by a simple vote in Parliament, and its terms did not prevent transfers of land from one category to the other (which had led, overall, to some shrinkage of the White area). The new act allocated, supposedly for all time, 45 million acres to each race, when Africans outnumbered Europeans by over twenty to one. Smith rejected criticism, shamelessly declaring: "If this is regarded as discrimination, at least it is equitable."[19]

Other statistics from the later UDI period suggest that land provision was anything but equitable, and that the settler farming lobby maintained considerable influence over government policy. On average, each European farm was approximately 100 times the size of a land unit in the Tribal Trust Lands, and ten times the size of a farm in a native purchase area. In 1976, around 40 percent of all employees in Rhodesia worked on the 6,682 White farms, which in turn produced over a third of the country's foreign exchange earnings. Yet productivity on European farms, many sustained by government subsidies or loans, was variable; it was estimated that over 40 percent of land in European ownership was either not used or underused.

Iniquities regarding land drew scathing criticism from one British visitor. "An extraordinary feature of the Rhodesian countryside is that one may drive for over a hundred miles without seeing a single African village. The land has been enclosed by barbed wire, signifying that all these hundreds of thousands of acres belong to White men. Given the historical circumstances of the last century, the conquest of Rhodesia by Europeans was understandable. But that they should have put barbed wire round half the country's land area, and forbidden Africans to enter it (except as their laborers and servants) strikes me as an unbelievable act of theft and injustice. . . . A great part of the enclosed land is not even being farmed."[20]

Meanwhile, the Land Tenure Act affirmed that Africans had no right to live in a White area. The RF further regulated employment of Africans in urban areas and their access to schools and hospitals. In a definitive break with more liberal thinking of the 1950s, it was now argued—as it had been in apartheid South Africa for years—that separation, not partnership, would reduce racial friction. Some senior figures in the Christian churches disagreed, both European and African. The act directly impeded multiracial church services, as it was now illegal for one race to enter another's area. It was thus opposed by Abel Muzorewa, bishop of the United Methodist Church, and Donal Lamont, a Roman Catholic bishop, among others. But for the time being at least, the government could ignore this opposition.

In the wake of these changes, it seemed most unlikely that the new conservative government of Edward Heath in Britain would finally endorse Rhodesia's independence. Nevertheless, when Smith met a sympathetic Alec Douglas-Home (the former Earl of Home, now foreign secretary) in November 1971, they did reach an agreement. Or rather, the British, having had no bargaining power since 1923 and having long ago ruled out the use of force, capitulated. The agreed-upon formula envisaged a distant time when most of the population would be qualified to vote via property and educational criteria. Smith was delighted, content to accept "majority rule" with the knowledge that it could be both flexibly interpreted and indefinitely postponed. But he had a problem: he had already conceded before the UDI that any constitutional settlement with Britain had to be seen to be acceptable to a majority of Rhodesians.

The eminent British barrister and judge, Lord Edward Pearce, was selected to travel to Rhodesia to test public opinion of all races in the breakaway colony. He arrived in mid-January of 1972. There were strong indications that he would discover widespread rejection of the proposed deal. Africans resented the exclusion from negotiations of their political leaders (many of whom were in detention), and they mistrusted the continuing White regime. In December 1971, the bishop Abel Muzorewa had stepped into the limelight, at the head of a new organization, the African National Council (ANC). This was a conscious echo of the long since banned African National Congress, and support for it spread with astonishing speed across the country. At last, Africans were being consulted about their future, albeit still not by their own government but by a foreign one. As early as January 28, Muzorewa stated the ANC's uncompromising position. "No settlement of the Rhodesian problem can be achieved without the active participation of the African people, through the leaders of their choice, in the actual process of negotiation."[21]

Thereafter, Pearce's commissioners heard fervent African criticism of a proposed deal in which the qualifications for voting would continue to be out of reach for so many. Furthermore, the Land Tenure

Act would remain in place. Imaginative attempts to sway African opinion fell flat. Having offered voters a big feast, one incredulous district commissioner lamented, "I slaughtered beasts for them, but still they rejected the proposals."[22] We may note in passing that this episode signified the end of the Centre Party's prominence, notwithstanding its commitment to multiracialism. When Pat Bashford, its European leader, declared the party ready to accept the Smith-Home proposals, Ronnie Sadoma, an African Centre Party member of parliament (MP), demurred. "I have discovered that the Africans whom I represent are definitely rejecting them. My conscience can no longer allow me to go on like this. Therefore, I want to join the ANC and be an independent MP."[23]

When Pearce presented the commission's verdict on May 4, 1972, Smith was shocked. Pearce's report concluded that "the people of Rhodesia as a whole do not regard the proposals as acceptable as a basis for independence." Observers noted that the Pearce commission "laid a number of long propagated myths to rest, including the belief that the Rhodesian Africans were apolitical, pleased with European administration and, in Mr. Smith's own words, 'the happiest Africans in the world.'"[24] The ANC had suddenly emerged, according to the report, because of "a potential desire among a majority of the people for leadership in a rejection of the terms, and in a protest against the policies of the last few years." One such policy was to arrest and detain both Garfield Todd and his daughter, Judith. While there had been some intimidation of Blacks during the commissioner's visit, there was no doubt that African rejection of the proposals by a substantial majority was "a genuine expression of opinion."[25] Yet this rebuff was not a vote for liberation through guerrilla warfare; rather, it could be interpreted as an indication that, as had been the case in the 1950s, many if not most politically conscious educated Africans yearned for participation, partnership, and genuine progress toward multiracial government.

Diehard Whites were incredulous. They had been unable to perceive that, for Africans, "mistrust of the intentions and motives of the government transcended all other considerations. Apprehension for the future stemmed from resentment at what they felt to be humiliations of the past. . . . One [African] summed it up by saying 'we do not reject the proposals, we reject the Government.'"[26] In a remarkably small-minded outburst, the RF party chairman, Des Frost, warned that "the Africans must realise there are limits as to how far the tolerance of the whites will stretch."[27] There were some signs that African nationalist "tolerance" was already approaching breaking point.

International Efforts to Find a Solution

Three pressures of varying intensity combined to push Smith toward the political concessions he had resisted for so long. The first pressure was the intensification of violence, primarily from two rival African guerrilla organizations. Under the pressure of a state of emergency and proscription after 1958, and especially following the RF's election victory in December 1962, rivalries had assumed a new and damaging shape. By the 1970s the two main groups were, to a large extent, distinguished by ethnicity. ZANU was based across the eastern border in Mozambique, along with its military wing, the Zimbabwe African National Liberation Army (ZANLA). ZAPU was based in Zambia to the north, along with its military wing, the Zimbabwe People's Revolutionary Army (ZIPRA). Leadership of the mainly Shona ZANU was fiercely contested, with Ndabaningi Sithole eventually replaced by Robert Mugabe (who enjoyed the support of the Tanzanian president, Julius Nyerere). In contrast, Joshua Nkomo's leadership of the largely Ndebele ZAPU remained secure, his patron being Kenneth Kaunda of Zambia. ZANLA's December 1972 attack on a tobacco farm owned by an unpopular White settler is widely adopted as the take-off event of the liberation war. For a while, the regime could contain the violence, but by mid-decade there was a significant intensification of pressure on Smith's government.

The second pressure was economic. Although Rhodesia's economy initially stood up well to sanctions, in time it came under strain. Moreover, with the fall of Portuguese colonial power in Mozambique in 1974, it became increasingly dependent on South Africa. This was a relationship, potentially a stranglehold, which the apartheid regime was quite ready to exploit for its own purposes. When the Rhodesian economy became skewed by the need to enable the security forces to sustain a long, drawn-out war against guerrillas both inside and outside the country, the strain on business and finances intensified. There was no better indication of the declining health of White Rhodesia at this time than the loss of White manpower, not to the war, but to emigration. The early years of the UDI had witnessed a rise in White immigration; by 1973, there were 270,000 Whites in Rhodesia (nearly half of them living in the Salisbury area). In 1975, liability for military service after two years' residence proved a deterrent for prospective new immigrants. But it was the *emigration* of many Whites already in Rhodesia that gave the strongest signal that the regime could not wage war indefinitely and would eventually have to make a political deal.

The third pressure was diplomatic. Smith could afford to be contemptuous of the British. In contrast, he was shocked and dismayed by far more insistent pressure from South Africa, which was in more than one sense his closest neighbor. And in the context of global Cold War, he also had to bend to the United States, which saw the various problems of the region through the lens of the contest between communism and the free world. Smith, a man who saw everything in black and white, struggled to make sense of others' motivations, especially when John Vorster's apartheid South Africa and Jimmy Carter's progressive United States were aligned. But these international developments were beyond Rhodesia's control.

The fact that Smith was so slow and reluctant to acknowledge reality amounted to a self-imposed pressure. He continued to believe that the guerrillas could be beaten, that most Black Rhodesians would unconditionally support his regime, that White morale was unbreakable, and that South Africa (and the United States) would never abandon Rhodesia to "Marxists." Presenting himself as a frank and consistent man of principle, he railed against the treachery, deceit, and intrigue of all those who sought to influence the direction and destiny of his country.

* * *

1975 witnessed a détente exercise. This was apartheid South Africa's attempt at a rapprochement with Black Africa. John Vorster, the prime minister and subsequent president of South Africa, sought to cooperate with Zambia's Kenneth Kaunda to get Smith to work out a compromise settlement in Rhodesia. This would involve both Muzorewa and Nkomo.

The initiative was prompted by the collapse of the two vast Portuguese colonies and the fear that each would become a regional base for world communism. Nothing could have been worse for South Africa than Rhodesia also succumbing to militant African nationalist forces supported by Russia or China. An unlikely quintet was born, comprising Vorster and Smith, plus Kaunda, Nkomo, and Muzorewa. Vorster would persuade Smith to talk; Kaunda would persuade Muzorewa and Nkomo to unite. The desired outcome was a compromise settlement that would please all but the extremists.

The Pretoria Agreement was signed on August 9, 1975, by Vorster and Smith, as well as Mark Chona, Zambia's representative. The plan was to bring together the Rhodesian government and the ANC in the hopes that proposals for a settlement would emerge from such a meeting.

But this was a futile exercise, in part because any settlement would have been ignored by an increasingly militant and capable ZANU, now operating under Robert Mugabe; but also because Smith did not yet recognize that he had to accept any settlement that sidelined him and his party. Smith was dismissive of what he termed "Vorster's détente capers," especially when his own security forces were reporting unprecedented success against the guerrillas. Smith later lamented that "South Africa, however, controlled our lifeline," and they would exploit that fact by withholding supplies and interrupting trade.[28]

The high point of this episode was the near-farcical conference held at Victoria Falls in August 1975. According to Smith, this was the brainchild of John Vorster, who was determined to be in the foreground in order to gain maximum credit for any resulting success. The meeting was held not in the grand Victoria Falls Hotel, but in a railway train parked on the bridge across the Zambezi. The river marked the border; the bridge straddled the river. Smith would not travel *outside* Rhodesia to discuss Rhodesia's affairs, and the African leaders would not meet *inside* Rhodesia for fear of being arrested. Parked on the bridge, this train could be half in Rhodesia and half in Zambia. The line of the border was extended to bisect a long table running down the middle of the carriage. In this "jamboree," Smith wrote afterward, "there were buffet saloons attached to both ends, loaded with every conceivable kind of drink. This worried me. There were six [people] on our side" [of the conference carriage]," he added, "and about forty on theirs, packed in like sardines."[29]

Here, the Vorster-Kaunda strategy was to bring the two sides together to agree to send representatives to Salisbury to negotiate a new constitution. There were supposed to be no preconditions for these "talks about talks," but Muzorewa (ANC) began by insisting on agreement on one-man, one-vote. On this issue, Smith would not budge. The railway carriage conference amounted to less than three hours of actual discussion. Smith was not prepared to give anything away, and there was no agreement among the African leaders present, including Sithole (ZANU) and James Chikerema of the Front for the Liberation of Zimbabwe (FROLIZI), a small force comprised of exiles from ZAPU and ZANU. After this non-event, Nkomo's comment said it all. At the times for refreshment, he noted, the tea and coffee came into each side from their own ends of the train; but "nothing came across the line, not even ideas."[30]

This strange gathering served only to enhance the uncompromising position of Robert Mugabe (ZANU), who had not attended. ZANU's guerrilla war intensified. Under stress, Smith held talks with Joshua Nkomo in February 1976. Before the talks collapsed, Nkomo tried to alert Smith to the scale of the danger he and his fellow Whites were in by referring to the dramatic events in Angola, Rhodesia's ex-Portuguese neighbor to the west. "The Portuguese had to run out of Angola because of their stubbornness," Nkomo told Smith. "We hope people in Zimbabwe realise that unless they think fast, they may have to run out in their pyjamas."[31]

Meanwhile, the RF's governance came under verbal as well as physical attack. The ongoing crisis did not silence critical voices of White liberals within Rhodesia who sought to sustain the moral debate, which had dominated the late 1950s. In August 1976, Donal Lamont, bishop of the Catholic Church in Rhodesia, roundly castigated Smith's administration. He focused on inequality, the intensification of racial discrimination, and intercommunal discord:

> As a Catholic bishop, I cannot be silent while civil discontent, racial tension and violence are so much in evidence and daily on the increase. Conscience compels me to state that your administration, by its clearly racist and oppressive policies and by its stubborn refusal to change, is largely responsible for the injustices which have provoked the present disorder; and it must in that measure be considered guilty of whatever misery or bloodshed may follow. Far from your policies defending Christianity and Western Civilisation as you claim, they mock the law of Christ and make communism attractive to people.[32]

Shortly afterward, Lamont was arrested, charged with not reporting the presence of guerrillas to security forces, tried, and sentenced to ten years in prison with hard labor. In March 1977, he was deported. His real offense had been to denounce injustice and to hold the beleaguered White government morally responsible for the conflict unfolding. Yet the White wife of a college principal considered he had got off lightly. She asked Denis Hills over tea, "What sort of a churchman is Lamont? I have a son in the army fighting these Black murderers. If the Bishop sides with terrorists, he deserves to have his throat cut."[33]

International diplomatic pressure, meanwhile, was unrelenting, and by the end of 1976 it appeared to have succeeded in breaking Smith's resolve. In September, he made a radio broadcast that stunned his White listeners. He announced that Rhodesians would see majority rule—not in a thousand years, as he had recently claimed, but after just two years of an interim power-sharing government. How had this change come about, and how significant was it?

Henry Kissinger could congratulate himself. The US government, of which he was secretary of state, was tied firmly to South Africa during the Cold War. In South Africa, Vorster was anxious to secure his strategic goals. It was after a meeting with Vorster that Kissinger persuaded Smith to make that potentially game-changing concession. The American stressed the growing threat from the guerrillas and told Smith that no one would ride to White Rhodesia's rescue militarily. Smith later recalled that Kissinger repeatedly apologized for insisting on a concession so horrid, while insisting that he was actually hawking a British plan (hence "Anglo-American" proposals). Included in the package of five points were a racially balanced council of state (to usher in a new constitution) and a council of ministers, with Africans in the majority. This deal, Kissinger predicted, would bring an end to the guerrilla war, the lifting of sanctions, and access to a trust fund for economic development.

Under additional pressure from a growing economic crisis, including increasing loss of White manpower through emigration, Smith revealed in his September 24 broadcast that he had signed up to responsible majority rule. But there was considerable ambiguity as to what this meant. Smith judged that the process could see the Whites retain control of all essential government portfolios, as the United States and South Africa intended, and have a White chair of the council of state. If there were no agreement on the details of a constitution in two years, this interim arrangement could carry on (though with sanctions lifted and recognition obtained). Furthermore, Smith, in a devious move, told Vorster that no constitutional changes of this order could be introduced in Rhodesia without endorsement from a two-thirds majority in the still White-dominated parliament.

Even so, Smith hated the situation in which he and his country had been placed. "Rhodesia was to be the sacrificial lamb which would buy for South Africa peace and acceptance of their apartheid policy"— acceptance, that is, by Kaunda and the presidents of other front-line African states. Smith insisted that he had no option but to go along with the Anglo-American plan. "Vorster placed the proverbial pistol to our head.... We were faced with his threat to cut off our supply line.... Kissinger's proposal seemed to be the only glimmer of hope." So he complied with Vorster's "escapade into détente," which was designed to secure a pliant, moderate African regime in Rhodesia, and to avoid a militant, Marxist one. Though he hoped to manage any transition process for White Rhodesians' benefit, there was no disguising how disturbing for Smith this shift in his public stance had been. When he was subsequently asked about the later Internal Settlement of March 1978, "Wasn't that occasion an emotional and traumatic experience?" Smith answered, "No." That experience had come in 1976, when he had to accept Kissinger's Anglo-American proposals.[34]

The follow-up to Smith's concession was the Geneva Conference, involving all parties to the dispute, from October to December 1976. This turned out to be another largely pointless, if not farcical, occasion. Smith had no strategy but to adhere to what he had agreed with Kissinger, the package of five points that he deemed non-negotiable. Front-line presidents Nyerere and Kaunda had not been deceived by what Kissinger had offered (and Smith had accepted): they realized that the Whites' interpretation of majority rule was no more than a formula for denying power to Black nationalists. They therefore rejected the proposals. Prior to the conference, in a political move of some lasting significance, Nkomo (ZAPU) and Mugabe (ZANU) agreed to present themselves as united in a Patriotic Front (PF). This was an embryo broad political leadership of the nationalist movement, though it excluded both Muzorewa and Sithole. The PF set itself to oppose the Anglo-American proposal and to make demands of its own, including the release of all political prisoners and the abolition of all restrictions on political activity.

Almost two decades after his fall from power, Garfield Todd was allowed to attend the Geneva talks as adviser to Nkomo's delegation. By this time, Nkomo's status was diminishing among both moderate and radical Africans. He had been in detention during the Pearce commission's inquiry, which saw the emergence of Muzorewa as a political rival; and, subsequently, he appeared reluctant to participate fully in the liberation war. Nevertheless, the fact that he was still a central player serves to remind us of earlier possibilities. In 1975, Nkomo had asked Ian Smith to allow him to have Todd as his adviser at their talks. Smith had said this was not possible, even that late in the day, because Todd was "a top security risk"—a "non-person," moreover, who for more than four years had been barred from straying more than 800 meters from his farm.[35]

Britain's former ambassador to the UN, Ivor Richard, was out of his depth as chairman of the Geneva gathering, which, despite bringing together the right people, could find no consensus. Perhaps his was an impossible task. Weeks passed without any fruitful discussion. Smith would proceed only on the basis of the five points; the nationalists remained divided. "All participants said their piece, restated their positions and retired to fight or intrigue."[36] In mid-December, Smith snidely declared: "This conference is about to make history by adjourning before it has actually commenced."[37] Robert Mugabe, now the acknowledged leader of ZANU and its forces, offered a more profound comment: "We shouldn't worry about the Kissinger-British proposals. They can put in any puppet government they want, but a puppet government cannot contain us."[38]

Meanwhile, on the domestic front, Smith and the RF maintained the superstructure of White power and privilege. In April 1976, a government-sponsored commission recommended some progressive reforms. The commission, which included moderate Africans and was chaired by a former high court judge, Sir Vincent Quenet, had been set up to investigate aspects of racial discrimination. Among its bold recommendations was an amendment of the Land Tenure Act, which the cautiously worded report identified as the primary cause of racial friction. Its proposal was to open all land until now designated European (except in residential/urban areas) to possible African purchase. The commission also recommended a return to the common roll for voting. But its report was strangled at birth. There was no common position among members of the RF, but enough were horrified. Smith ruled out changes to either the Land Tenure Act or the voting system. It was as if there had been no earlier moral challenge to their racism, no liberation war, and no need to indicate to world opinion that changes were in hand. Deeply rooted White complacency persisted.

Toward an Internal Settlement and Endgame

After Geneva, Ivor Richard brought revised British proposals to Salisbury. According to these, a resident British commissioner would head a multiracial security council and, very shortly, cede authority to an African government effectively under the control of the Patriotic Front (which was recognized in January 1977 by the Organisation of African Unity as the sole legitimate liberation organization in Rhodesia). It was inconceivable that Smith would accept such a plan. Later, Smith said of Richard's promotion of such an improbable scenario, "I could not believe he was serious."[39] Instead, Smith announced he would proceed with his own plans for a transition to majority rule.

Before long, however, he had to respond to a new Anglo-American initiative. Prime Minister James Callaghan believed that a joint effort with the United States (whose newly elected president, Jimmy Carter, was eager to promote human rights across the world) would have a greater chance of success than Richard's solitary mission. Thus, David Owen, British foreign secretary, and Andrew Young, US secretary of state, combined to produce a different strategy for a settlement. Whereas Kissinger's plan was to establish an interim government (for two years) and let it work out details of a new constitution, the Owen-Young plan was to seek broad agreement on the essentials of a new constitution first, and then to decide on transitional arrangements.

This, too, failed to achieve its objective. The plan could not locate enough common ground for Smith, on the one hand, and the PF, on the other. Perhaps a new conference could have been convened on the promise of, for instance, a government elected on the widest possible franchise, and an independent judiciary with a justiciable bill of rights. But how were the security forces of an independent Zimbabwe to be instituted and deployed? Unsurprisingly in the context of a war being waged, there was unbreakable deadlock. The PF insisted that their forces should take control (having forced Smith to negotiate) and argued that the White security forces would block meaningful majority rule. The PF also refused to accept that an interim administration should involve either a British commissioner or a neutral peacekeeping force. For his part, Smith distrusted Owen, accused him of making concessions to terrorists who lacked unity and discipline, and stressed that if the existing Rhodesian security force was disbanded, the country would collapse because the Whites would abandon it.

Smith had always regarded settlement initiatives from outside Rhodesia as unsympathetic, if not ill-intentioned, interference in his country's internal affairs. The latest being no more acceptable or practicable than those that preceded it, he stood firm against participating in a conference on the Owen-Young plan. Instead, he resumed his own search for African partners and, with them, a formula for resolving the illegal republic's prolonged political crisis. Late in 1977, his followers continued to whistle in the dark. A dozen years of the UDI were to be celebrated. On November 10, an independence ball was staged in Salisbury, but this amounted to "little more than a group of middle-aged conservatives honouring an event which had nearly caused the ruin of a nation." Even so, the republic's new national anthem, written in 1974, was sung (to the familiar, if singularly inappropriate, tune of Beethoven's "Ode to Joy"); and Prime Minister Smith was cheered when he toasted "twelve incredible years."[40] "Let us hope that with 1978 a new era is about to begin. . . . We should grasp the opportunities open to us to end our dispute, to the benefit of all our people," said Smith in his 1978 new year message.

What opportunities, though? Smith renewed his search for prominent Africans who could agree to, and deliver, a satisfactory formula for the country's future. He spoke primarily to Muzorewa, head of what was now the UANC (United ANC), which by this time included both James Chikerema, former radical of the Salisbury City Youth League (CYL), and Elliot Gabellah, an accomplished and well-respected chief from Matabeleland. Smith held additional talks with Ndabaningi Sithole (no longer head of ZANU), and some favored chiefs, such as Chief Chirau. It was these people who, in this Internal Settlement, eventually agreed to the creation of a transitional government on March 3, 1978, based on eight constitutional provisions. The main sticking point had concerned White representation in the new parliament. It was decided that there would be twenty-eight seats (out of a hundred) reserved for Whites elected on a separate roll, as well as a blocking mechanism that would require approval by three-quarters of MPs (including at least six Whites). These arrangements would last for ten years. There was no indication as to how the new government would tackle issues relating to the ownership of land.

But neither the United States nor Britain would recognize such a transitional government. They insisted that Rhodesia accept plans for a new conference where all parties to the conflict would gather, including the PF, which predictably rejected the so-called internal settlement. This deal was criticized from within, too, in a sign of continuing differences of opinion among Whites. Byron Hove, a European lawyer and minister in the new Rhodesia administration, was sacked in April 1978 for advocating a program of substantial reform. "To win over the Black people, we have to be seen to be making changes," he insisted. "We have to do something." After flying to London, he declared his own administration's Internal Settlement a sham. Of Smith, he declared, "He believes in the substance of power remaining in white hands, with the shadow of authority passing to blacks. That is his majority rule."[41]

The new transitional government, led by an executive council including Muzorewa, Sithole, and Smith, lacked credibility on several levels. The one African nationalist figure who could have given it authority was Nkomo, Smith's preferred partner all along—at least during the five years since he realized, belatedly, that talking to Nkomo might have been more sensible than imprisoning him. Kissinger would have approved: "If I could have picked someone from the beginning," Kissinger remarked in 1977, "it would have been Nkomo. Nkomo is the best."[42] Nkomo was a known moderate who was ready to make compromises, yet also the leader of ZAPU and its armed wing ZIPRA, which he had been holding back but could unleash. It would be a political masterstroke if Smith could bring on board such a significant figure: an act which would, moreover, split the PF and isolate Mugabe's ZANU. But Nkomo kept his distance. Smith continued to engage with him—they met secretly in Lusaka in August—and even offered him chairmanship of the new executive council. Nkomo declined. "I want to come home," he responded. "But after all those years in detention, prison and exile, I can't come back to a shadow of what we have been fighting for."[43] Nkomo knew that any durable settlement had to be with the PF as a whole, and especially with Mugabe, who would continue to obstruct any alternative. Smith's long-overdue attempt to enter a working political alliance with the man who had personified moderate African nationalism since the early 1950s was frustrated. Nkomo observed later: "I found Smith a tired man, a battered man. He told me he wanted to surrender power, to hand the whole thing over."[44]

Unsurprisingly, John Ngara, an African Marxist, depicted the settlement as a way "to perpetuate the repressive regime through the cosmetic involvement of some Africans." His judgment of the Africans involved was severe. He was dismissive of the urban educated Africans in the UANC as comprising academics, professionals, and businessmen who favored private enterprise while harboring their own doubts about majority rule. He was disdainful, too, of the Zimbabwe United People's Organisation (ZUPO), sponsored as a party in 1976 by the White regime, as speaking only for ill-educated chiefs, paid employees of the government whose priority was law and order. This harsh critique carries some weight. But it was not entirely reprehensible that some members of the variegated African middle class and chiefs chose to identify with a regime that "sustains and guarantees their existence."[45] Not every African was a revolutionary socialist, active or armchair. The more important point is that both parties to this Internal Settlement were weak. The White regime had chosen a course that was unsustainable; the Africans appended to it were unproven as representatives of the Black majority. Neither could stop the war.

The new administration carried on, very much as before. There was no repeal yet of the Land Tenure Act. Smith, fearing White resistance to such a move, maintained that the government could not spare the time needed for a proper review of such complex questions. But its African nationalist opponents waged war against the White settlers and their transitional government, more seriously and effectively now, especially from ZANU bases in the east. 320 White farmers were killed between 1973 and 1979: "Every farm was a target."[46] ZIPRA was having more of an impact, too, out of Zambia. It shot down a civilian plane in September 1978, which caused Smith to label Nkomo "a monster." By this time, the war against ZANLA and ZIPRA, within Rhodesia and beyond its borders, was a daily reality. The internal security situation became increasingly grim, with White farmers complaining that their workers were intimidated or killed by guerrillas. And the state's security forces were hemorrhaging White personnel. Through emigration, Smith recalled, "we were losing one territorial company of our fighting men per month. This was an intolerable situation."[47] There was a net loss of 13,000 Whites between June 1978 and February 1979, a span of a little over half a year.

By 1978, Robert Mugabe was firmly established within ZANU—and in the public consciousness—as the personification of fighting to the end, eschewing compromise. His ZANLA was inflicting real damage on the Smith regime and emerging as a political force over an expanding area of the country. Nkomo's ZAPU were less effective, partly because Zambia was a far harder base from which guerrillas could operate; the Zambezi River provided a strong natural line of defense for Rhodesia, compared to Mozambique, with its porous border of mountain and forest. Even so, according to Nkomo in his memoir, ZAPU shot down around thirty Rhodesian warplanes and helicopters, causing the resignation of a minister of defense. Nkomo claimed that Smith's cover-up of these losses was one of his greatest propaganda successes of the war. Yet it became increasingly clear to all concerned that the interim government did not have the means of defeating the guerrilla campaigns adopted by the two wings of the PF.

Still, 1979 began with a referendum for Whites on the March 1978 constitutional proposals, which remained unratified . . . and in which every instrument of White power other than parliament would remain under White control. 85 percent of participants approved. Meanwhile, after ten years in place, the Land Tenure Act was at last repealed, only to be replaced by economic hurdles to ensure most Blacks remained separated from the White community (for example, access to different schools and hospitals had to be purchased).

On April 20, a general election was held. Smith's RF won every White seat (though a dozen of its MPs, outraged at the course of events, had left his party to form a more extreme alternative). Muzorewa and the UANC won 67 percent of the valid votes cast by Africans. The elections were not entirely free and fair, but observers concluded that the result did express the will of most African people. "A black leader who promised peace was considered worth having."[48] The election undoubtedly represented something of a victory for the Whites, in two respects.

Arrangements that kept them in key positions of power had been endorsed. In addition, their rebellious state was still seen to be functioning, despite the war. While the guerrillas (of whom there were over 12,000 in the country by now) had tried to persuade Africans to boycott the election, the government had urged them to turn out and vote. About 1.8 million votes were cast; only 18 out of 932 polling stations were attacked. It is of some interest that, before this election, Chief Ndiweni broke from Chief Chirau's group to form the United National Federal Party. This advocated a federal system for future African self-government that would safeguard the position of the Ndebele (of whom Ndiweni was a chief for many years), and would thus regulate the postindependence relationship between Zimbabwe's two major ethnic groups. Yet nothing came of this potentially significant initiative.

On June 1, Abel Muzorewa became first prime minister of Zimbabwe-Rhodesia—a clumsy name that seemed only to signify unfinished business—with Smith as minister without portfolio. But Muzorewa proved inept. Vain and shallow, he had been catapulted to the fore during 1971–1972 when others were in detention. Since then, he had served the purposes of various political forces who needed a respectable figurehead. He was at his most absurd when claiming in October 1978 that all racial discrimination was finished. As prime minister he was out of his depth, hopelessly indecisive. His ham-fistedness was evident in, for example, inviting 1,000 Vietnamese "boat people" to a country with an African unemployment rate of 50 percent; and in seeking, with terrible timing, to wipe out groups of Sithole's mutinous auxiliaries during an amnesty program.

Yet the one diplomatic goal that Smith had sought for over a decade eluded him. There was no recognition of Rhodesia, by any country. The Internal Settlement was not thought by foreign governments to be a manifestation of majority rule; and in any case, the PF sustained its liberation war against this new regime. The August 1979 Commonwealth Heads of Government meeting in Lusaka confirmed the complete international isolation of a country whose government still so closely resembled that of the former White self-governing colony. In Lusaka, pressure was put on the new British prime minister, Margaret Thatcher, by influential Commonwealth individuals such as Michael Manley of Jamaica and Australia's Malcolm Fraser. But it was probably Kenneth Kaunda's dogged insistence that ensured that Muzorewa's Zimbabwe-Rhodesia was not recognized and that the British agreed to host a constitutional conference in London for all parties to the conflict. This would start in September at Lancaster House . . . where Zimbabwe would be born.

* * *

Why did Ian Smith agree to engage in peace talks? There were few options for the Whites of Rhodesia beyond the choice of staying or leaving. Their government was simply committed to holding what they held ... until a new order was imposed on them. In his memoir, Smith presents the liberation war as little more than an irritant, while highlighting atrocities carried out by guerrilla forces. But his portrayal needs fleshing out. The far more convincing verdict of two White reservists is that

> from 1965 to 1972, the guerrillas had managed to apply pinpricks to white rule. In the second phase, from 1972 to 1976, there had been a large degree of African mobilisation, particularly in Mashonaland, but the government had managed to contain the burgeoning conflict with the reluctant and erratic support of South Africa. In the following three years, 1977–79, the war would grow to engulf the whole country and to destroy the Rhodesian government's resolve to fight on.[49]

Resolve as well as capability was worn down. The political turning point in the 1970s was Smith's public acceptance of majority rule in his broadcast on September 24, 1976. The primary pressure on him then was diplomatic, not military. Vorster was leaning heavily on Smith for a ceasefire, with a goal of obtaining a negotiated settlement in the region. Smith was bitter about this intervention: "We were on the brink of dealing a knock-out blow. We had them on the run."[50] At that time, Smith later insisted, "the security forces were having great success in the war against the terrorists and their kill-rate had reached the highest peak ever."[51] A credible independent estimate, moreover, was that "in March 1976, the Rhodesian government appeared to be on top of the war."[52]

The full-scale war took off only after Smith's political concession to Kissinger. The subsequent Geneva conference may have fueled a sense that Smith's Rhodesia was weakening and vulnerable, although the White regime was still in place. Thereafter, in the period between 1977 and 1979, the military factor did become decisive. For Smith, the main purpose of any internal political settlement was to end the war. He mistakenly thought his deal with African moderates would stem the flow of new recruits into ZANLA and ZIPRA and even bring in Nkomo. But the time had passed. And to Smith's chagrin, although majority rule appeared to have been secured, Muzorewa's elevation to prime minister of Zimbabwe-Rhodesia did not end the war. With Whites allowed to continue in power, the war intensified behind the façade, to the extent that the Rhodesia elections planned for December 1978 had to be postponed to the following spring. The reality was that only Mugabe could end guerrilla hostilities, and any settlement that did not include the PF would not persuade him to—nor would it earn international recognition and all the benefits that would bring.

The Rhodesian security forces could not defeat the increasing number of guerrillas. It had been estimated in March 1976 that there were no more than 700 guerrillas left in the field. A year later, there were three times as many. Take-off came from mid-1978, so that during 1979 guerrilla numbers grew from 10,000 to over 15,000, by which time over 90 percent of the territory was under martial law. The Rhodesian economy was under increasing strain by this time, and tax collection was breaking down. Above all, their own dwindling numbers ruled out a victory for the White minority. Though the UDI had seen an influx of new immigrants, in 1978 net emigration was 13,709. As one British academic neatly put it, "Rhodesia has always been a country of impermanent white residence."[53] From 1976 to 1978, almost 50,000 emigrated, approaching a fifth of the entire White population. The greater number who stayed cast their votes in April 1979 in a delayed general election, contrasting with the thousands of people who had already voted with their feet. The Whites who remained included some of that persistent minority of liberal-minded Whites who had never voted for the RF. But the rising number of both guerrillas and White emigrants were parallel indications that the time of White minority rule was approaching its end. Morale in the security forces could no longer be taken for granted. By 1978, 80 percent of their number were Black. But what were they fighting for, now? Smith found himself with no option but to talk.

* * *

What, then, brought Robert Mugabe to the negotiating table? To his disappointment and frustration, the regime's ability to hold the election in April 1979 demonstrated that the Rhodesian state could still function. As Samora Machel told Mugabe, contrasting the Rhodesia situation with the collapse of Portuguese rule in Mozambique: "We FRELIMO secured independence by military victory against colonists. But your settlers have not been defeated, so you must negotiate."[54]

Through the 1970s, African opposition to the White regime remained undiminished. For town dwellers in particular, privilege was at its heart. Herbert Chitepo, barrister-turned-guerrilla leader, identified privilege as fueling resistance to White rule. He wrote in 1973 that the incipient war of liberation was designed to do such damage to the Rhodesian economy that the Whites would have to yield. It aimed to break "the morale of the Whites, most of whom had come to Zimbabwe lured by the prospect of the easy, privileged life promised by the regime."[55] Such a life largely excluded Africans. Those who acquired the conventional trappings of European civilization, primarily through education, were generally not acknowledged as having done so. Many politically conscious young school-leavers were not absorbed into the White world; rather, they were "unwanted in commerce and industry, unwelcome in the civil service, and generally cast away by the controlling white society."[56] Another ceiling of privilege lay in the franchise. Whatever their achievements and attitudes, Africans were too often not recognized as capable of partnership or even cooperation. They had not, in the settlers' estimation (and it was they who were empowered to judge), progressed far *enough*. In short, Smith's government largely closed the door on African aspiration. But this was a door that, in due course, mission-educated African nationalists and their tens of thousands of supporters were to rattle and, ultimately, force open.

Layers of segregation persisted. Holderness wrote of the industrial color bar: "It is no advertisement for European civilisation that Europeans should have to secure themselves by preventing employees of another race from doing work which they were capable of doing."[57] Vambe's critique was wider ranging. "If a society has to depend on its survival solely on machine guns," he wrote in 1972, "rather than on its attractions of freedom, justice and the enduring foundations of respect and loyalty between its people, then it is clear that its architects have failed to subscribe to the values on which Western civilisation was founded."[58] On the other side of the Atlantic, the writer James Baldwin had observed that a Black's experience "cannot possibly create in him any respect for the standards by which the white world claims to live. His own condition is overwhelming proof that white people do not live by these standards." He had asked: "How can one respect, let alone adopt, the values of a people who do not, on any level whatever, live the way they say they do, or the way they say they should?"[59] His critique of the southern states in the United States could also be applied to Southern Rhodesia.

Rhodesian Africans hoped that attending the White man's schools would enable them to share in the White man's world. But access was denied. They could neither socialize with the Whites nor vote with them (aside from a select few). Mission schools thus offered more than they could deliver. Their education might fulfill, but it could also frustrate. Christianity had the potential to break barriers and did so at times, but it did not dissolve them. During the liberation war, Vambe wrote about the shallow and self-destructive hypocrisy of an un-Christian White etiquette, which sustained remoteness and lacked empathy. "I suggest that it is conceivable that had the majority of Europeans in Southern Rhodesia been able to exercise elementary patience and civility towards their fellow African citizens, we might have been able to learn to know and trust one another as human beings, surely the first and most vital step on the difficult road to the democratic building of a nation."[60]

Such was the fuel of protest and intensifying opposition in the colony. Leading African nationalists were effective at garnering sympathetic world opinion. What mattered more, however, was the situation beyond the towns and suburbs of the colony, where African farmers' grievances over land loss, forced migrations, and top-down intervention in land use had accumulated over the past decades. And it was in the rural areas that the war was being fought.

Here, across the territory, wrote Terence Ranger, "a consistent peasant political ideology and programme, developed from the 1940s . . . contributed powerfully to the ideology and programme of the rural guerrilla war."[61] Peasants fought not only for the recovery of their lost lands, but for "a state that would back black farming against white, rather than the other way round," and one, moreover, that would not interfere with peasant production.[62] The guerrillas knew how to attract peasant support. "We did not tell the peasants about socialism," one fighter recalled; another explained "that you do not talk about the capitalist state or the socialist state to them: what mattered to them was how to do away with their grievances at the present time."[63] Peasant support entailed not only providing guerrillas with food and shelter and information but also participating in attacks on soft targets: for example, rustling White farmers' cattle. Meanwhile, the role of religious beliefs, old and new, in African resistance was complex. There were numerous instances of Christians, European and African, committing themselves to the armed struggle. Yet some fighters were hostile to Christianity: "We don't want to hear about Jesus. Jesus can do nothing." And a significant ideological contribution to the cohesion of resistance, echoing that of the mid-1890s across Mashonaland and Matabeleland, was that of Indigenous spirit mediums, the "traditional" protectors of the land.[64]

The guerrillas had a powerful cause and a simple message, and it appears that their propaganda was far more effective than the White regime's. Years of association with communist China proved especially fruitful for ZANU. Maoists provided would-be African guerrillas with both confidence and capacity: "A sense of audacious possibility, as well as techniques for reaching the Zimbabwean grassroots," in the words of Julia Lovell, professor on modern China in London.[65] Rex Nhongo, ZANLA commander, recalled: "In the Soviet Union, they had told us that the decisive factor of the war was weapons. When I got to Itumbi [Tanzania], where there were Chinese instructors, I was told that the decisive factor was the people."[66] Mugabe's guerrillas were indeed in touch with the Zimbabwean peasantry for whom they fought. Their political aspirations were spread by word of mouth in local meetings; many speakers may themselves have been ill-educated, but they came from and knew their people.

Meanwhile, White strategy during the conflict alienated increasing numbers. Methods could be gruesome. They included the injustice and pain of collective punishments, such as hut burning, the slaughter of cattle, and the uprooting of many thousands into "protected villages," where they were uncomfortably contained within wire fencing. These were "desperate places, rife with poor hygiene, disease and abuse by government workers." Rhodesian special forces resorted to biological and chemical warfare, as well as routine brutality against civilians. "ZANU needed every ounce of Maoist discipline to survive the insurgency."[67] By 1979, the activities of auxiliaries (ill-disciplined private armies loyal to one or another African leader in the interim government) often involved looting and intimidation, not security.

Even so, especially away from the rural areas where the guerrilla war was most intense, Africans perceived their own reality in a range of ways, dependent in part on their own situation in the White man's colony. Not all were in active revolt. The order forged by White rule in the first half of the twentieth century offered, as we have seen, not just material goods but some opportunities. Many among a new generation had found employment, income, and purchasing power in the world of the White settlers. In this context, resentment and grievance could fall short of total alienation and a decision to take up arms. Numbers of Africans, especially in the towns, had a stake in, and would bear, the status quo, so long as government by honest officials could provide order, jobs, schools, and hospitals. Up to a point "good government" remained possible. The Rhodesia-Zimbabwe of the Internal Settlement had its activists and supporters, notwithstanding the extent to which it fell short of Black majority rule in practice. In part, it reflected "the considered hope of teachers and mature individuals that a moderate government will prevail—with less honour and glory but with less bloodshed."[68] "Only youth is reckless," observed Hills. "The middle-aged wage or salary earner has too much to lose by challenging authority."[69] There was something of a generational divide: older Africans (with jobs) were more likely to be acquiescent; younger Africans (especially the unemployed) to be more impatient, radicalized, and drawn into active resistance. Nonetheless, many young men volunteered for the security forces and police, albeit in pursuit of employment rather than through heartfelt loyalty to the White man's cause. At the height of the liberation war there were three times as many Blacks as Whites in the full-time police, and they were not conscripts.

In the countryside, where the liberation struggle was grounded, no areas of Zimbabwe were fully and continuously under the control of the liberation movements during the war. While peasant support for the guerrillas did not flag, the fighters of ZANLA and ZIPRA were not capable of defeating the organization, equipment, and firepower of the Whites' forces in an overthrow of the settler state. All Africans in the rural areas were not equally committed to the liberation war. This engendered some intra-African violence. For example, peasant farmers evicted from native purchase areas opposed fellow Africans who replaced them as purchasers of their lands. There was resentment, too, of small businessmen who were perceived as profiteers, and violence against the many Africans, often migrants, who sustained settlers by working on White estates . . . land that Indigenous Africans regarded as their own. Though such antagonisms were not a decisive feature, the guerrillas fought in the name of an as yet only imagined nation.

When the nationalist movement turned to violence in the 1970s and liberation war ensued, circumstances intensified rivalries. The largely Shona ZANU was based across the eastern border in Mozambique; aligned with China, it sent guerrillas into predominantly Shona areas. The largely Ndebele ZAPU aligned with the USSR, was based to the northwest in Zambia, and operated largely in Matabeleland. It was the view of the Front for the Liberation of Mozambique (FRELIMO), which assisted ZANU guerrillas in the east of the country, that ethnic rivalries among Zimbabweans were exacerbated by the Sino-Soviet split. Mugabe (ZANU) played no part in the 1975 Victoria Falls talks; Nkomo (ZAPU) did. To be sure, in Geneva the following December, the two leaders presented themselves as a PF, but the two wings remained separate in practice and military strategy. It had originally been pressure from White proscription that divided the African nationalist movement in 1963; this split increasingly assumed the character of ethnic rivalries in response to RF intransigence in the 1970s.

As Alois Mlambo points out, tensions between the two major guerrilla groups actually worsened during the conflict. "Some of the bitterest armed clashes during the years of the liberation struggle were between ZANLA (ZANU) and ZIPRA (ZAPU) fighters when they met in the field, testifying to the deepening hostility between the two groups."[70] Under pressure from the White regime, and in competition for the spoils of victory, ZAPU and ZANU increasingly represented two rival ethnic cultural identities. Before March 1980, the uneasy, opportunistic PF alliance of late 1976 would break, leaving ZANU-PF and PF-ZAPU to contest the first election of independent Zimbabwe.

We may take into account some personal first-hand observations of Peter Godwin, from when he was a reluctant young White recruit into the security services—observations that arose from the varying degrees of colonial contacts with Indigenous Africans. "Life in the tribal reserve was grindingly hard," wrote Godwin. Men and woman struggling to eke out a living from the land were not likely to leave homes and resist a remote enemy that was in many cases completely unknown. "I drove all over the district," Godwin continues, "even to villages far from the road which had never been visited by a white man before." Later, an African guide took him to a village, where he met the African's wife. "She gave me a brisk once-over. . . . I was the first white man ever to set foot in their village." Such was the remoteness of some Africans not only from the liberation war but from the Whites who ruled them and shaped their lives. The emergence of political consciousness and growing radicalism among African peasant farmers over the decades, which Terence Ranger identified, was not universal.

Not all Africans were quite so distanced from the White community, and an equally telling recollection comes from when Godwin, as a boy, accompanied his mother, a doctor, into villages to perform free vaccinations (often against the will of local "witch doctors"). "Grand tours to inoculate people against smallpox, diphtheria, tuberculosis and polio," he recalled, "had become part of our dry-season routine, and there is no doubt they saved thousands of lives. The same lives that the guerrillas would later claim we were trying to snuff out with hard-sell contraception."[71] If the visit of a White woman doctor and her child was an African's direct experience of colonial rule, it was not likely to alienate them from it.

The spread of the liberation war, as it entered its third phase, raised questions of ultimate political loyalty, but it did not make choice any easier. In *Rebel People,* published in 1978, Denis Hills offered the concise and fair-minded insights of an experienced European writer, teacher, and traveler. Hills was in Rhodesia when the violent conflict of the liberation war was already a reality but mostly heard about rather than experienced. Hills's overall verdict was humane and sympathetic toward both European and African. "Rhodesia's problem is an emotional and divisive one. Among the protagonists the best and the worst emotions are inter-tangled. . . . To commit oneself to one side or the another is to take a painful decision: a decision that has split families and friends, white, black, and coloured alike."[72] For some, perhaps, growing war-weariness meant that the return of order, personal security, and any administration that would reopen schools and clinics was a greater longing than victory for one side or the other.

* * *

The agreement to talk at Lancaster House arose from the reluctant recognition of both Smith and Mugabe, and their respective wartime colleagues, that neither side could prevail through armed conflict. But this apparent stalemate signified different processes and outcomes. On the one hand, the RF government of Ian Smith had brought about their own demise: they were responsible for provoking a war of resistance in which they could not triumph. Their direction of political travel since 1962, and especially since 1965, was proving to be a cul-de-sac. It is thus with Ian Smith and the Rhodesian Front that responsibility for the disruption and bloodshed lay, and not with that minority of Whites who had sought a progressive alternative path.

On the other hand, while there was frustration at inability to achieve a military victory, the massive accumulating weight of grievance-based support which the guerrillas enjoyed across the regions of the territory was enough to make White rule unsustainable and shortly secure the political success of Black majority rule. As noted previously, ZANU and ZAPU did prove able "to destroy the Rhodesian government's resolve to fight on." From its birth at the turn of the century, the colonial state had depended on a degree of African acquiescence and participation, willing or otherwise. After a decade and a half of intransigent White supremacist RF government, sliding into years of dislocation from the swell of violent opposition to it, that age was gone.

It is fitting to close this chapter with a glance back to the 1950s, when the White consensus had been challenged and White choices for the way ahead had to be made. Consideration of the painful decision facing every African in the late 1970s presents the period two decades earlier in a fresh and revealing light. It serves to confirm that there was a readiness among most Africans *then*, if not up to the time of the Pearce commission of 1972, to accept gradual progress toward a genuine, power-sharing, multiracial Rhodesia . . . before attempts to adopt it were torpedoed by White reactionaries. The next chapter explores the consequences that ensued when the RF opted for unapologetic racism.

Notes

1. Quoted in R. West, *The White Tribes of Africa*, 78.
2. Vambe, *An Ill-Fated People*, 247.
3. Keatley, *The Politics of Partnership*, 476.
4. Quoted in Leys, *European Politics*, 275.
5. Todd, *Rhodesia*, 44.
6. Clutton-Brock, *Cold Comfort*, 61.
7. Quoted in Hancock, *White Liberals*, 25.
8. Caute, *Under the Skin*, 27, 28.
9. Quoted in Todd, *The Right to Say No*, 102.
10. Godwin and Hancock, *Rhodesians Never Die*, 44. Italics added.
11. Quoted in Lapsley, *Neutrality or Coercion?* 12.
12. Quoted in Lapsley, *Neutrality or Coercion?* 16.
13. N. Sithole, *African Nationalism*, 8.
14. Dangarembga, *Nervous Conditions*, 16.
15. Grant, *The Africans' Predicament*, 4.
16. Quoted in Meredith, *The Past*, 234.
17. Blake, *A History*, 366, 397.
18. Quoted in Godwin and Hancock, *Rhodesians Never Die*, 69.
19. Quoted in February, *African Perspectives*, 86.
20. Hills, *Rebel People*, 202.
21. Muzorewa, *Rise Up*, 104.
22. Quoted in Muzorewa, *Rise Up*, 101.
23. Quoted in Muzorewa, *Rise Up*, 105.
24. Grant, *The Africans' Predicament*, 19.
25. Quoted in Meredith, *The Past*, 99, 100.
26. Pearce Report, Appendix 4.
27. Quoted in Meredith, *The Past*, 96.
28. Smith, *Betrayal*, 175.
29. Smith, *Betrayal*, 178, 179.
30. Nkomo, *My Life*, 155.
31. Quoted in Meredith, *The Past*, 220.
32. Quoted in Meredith, *The Past*, 235, 236.
33. Quoted in Hills, *Rebel People*, 132.
34. Smith, *Betrayal*, 228, 248.
35. Grace Todd, quoted in Woodhouse, *Garfield Todd*, 402.
36. Verrier, *The Road to Zimbabwe*, 201.
37. Smith, *Betrayal*, 222.
38. Quoted in Meredith, *The Past*, 266.
39. Smith, *Betrayal*, 222.
40. Meredith, *The Past*, 321.

41. Quoted in Meredith, *The Past*, 336, 337.
42. Quoted in Moore, *Mugabe's Legacy*, 63.
43. Quoted in Meredith, *The Past*, 334.
44. Nkomo, *My Life*, 189.
45. John Ngara, "The Zimbabwean Revolution and the Internal Settlement," in *Marxism Today*, November 1978, pp. 343–349.
46. Walker, *Mugabe and the White African*, 22.
47. Smith, *Betrayal*, 260.
48. Meredith, *The Past*, 365.
49. Moorcraft and McLaughlin, *The Rhodesian War*, 46.
50. Quoted in Moorcraft and McLaughlin, *The Rhodesian War*, 40.
51. Smith, *Betrayal*, 175.
52. Meredith, *The Past*, 42.
53. Richard Hodder-Williams, in Morris-Jones, *From Rhodesia to Zimbabwe*, 61.
54. Quoted in Moorcraft and McLaughlin, *The Rhodesian War*, 166.
55. Quoted in Meredith, *The Past*, 142.
56. Shamuyarira, *Crisis*, 123.
57. Holderness, *Lost Chance*, 151.
58. Vambe, *An Ill-Fated People*, 234.
59. Baldwin, *The Fire Next Time*, 28, 82.
60. Vambe, *An Ill-Fated People*, 216, 222.
61. Ranger, *Peasant Consciousness*, 284.
62. Ranger, *Peasant Consciousness*, 177.
63. Quoted in Ranger, *Peasant Consciousness*, 178, 179.
64. Quoted in Ranger, *Peasant Consciousness*, 209.
65. Lovell, *Maoism*, 218.
66. Quoted in Lovell, *Maoism*, 218.
67. Lovell, *Maoism*, 219.
68. Hills, *Rebel People*, 168.
69. Hills, *Rebel People*, 130, 170.
70. A. Mlambo, *A History*, 255.
71. Godwin, *Mukiwa*, 94, 253, 359.
72. Hills, *Rebel People*, v.

8

Legacy: Zimbabwe

THE WIDER RECORD OF DECOLONIZATION IN BRITISH AFRICA before 1980 demonstrates that colonial rule usually ended badly, leaving in its wake troubled, ill-formed states barely capable of assuming the range of responsibilities they inherited. Throughout the continent, there was no formula for decolonization. This was partly because for many years none was sought, since this process, to which the British were notionally committed, was always expected to take place at some time in the (distant) future. There was nonetheless a proud if underlying assumption that one day there would be a seamless transition from colonies toward independent states, each exercising Westminster-style multiparty representative democracy—which the British believed, and taught their subjects, was the finest form of government. It was never clear *how* colonial rule, which bore little relation to that model, would evolve toward the professed goal. In British East Africa, for example, tentative preliminary steps were taken, as when prominent individual Africans were selected to join legislative councils (embryonic national assemblies); or when, after World War II, an element of popular participation was introduced into local government.

But starting in the early 1940s, the emphasis was on economic development rather than constitutional change—understandably so, since a sound and expanding economy could serve parliamentary democracy, not least by producing over time a nation of taxpayers who could hold their representatives to account. One indication of the sluggish pace at which colonial officials believed they could attend to constitutional change emerged in a conference of East African governors held in London in 1959. They agreed that they probably had around twenty more years in which to prepare Tanganyika, Uganda, and Kenya for independence; in fact, these milestones were reached in 1961, 1962, and 1963, respectively.

Last minute discussion of constitutional arrangements for representative government preceded transitions to independence. But African understanding of power and its exercise owed far more to the actual experience of having been administered by a caste of Europeans in top-down, authoritarian, no-party rule. The familiar reality of autocracy came to be closely imitated by incoming African leaders when it was time to lower the union flag. British rule in some instances could claim to have been a latter-day "enlightened despotism." But it was despotism, nonetheless. Privileged rather than corrupt, it had delivered "good government" at some times and in some places. In contrast, there was little prospect that successor African regimes would be capable of delivering development and conflict resolution. Elections as periodic political practices had almost no place in the colonial period experience. For example, in British East Africa, the number of territory-wide one-man, one-vote elections, prior to independence, was: Uganda, one; Kenya, one; Tanganyika, none. Moreover, the rules and accumulated customs—the *culture* of democracy that was entrenched and universally valued in the mother country—was not readily exportable from Britain.

Africa's new postcolonial states may have been "pressed into a corset of representative government, a form alien to their own traditions and unprepared by colonial paternalism. Their colonial masters, afraid of their incipient nationalism and contemptuous of their abilities, had not taught them much."[1] Elections were not regarded by the British as a schooling in democracy. Rather, they were introduced only in the final throes of colonial rule, with one primary purpose: to determine which leader and party would come to power in their place. African democracy was neither organic nor evolutionary.

Perhaps the greatest challenge, though shelved for many years during colonial rule, was demographic. It is a commonplace criticism of European powers at the time of the "scramble" for Africa that the established colonial boundaries bore no relation to ethnic diversity on the ground. Most obviously problematic in the long term were colonies that drew into a single colonial state peoples distinguished from each other by patterns of economic life, language, custom, culture, or religion. This was the case in Uganda, where a range of northern tribes had nothing in common with the Baganda, the dominant kingdom to the south. Disinterested colonial administrations, positioned above such diversity and enjoying a monopoly of force, could cope with, contain, or exploit difference. Yet historic cleavages emerged, albeit redefined or distorted by the experience of colonialism, in almost every instance at the prospect of majority rule. They challenged the stability of new states. In several cases, political tribalism—the exploiting of ethnic differences—was to be a hallmark of the early years of independence.

Economic "backwardness"—what Walter Rodney famously and bitterly dismissed as "underdevelopment"—was another inheritance across the continent.[2] To be sure, colonial economies had often provided the means (cash crops such as cotton or coffee, for example) by which small farmers could earn enough income not only to pay taxes but also to buy imported goods that raised their material standard of living. But the export of a range of raw materials did not amount to substantial local economic growth (for which colonial rulers had neither the ambition nor the means), and neither did transport and communications, which primarily linked sources of raw materials with ports from which they could be shipped. Typically, at independence, there was only a small African middle class, comprised of an educated elite with some experience in bureaucracy or professions. There was no confident, dynamic, bourgeoisie of capitalists, entrepreneurs, and businessmen whose prosperity and ambition might form the core of a thriving civil society able to play its part in government or to challenge misgovernment.

The significance of this commonly overlooked fact cannot be overstated. African states newly installed in the late 1950s and early 1960s were not nations of taxpayers. This was as much a political disadvantage as an economic one. As it evolved in Western countries such as Britain, representative democracy came to rest on two levels of accountability. The first and more obvious was the electoral level: periodically and predictably, people had the opportunity to vote into office the party, often the alternative government, of their choice. The second level of accountability was financial. The people were taxpayers, and years of revenue bargaining had seen governments authorized by representatives of the taxpaying public to spend revenue on agreed projects. Governments were constrained to act and spend on behalf of the people who elected and funded them (and their policies) . . . and to whom they remained accountable.

In no postcolonial state of British Africa did such twin relationships apply. Nowhere were "the people" sovereign except in name. Elections could be and were manipulated by those in power. Thus in East Africa, during the fifty years following independence, no general election in Kenya, Uganda, or Tanzania saw the loss of power by an incumbent president standing for a further term; and only one election (in Kenya, 2002) saw a ruling party replaced. Meanwhile, central governments came to be funded by borrowing, taxes on companies and consumption taxes, along with customs and excise, not by income taxes raised equitably from the Indigenous community. This was not entirely the fault of African regimes: they could not raise income taxes on people who had no taxable incomes. In 1962, fewer than 10,000 people in Uganda paid income tax, out of a population of around seven million; forty years later, just 1 percent of the population paid income tax.[3]

New African governments adopted other strategies, not inclined to focus on economic development and having little to gain from the prosperity of the masses. Their members, who were effectively unaccountable, were tempted to reward themselves and their dependents from central government revenue, foreign aid receipts, or privileged access to priceless assets. Opportunities for corruption were plentiful. Michaela Wrong memorably titled her 2009 study of politics in postindependence Kenya *It's Our Turn to Eat*. In the years following the departure of the British, Africans came to regard their own governments as negatively as those of the colonial period, or even more so. These were not responsive and replaceable agencies trusted to work for the common good, but oppressive instruments operating in the exclusive interests of those in power.

In many cases, and long before the birth of Zimbabwe, former British postcolonial African states proved dysfunctional, in some instances tragically so. They acquired constitutions upon formation. But they could not as easily acquire "constitutionalism," that reverence for impersonal practices and procedures that trumps political ambition. Moreover, constitutions fell short as instruments of nation-building. They could be ignored, as the politics of identity saw individuals and groups competing for wealth and power without inhibition. Financial mismanagement and intolerance of opposition were frequent characteristics. The tyranny of Idi Amin following his 1971 military coup in Uganda is best known in the West for the expulsion of around 50,000 Asians in 1972, but his regime resulted in around a quarter of a million African deaths. This was part of the terrible aftermath of the *Pax Britannica*, a consequence of the failure and inability of the metropolitan authority to devise transitional arrangements for long-term economic development and political stability in territories, such as this one, which they had arbitrarily carved out.

African politicians everywhere were in a hurry for power; during the Cold War period of the late 1950s and early 1960s, Britain, for its part, was in a hurry to depart with minimal cost and with some dignity, without driving successor regimes into the welcoming arms of the Russians or the Chinese. The emergence and durability of the commonwealth represents a success of sorts, but few of its African member states have been characterized by prosperity and conflict-free political stability.

Though it was easy enough for the British to agree to let go of former colonies, the 1960s and 1970s demonstrated how hard it was to transfer power to governments capable of managing a host of challenges arising from the precolonial as well as colonial past. It would be harder still in the case of Rhodesia. This was a settler colony, and its reactionary regime did not even aspire to prepare its Africans for majority rule. During the early 1960s it chose instead to take Rhodesia in a direction that would render a newly independent Zimbabwe a particularly flawed polity.

Aftermath of Rhodesian Front Rule and the Liberation War

Britain was involved in several attempts to find a formula for an independent Zimbabwe: In the early 1960s; shortly after the Unilateral Declaration of Independence (UDI); at the time of the Pearce commission; and then through such intermediaries as Henry Kissinger and Andrew Young. Nothing came of these attempts. The settlers looked in horror at what was taking place following decolonization elsewhere in Africa, and they saw no reason to make the concessions demanded by nationalists, as long as they had support from South Africa (and Portugal) and as long as the outcome of the liberation war remained in doubt. In contrast, when the Lancaster House gathering was convened, all agreed that there was an urgent need for a settlement. For the first time, all parties to the conflict (including the Patriotic Front [PF]) were participating. It should be recalled that the priority at Lancaster House was not discussion of what the future would look like, but how to stop the fighting. Many years after the birth of Zimbabwe, Lord Renwick, one of the British participants who had been closely involved at Lancaster House, made a remarkable admission regarding what had happened there. "We didn't actually negotiate the constitution in any detail . . . we simply dumped on the table a document that epitomised the kind of classic independence constitution on the basis of which we had granted independence in every other case."[4] *Dumped* was the word choice he used. It was perhaps in recognition that comparable constitutions had not ushered in political stability in other cases, and could be ignored, that the British did not "actually negotiate" Zimbabwe's constitution.

Certainly, it is hard to think of what else the British could have done in 1979, seeking an exit strategy to get the Rhodesia problem off the incoming Thatcher government's agenda. As for the African political elite on the verge of power, they did not much care about terms and conditions. They would be free agents before long. Britain's considerable triumph was to bring the liberation war and White minority rule to an end. There was little they could do to ensure either democracy or good government thereafter. In Zimbabwe, those in power soon learned how to remain there, elections or not. The constitution that the British persuaded all parties to sign could not guarantee stable representative parliamentary democracy on the Westminster model.

The consequences of coming to power on the back of a guerrilla war campaign were very damaging. Triumphalism on the part of Mugabe and Zimbabwe African National Union—Patriotic Front (ZANU-PF) arose from "winning the war" and "liberating the people." This was part myth, of course. They had withstood but not beaten Rhodesia's forces; and it was the British, especially Lord Carrington as chair at Lancaster House, who had brought about peace and independence. ZANU-PF claimed something like a "divine right" to rule, disdainful of any Zimbabwean critics who had not actively sided with them in the war, and dismissive, too, of others who had fought but were now seen as a threat to their newly gained power. A pitiless, domineering mentality imitated that of the Rhodesian Front (RF)—for example, in the suppression of independent trade unions and scorn for academics and intellectuals. Notwithstanding its claim to be bringing in socialism, this was a self-righteous, top-down government "seeing like a state." While courting coalition, it was intolerant of political debate, incapable of tolerating diversity, and left no space for that compromise and respect of difference that are at the heart of a functioning democracy.

There was more to this merciless mindset than the corrupting impact of the fighting; or rather, there was a separate aspect of the liberation war that helped to shape it. Julia Lovell observes that the close association of Robert Mugabe and Zimbabwe African National Union (ZANU) with Chinese communists over many years did more than influence Zimbabwe African National Liberation Army's (ZANLA's) tactics and its senior commanders, such as Josiah Tongorara, on the battlefield. "The Maoism that men like Tongogara studied in the 1960s helped bequeath ZANU a conspiratorial, totalitarian political template, in which the party—and the man at the top of the party—are always right; in which those defined as 'enemies of the people' (as defined by the party) can be annihilated; and in which military interests rule supreme."[5] This transformation in the way that key African political figures in Rhodesia perceived their world and framed their ambitions was a tragic consequence of Whites choosing not to talk to African nationalists in the late 1950s, but to demonize them.

While there was democracy in name, and political parties could compete for power at elections, the party in power in the new Zimbabwe insisted that no others had a right to govern. Its rallying cry was "unity," not "democracy." The latter would have opened it up to legitimate political challenge from any quarter: from rival former combatants, for example, or indeed from those who had been willing to compromise with a White rule that had brought them new chances and choices. Another alternative political motto, "liberation," would have required the recognition of all others who had played their parts in the struggle. It was shrewd instead to proclaim the politically self-interested concept of "unity." It was stated unequivocally in 1981 by the party's publicity secretary. "ZANU-PF is aiming at a situation where there is no separation between party and state. . . . We are convinced . . . that before the middle or end of next year, it will be impossible for any other party to operate on the ground."[6]

A nonviolent means of fabricating unity and keeping control was the media. This former arm of White rule became an arm of ZANU-PF. It was, in short, repoliticized. Control of information and the ability to impose a self-serving narrative were invaluable. Therefore, no official mention was made of government atrocities in Matabeleland in the early to mid-1980s. The government thus enjoyed impunity over the massacre. Meanwhile, South Africa was routinely demonized (not entirely without grounds) as the primary force of destabilization in the region. More generally and following the pattern of other recently independent African states, the media enabled Robert Mugabe's incumbent government to dominate election procedures and discourse, and so to remain in power. The Official Secrets Act and the Law and Order (Maintenance) Act were just two measures inherited from the White regime that could be used to block the spread of information and to intimidate journalists.

In part through the waging of war, an authoritarian RF government had installed several coercive laws and organs that ZANU-PF could readily employ. The White colonial state had been established though violence. Six decades later, Ian Smith's RF government had responded to guerrilla challenges by unleashing the weapons of the state against Zimbabwe African People's Union (ZAPU) and ZANU. In 1982, following "liberation," senior former members of Zimbabwe People's Revolutionary Army (ZIPRA) were detained and charged with treason. When six of the seven were found innocent by the courts, they were immediately detained under inherited RF emergency regulations. ZANU-PF in government could also turn on its own. In 1983, nine provincial officials were detained and tortured for refusing to agree to the removal of a dissident as mayor of Gweru. As for veteran nationalist leaders, Joshua Nkomo went into exile in 1983, alleging threats to his life; Bishop Muzorewa was detained for ten months starting in 1983; and Ndabaningi Sithole went into exile for most of that first decade of Zimbabwean independence.

The White farmers' annual congress in July 1979 had hosted a somewhat chilling indication of the direction in which majority rule would go. Francis Zindoga was Bishop Muzorewa's newly appointed minister of law and order in the Internal Settlement government of Zimbabwe-Rhodesia. His priority was clearly order, not law. He assured the assembled farmers that he would be tough against stock thieves and "terrorists." "Ladies and Gentlemen," he said, "this is Africa. What was done in white Africa and was criticised abroad, if it is done in black Africa, there is no criticism. Therefore, the measures we intend to take are stiffer than the measures fourteen years ago."[7]

The constitution itself had been used as a flexible device to be manipulated solely in the interests of the White minority. Embryonic African political parties were successively banned. Generations of Southern Rhodesian Africans had no opportunity to cultivate political compromise and conciliation. Even before the liberation war, Robert Tredgold observed that while White Rhodesians were quick to condemn unconstitutional steps taken in the newly independent African states elsewhere, "they seem quite unable to see that their own government is in the same case. . . . It has given itself power to amend the [1965] constitution at will."[8] He saw that the state was turning into an instrument of extrajudicial repression, and this did lasting damage. In the 1970s, the RF regime took on a war footing. Although doughty Whites lived their lives much as before for several years after the UDI, eventually enough men were drafted into service with the security forces for the state's general functioning to suffer. The financial and economic costs of resisting the liberation were sizeable, but from those there might be recovery. The authoritarian state, a de facto one-party dictatorship that had survived for nearly two decades, was not so easily left behind.

Before 1979 and 1980, Africans in Rhodesia had experience only of an exclusive White rule in the form of a government becoming increasingly authoritarian and violent, permitting no dissent. Two illustrations from the late RF period will suffice. In July 1976, P. K. Van der Byl, minister of defense, was cheered in parliament when he said, "If villages harbour terrorists and terrorists are found running about in villages, naturally they will be bombed and destroyed in any manner which the commander on the spot considers to be desirable" and, he added, "one can have little sympathy for those who are mixed up with terrorists when finally they receive the wrath of the security forces."[9] By the later 1970s, the RF government had installed a chief justice, Hector Macdonald, a World War II veteran with limited, if any, qualifications for the role. His death sentences on "terrorists" were widely reported. In his words, "We are going to be obliged to resort to the most drastic penalties for relatively minor offences."[10] For its part, after 1980 the new regime's response to diversity of opinion would not be to entertain dialogue but to subdue by force, using the security instruments already at hand. As one African historian put, two decades after the end of colonial rule, "The culture of intolerance for political opponents seems to have been inherited lock stock and barrel."[11] Back in 1968, Tredgold had seen what was coming. "Bad majority government will succeed bad minority government, and the majority will have been habituated to the idea that the proper way to govern is ruthlessly to suppress all political opposition."[12] Given such a formative experience, it was not surprising that repression and the use of violence proved to be "the programmed default position" for the new governing elite, whenever they felt threatened.[13]

As David Moore, former professor at Johannesburg University, has recently documented in detail in *Mugabe's Legacy*, the lasting patterns of factionalism, conceit, and lies—and of Mugabe's brutal removal of rivals—were set during the last decade of RF rule. More broadly, the capricious and frequently deadly activities of all the protagonists of the later 1970s inured ordinary people to violence and desensitized them to the political use of physical force against opponents. The extent of this phenomenon is of course immeasurable, but it may have contributed to the muted response, just a few years later, to the massacre of Ndebele and to the periodic removal of political rivals by ZANU-PF. White rule had taught that the end justified the means. Harsh methods for achieving power and all devices for staying in power were among the new norms of political life. Both sides were brutalized by the liberation war. "Freedom fighters" terrorized villagers, butchered alleged "sell-outs," massacred innocent families, and desecrated churches. The White defenders of "civilization" tortured their captives, murdered civilians, burned villages, and dispatched prisoners. For the first time since the 1890s, a generation of Rhodesian Africans was reared on conflict, violence, and cruelty. As Nkomo observed, "All of us who lived through that war became hardened by it." The worst thing "was the callousness it bred. Death became a remote, impersonal fact," he added, and that was "the atmosphere in which, when the war at last ended, we had to create a new and peaceful state in Zimbabwe."[14]

One special instance of societal degeneration is worth noting. Among Mugabe's first ministerial appointments was a fellow Shona, Emmerson Mnangagwa. Years earlier, he was trained in China before operating as a ZANLA guerrilla. In 1965, after blowing up a railway locomotive, he was captured. Before his trial, at which he was sentenced to ten years in prison, he was tortured by the police. White officers hung him upside down by leg irons from butcher's hooks that ran along a track in the ceiling, and then batted his suspended body back and forth on the track from one end of the room to the other. Years later, during the first decade of Zimbabwean independence, Mnangagwa was minister for state security when armed forces were unleashed in Matabeleland. In November 2017, he cynically orchestrated a "popular" coup d'etat, replaced Mugabe as president of Zimbabwe, and had security forces fire on demonstrators. Mugabe and Mnangagwa were creatures of their times, each personifying the unintended consequences of politicized White reactionary racism, each thereafter opportunistically using the political means at their disposal.

As in other former colonies, democracy in Zimbabwe in 1980 had no historic roots deriving from the colonial period. Africans had been excluded, not just from voting periodically, but, just as important, from the experience of accepting fair election results, even election defeat. They were barred from acquiring that culture of democracy (including respect for the constitution) without which the mere holding of an election readily becomes the cynical device of a ruling elite. There was democracy, but only in three narrow senses. Africans now ruled themselves for the first time since the 1890s. There were one-man, one-vote elections and all the trappings of parliamentary procedure. Furthermore, a written constitution provided for periodic general elections. But this was not enough. The corrupted legacy of settler rule meant that "good government" would prove elusive.

In retrospect, the Zimbabwe-Rhodesia election of April 1979 is of particular interest as a harbinger of political interference in democratic processes to follow. Bishop Muzorewa was elected, with a large majority, on a sizeable turnout. There was, however, much intimidation in the rural areas by Muzorewa's and Sithole's "auxiliaries." To be sure, the bishop was not elected *because of* this intimidation. He had come to prominence at the time of the Pearce commission, and there is little reason to suppose that he was anything other than a popular choice among many Africans at that time. But the report of a group of observers led by

Lord Chitnis, a British liberal peer, was scathing. The electoral process, the group concluded, was "a blatant attempt to perpetuate a fraud and justify a lie." The election was "nothing more than a gigantic confidence trick designed to foist on a cowed and indoctrinated black electorate a settlement and a constitution which were formulated without its consent, and which are being implemented without its approval."[15] Thus, while much of the interference may have been unnecessary, the precedent had been set at this first election held in the country on a mass franchise. The gist of the group's verdict would be equally applicable on comparable occasions in Zimbabwe in the future.

As for the post–Lancaster House election of March 1980, it would have been unrealistic not to expect some intimidation from all sides. The scale of preemptive interference by the established forces of the White regime was nonetheless remarkable, even though they expected Muzorewa, their candidate, to win. Martial law allowed Rhodesian forces to destroy crops, huts, livestock, and personal property if they suspected villagers of collaboration with guerrillas. The printing presses of a Catholic agency that had opposed the RF were blown up. Two attempts were made on Mugabe's life. Most Whites and foreign observers did not believe that ZANU-PF could secure the fifty-one seats needed to win an outright parliamentary majority. "Others apparently recognised that Mugabe was the man to beat—by any means."[16] In one sense, the latter were right. When Mugabe arrived in the capital in late January, he was greeted by a crowd variously estimated to be between 250,000 and a million. Meanwhile, observers from the commonwealth enumerated violations of proper procedure: the deployment of the Rhodesian forces against the guerrillas, the presence of South African forces during the transition, perceived British partisanship, and the governor Lord Christopher Soames's threat of disenfranchising parts of the country. Such were the measures used by Whites to try to secure the victory of the incumbent prime minister.

Interference by guerrilla forces was also widespread. In his report, however, David Glendenning, who supervised the election in the east of the country, concluded this had not determined the outcome. "Despite the fact that intimidation by 'presence' may have increased the ZANU-PF vote by some number, perhaps by 10%, I have no doubt whatever that the result of the election accurately reflects the opinions of the electorate. It was the authentic voice of the African people."[17] The collapse in Muzorewa's vote had arisen from his failure to stop the war. As in 1979, the most popular leader was elected. But a pattern had been established. Outcomes in the future would not be left to chance.

Diehard Whites were quick to accuse Africans of resorting to what they termed tribalism in political competition, but incapable of recognizing their own responsibility for its emergence. Of minimal significance up to and including the 1950s, political tribalism sprouted among African activists in the pressure cooker of repression, detention, bans, and the ensuing battles for loyalty and leadership: in short, in their struggle for survival. It emerged as an aspect of Africans' response to the reality and policies of the White police state. Ever self-righteous, the RF passionately condemned a situation that they had played a huge part in creating.

Zimbabwe itself was a postcolonial African state of its time, and its peoples could barely be described as a nation. In Sara Rich Dorman's analysis, the political conflicts that emerged twenty years after independence were "very much the result of the flawed nation-building project initiated in 1980." [18] African nationalism had played its part, from the rebirth of the ANC in 1957 through the years of guerrilla fighting, but calls for unity thereafter were in part the rhetoric of a nationhood that did not exist. There were huge inherited contradictions, conflicts of interest along racial, ethnic, and class lines. It might have been otherwise. Some internal tensions were inevitable. Yet in the 1950s and even later, a range of White liberals had wanted to steer Southern Rhodesia—and an African population broadly as yet acquiescing in conciliation and compromise—toward a nonracial nationhood. The fracturing of the African nationalist movement, it should be stressed, manifested itself in 1963—that is, only after the White minority had irreversibly rejected dialogue with the African political elite by declaring a state of emergency and banning African political activity. From then on, ready-made ethnic loyalties fed competitiveness in the do or die struggle for freedom from colonial rule and the hopes of replacing it.

Zimbabwe, 1980s

It was hoped by all sides that the Lancaster House conference from September to December 1979 would bring lasting peace to the region; an internationally accepted political settlement based on a new agreed constitution for independent Zimbabwe; and the end of sanctions. In reality it could do no more than close one chapter of the territory's history and open a new one. Much could have gone wrong. But the chairing of the conference by Lord Carrington, the British foreign minister, was masterful. And the fact that being part of a settlement was preferable, for all sides, to walking away, helped to bring about this long sought after success.

No such conference and no such agenda would have been required if, two decades earlier, most White settlers had chosen to follow Todd's direction and worked with, rather than against, African political leaders to take irreversible steps toward majority rule. Nevertheless, after 1980 it appeared for a while that all was well for the Whites who remained. Albeit on a separate roll, the Whites would hold a fifth of the seats in the new parliament (and they did so until 1987). With the arrival of universal suffrage, they would not have profited from a common roll; and while the 20 percent limitation clearly ruled out any return to power, they did enjoy recognition and a voice at least comparable with that granted to Africans in the days of the federal parliament. This, however, was a mixed blessing. It has been argued that "the existence of those seats, and the behaviour of their Rhodesian Front occupants, became the single most important impediment to racial reconciliation in the early 1980s." Whites—many of them supporters of Zimbabwe in little sense other than that they had stayed rather than emigrate—did not use their platform to seek compromises founded on reconciliation. Rather, they remained "cocooned in little white islands within Zimbabwe." Ian Smith, rendered no wiser by his fall from power, chose to exploit the political space that, remarkably, he still enjoyed, by fighting the 1985 general election "as if nothing had changed."[19] Self-isolation left Whites failing to recognize how the liberation war had generated and intensified interracial hostility.

Land was the biggest issue of all, and one that highlighted a wider reality. At ZANU's first press conference in 1963, Ndabaningi Sithole had made the abolition of the Land Apportionment and Land Husbandry Acts a priority. If the Whites had been vanquished in the war (by forces of an African movement driven by left-wing ideology), political independence and economic transformation intended to benefit the mass of farmers and workers might have been possible. Instead, there was, as one political economist critic wrote at the time, "A neo-colonial pattern, where growth and social mobility are at the expense of continued economic inequality."[20] Land was the country's primary asset, and it was the one that embodied a gross inequality originally based entirely on race. There was more to this question than the grievances of loss and injustice: land had been the foundation, literally, of White supremacy. The Land Apportionment Act of 1930 had formalized dispossession on a huge scale. The RF's Land Tenure Act of 1979 legalized a half-and-half division, which was an affront to Africans who outnumbered the Whites in a ratio by now approaching thirty to one. At independence, around 6,000 White farmers occupied over 15 million hectares, well served by government-funded infrastructure, while millions of Africans remained packed in the reserves.

There were three imaginable futures. Up to the middle of 1979, it appeared that the guerrillas might win their war and "liberate" the land by driving from it the Whites who had not already fled. However, the ZANU-PF and ZAPU forces did not defeat the RF government and could only force it to the negotiating table. Here was a second possibility: that a deal of historic significance could be thrashed out which entailed the gradual, peaceful transfer of land ownership from White settlers to Africans. Land was indeed on the agenda for this London conference but, as one observer noted, "Opinion between the negotiating parties moved between extremes, from 'all land belonged to the state,' to 'maintaining the status quo.'"[21] It surprised no one that the issue very nearly brought proceedings at Lancaster House to a premature end. The African delegations sought to undo the injustice, but since they did not come to London as victors, they were not in a position to dictate peace terms or have recognized any right to confiscate White-held properties.

It was only when, at the last minute, British and US governments issued ill-defined promises of funding that the principle of "willing seller, willing buyer" was accepted (with sales to be at market prices and in foreign currency). It was even envisaged that funding would be available to assist incoming African farmers to establish themselves. This was an unrealistic, uncosted, and ultimately unrealizable compromise, but Europeans and Africans could sign up to it (if without enthusiasm, especially on the part of the Black negotiators). But this third, default outcome was no solution. Africans could not afford or were reluctant to buy from Europeans lands that the latter had expropriated. At a preelection meeting in 1980, Bishop Muzorewa was addressing a crowd on this issue when attention turned to the future of one particular White estate. A ZANU-PF negotiator who was present later recalled a telling exchange. "The bishop said, 'No, it is not allowed to take Bob Richards' farm without having to pay compensation. You have to buy it from him.' We said, 'What about Bob Richards himself? Who did he buy it from?'"[22] As for the Whites, most were *not* willing to sell land, other than some less productive, marginal areas of what they owned. In this respect, Lancaster House did little more than provide White farmers with a further decade of privilege and prosperity.

We may note here that a history of land seizure and White settlement did not in itself present an insuperable problem. It had been solved in the case of Kenya. To be sure, the Whites there were a much smaller minority, they had taken possession of a smaller proportion of African land, and they were never the governing authority as their counterparts were, since 1923, in (Southern) Rhodesia. Nonetheless, given time, a readiness to compromise, and determination to end the war, a deal along Kenyan lines might have been agreed to between the Rhodesian and Patriotic Fronts. The obstacle that proved insurmountable was funding, which had to come from the outside. In 1962, the British had paid the government of Kenya £7.5 million and loaned it another £9 million for the purchase of White farms and the settlement of landless Africans on them. In this case, European settlers generally acquiesced. There was no White flight, and the contentious issue was to be intra-African: Who was going to get the land?

Twenty years later, however, neither Britain nor the United States was willing or able to provide the staggering sums needed to implement a comparable scheme in Zimbabwe. The British did provide £44 million, but this was only a fraction of what was required. Funding was suspended over charges of maladministration by the Zimbabwean government. And after the Labour Party came to power in Britain in 1997, the secretary of state for international development, Clare Short, absolved it as being "without links to former colonial interests" from any responsibility for land purchases in Zimbabwe.[23]

Even so, it was years before residual White land ownership was seriously challenged. The ZANU-PF government acquired some areas early, either marginal or abandoned by émigrés, and resettled around 50,000 African peasant families from congested communal areas on it. But White farmers who were not willing to sell did not have their lands confiscated by the new regime. This was in part because in the Lancaster House agreement, White large-scale farmers were protected in their ownership for ten years. The primary reason, however, was that this commercial farming sector was valued.

As in earlier years, the Whites were a diverse group, held together by a belief in "the Rhodesian way of life" but little else. Twenty years before, more prosperous White farmers had been among those in key positions in the political economy of the country, and they argued in favor of opening up both the politics and the economy of Southern Rhodesia on a nonracial basis. Subsequently, in the early years of Zimbabwe, many such farmers found themselves stakeholder partners with ZANU-PF. Indeed, two prominent Whites with farming backgrounds served in Mugabe's first cabinet: David Smith, as minister of commerce and industry, and Denis Norman, as minister of agriculture. Smith, though by no means a right-wing extremist, had been vice president of the RF and served in the Internal Settlement government of Bishop Muzorewa. Standing for election in March 1980, he was returned unopposed. By contrast, Denis Norman had had little interest in politics and no political experience. He became an unelected member of Mugabe's team and served in his government well into the 1990s. His was an altogether somewhat unlikely instance of multiracial representative democracy.

Some other farmers became party members, but they were the exception. For most, change was a threat rather than a challenge, and former attitudes persisted. Farmers were more secure in 1980 than they had been the previous year, when support from their own RF government had to be reduced at a time of numerous guerrilla attacks on farms and livestock. Now, promised ten years of statutory protection, with good working relations with the new government and enjoying a period of considerable prosperity, short-sightedness persisted. As one African academic put it somewhat mildly, "White farmers were generally reluctant to relinquish their colonially inherited privilege."[24] Resistance to multiracialism in all its forms would prove a costly mistake for Whites—for example in education, where Whites took steps to ensure their children continued to be schooled separately. When times changed and the climate deteriorated, they would be easy targets for politicians to brand them as self-interested segregationists who were not committed to the well-being of the country and all its people.

It was only about eighteen months before Mugabe, a Marxist in orientation, began to lose his conciliatory tone and target the White community. South Africa had sought to sabotage the Zimbabwean economy from the outset. Growing confrontation with the apartheid regime raised questions about the loyalties of fellow Whites in Zimbabwe. At the end of 1981, Mugabe accused them of collusion. "What baffles my government is that reactionary and counter-revolutionary elements—[which] because of their treason and crimes against humanity in Zimbabwe we could have put before a firing squad, but which we decided to forgive—have hardly repented."[25] The honeymoon with the White community was over. Declarations such as these impelled half of the remaining White population to emigrate during the first three years of Zimbabwe's existence.

Even so, at first there was little sustained pressure to disturb the remarkable coalition between ZANU-PF and commercial White farmers, especially when the economy was doing well. By around 1990, however, increasing land hunger prompted unauthorized occupations of White land. This led the government, no longer tied by the terms of Lancaster House, to pass a Land Acquisition Act in 1992, which authorized official compulsory purchase with compensation. It looked as though yielding to the political pressure of land hunger and the war veterans' demands for their just reward replaced the economic benefits of safeguarding visible relics of the White settler days as the government's priority. Nonetheless, lack of funds and continuing White resistance meant that little changed.

A new wave of land seizures at the turn of the century finally led Mugabe's government to offer to the war veterans and ZANU-PF youth activists its "organisational, logistical and coercive support . . . crucial distinguishing features of the post-2000 occupations."[26] These seizures were often accompanied by the singing of songs and the chanting of war slogans denouncing the Whites, which dated to the liberation war. This campaign—fueled by mass grievances, authorized by government, and prompting fierce criticism from Britain—proved to be the delayed turning-point. In the year 2000, there were 4,500 White commercial farmers occupying 11 million hectares (and producing over 70 percent of the country's agricultural output); by 2008, the number of White farmers was down to around 500. To this extent the settlers, an earlier generation that had indirectly brought Mugabe to prominence, found in him (as many had feared) their nemesis. Many years earlier, in 1960, Bernard Chidzero had issued a prophetic warning following the violent suppression of African protests during that year. "It is well for the European to stop and ponder. For what he does today may be perfected on him in turn by his present victims, who will have learnt lessons from him."[27]

Also in 1960, Whites had rejected the Quinton Report's proposal that the Land Apportionment Act should be scrapped. That policy could not therefore find its place in a broader program of gradual political, economic, and social reform. Instead, as we have seen, Whites soon afterward committed themselves to an alternative route, down the cul de sac. As a result, after independence they had to accept whatever treatment of them a frustrated Black majority government chose to administer.

* * *

In the 1980s, it was not the Whites who suffered most at the hands of Mugabe's government, but the Ndebele. A deployment of shocking force took place in Matabeleland, over several years, starting in 1982. As a response to the discovery of ZIPRA arms caches and some ZIPRA fighters resorting to a guerrilla campaign against the central government, Mugabe's Korean-trained Fifth Brigade slaughtered over 20,000 Ndebele. According to the Catholic peace and justice commission, "The presence of the 5th Brigade in an area in 1983 meant an initial outburst of intense brutality, usually lasting a few days, followed by random incidents of beatings, burnings and murders in the ensuing weeks, months, and years."[28] Mugabe took the opportunity to blame Nkomo and to remove him and other ZAPU members from his government, after which Nkomo fled the country for safety abroad. Mugabe had stronger grounds when accusing apartheid South Africa of backing ZIPRA dissidents to destabilize his rule. The Unity Agreement of 1987 brought a formal end to this division: ZAPU ceased to exist, and ZANU-PF ruled as an African de facto one-party state in succession to the White RF. As in other parts of Africa at this time, Black-on-Black violence received relatively little coverage in the Western press. When Idi Amin had come to power in Uganda, far more attention was paid by overseas observers to the fate of the Indians he expelled in 1972 than to his innumerable African victims who had nowhere to go. Similarly, Western opinion ten years later (largely White) appeared more concerned with the fortunes of "kith and kin" in Zimbabwe than with African victims of Mugabe's exercise of terror.

Whether and how an incumbent ZANU-PF government could withstand a strong, peaceful, and democratic challenge was tested in the elections of the year 2000. In the early 1990s, an externally imposed structural adjustment plan and a prolonged drought had combined to impoverish innumerable Zimbabweans. In the wake of strikes by workers and civil servants mid-decade, political opposition took shape in the Movement for Democratic Change (MDC). Emerging in 1999 under the leadership of Morgan Tsvangirai, this was a broad coalition of groups united against ZANU-PF. Had Zimbabwe been a working democracy, the MDC would have come to power in the 2000 elections. However, not only democracy but "good government" was jettisoned. The challenge posed by the MDC to those in power triggered tyranny and economic meltdown.

State violence was repeatedly unleashed against the MDC and its real or supposed supporters, especially following the 2008 elections (general, local, and presidential), which the Mugabe regime evidently lost yet denied losing. Meanwhile, in the wake of the chaotic land reform program, as well as the collapse of sectors in the economy other than agriculture, notably tourism, unemployment exceeded 80 percent in 2008. By this time, Zimbabwe's currency lost all value, with the official inflation rate of that year at 230 million percent. Following the intervention of the Southern African Development Community, the formation of a "government of national unity" restored some political calm and economic recovery. But this was not a harmonious coalition, and it did not mark any real transformation of the postcolonial state. Years later, Mnangagwa's early wanton use of violence against unarmed demonstrators in 2017 would be a mark of continuity, not change.

That decade of crisis, from around 1998 to 2008, was long after the birth of Zimbabwe. But in several respects it bore the hallmarks of a colonial legacy. There can be little doubt that it had its origins in the social, economic, and political after effects of ninety years of European settler rule. One such effect was the intolerance of opposition. ZANU-PF barely accepted the legitimacy of the MDC. In terms of personality, this was expressed by comparing Mugabe, the "father of the nation" who had led Zimbabwe's struggle for freedom, with Tsvangirai, who was not and had not. The politicization of the judiciary and civil service had antecedents in the White settler period, too, as did restrictive legislation such as the Public Order and Security Act of 2002, which was designed to block the activities of the opposition and to control the press. As we have seen, the land question, so divisive in the colonial period and left unresolved by Lancaster House, was finally weaponized when Mugabe identified it as the one he could use to appease the land hungry and target residual White privilege.

The liberation war helped to define Zimbabwean politics well into the fourth decade of independence. Mugabe's wartime colleagues were key figures in his political longevity. When ZANU-PF had to consider a possible successor to the nonagenarian Mugabe, two factions emerged, defined in part by the history of Rhodesia/Zimbabwe. In a struggle that persisted for three years, Grace Mugabe's so-called G40 political faction represented the women's league and the youth league. Its aim was to push for a transfer of power to younger leaders, "regardless of the fact that they were political novices and *lacked liberation war credentials*." In competition with them was a faction that represented the old guard and the military top brass. They were labeled "Lacoste" after the fashion brand that uses a crocodile as its logo—"the crocodile" being the treasured nickname of their nominee to succeed Mugabe, Emmerson Mnangagwa. By contrast with the G40, the Lacoste faction could insist that Mnangagwa had not only a unique record of loyalty to Mugabe but also "*unquestionable* liberation war credentials."[29]

Yet perhaps the past haunted the present most profoundly in the discourse of the great political confrontation of the earlier 2000s. Each side sought legitimacy and support by claiming to be the successors of Southern Rhodesia's African nationalist movement. ZANU-PF presented itself as the agency that had brought liberation, that was undoing the lynchpin of settler rule (inaugurated by Cecil Rhodes) through land reform; and that was standing up against neo-imperialism and especially British critics abroad. In contrast, for their part the opposition claimed to represent the unfinished struggle for human dignity (espoused by David Livingstone), human rights, and democracy—the cluster of liberal notions around which a loose multiracial coalition had briefly formed in the late 1950s.

By 2000, the ZANU-PF state in Zimbabwe resembled in many ways the later colonial state of the RF. Notwithstanding positive aspects in both cases, each governing party used the state as an organ of oppression. Government was not widely representative. It was self-perpetuating, largely indifferent to if not contemptuous of the needs of the masses. The RF had been accountable primarily to the White minority; ZANU-PF could not form a government that was genuinely and periodically accountable to a nation of taxpayers. Reality was out of step with rhetoric: in the former case, the rhetoric of "civilization"; in the latter, the rhetoric of "unity." Both were defined more by the demands they made on people than by the personal security and services they provided for those people. Longevity of those in power rested more on manipulation and coercion than on widespread consent or respect for procedure. In each, to oppose was to fall foul of a government that welcomed neither criticism nor compromise.

Notes

1. Landes, *The Wealth and Poverty of Nations*, 431, 504.
2. Rodney, *How Europe Underdeveloped Africa*.
3. Thompson, *African Democracy*, 380, 381.
4. Quoted in Thompson, *African Democracy*, 167.
5. Lovell, *Maoism*, 220.
6. Eddison Zvogbo, quoted in Dorman, *Understanding Zimbabwe*, 40.
7. Quoted in Godwin and Hancock, *Rhodesians Never Die*, 255.
8. Tredgold, *My Life*, 246, 248.
9. Quoted in February, *African Perspectives*, 85.
10. Quoted in Hills, *Rebel People*, 141.
11. A. Mlambo, *A History of Zimbabwe*, 257.
12. Tredgold, *My Life*, 251.
13. A. Mlambo, *A History of Zimbabwe*, 257.
14. Nkomo, *My Life*, 168–170.
15. Quoted in Martin and Johnson, *The Struggle for Zimbabwe*, 301.
16. Martin and Johnson, *The Struggle for Zimbabwe*, 32.
17. Quoted in Martin and Johnson, *The Struggle for Zimbabwe*, 328.
18. Dorman, *Understanding Zimbabwe*, 4.
19. Godwin and Hancock, *Rhodesians Never Die*, 264, 317, 318.
20. Lionel Cliffe, in Stonemen (ed), *Zimbabwe's Inheritance*, 9.
21. Norman, *The Odd Man In*, 60.
22. Ranger, *Peasant Consciousness*, 288.
23. Quoted in A. Mlambo, *A History of Zimbabwe*, 226.
24. James Muzondidya, in Raftopolous and Mlambo, *Becoming Zimbabwe*, 172.
25. Quoted in Meredith, *The State of Africa*, 627.
26. Raftopoulos, *Becoming Zimbabwe*, 212.
27. Chidzero, *Good Government*, 180.
28. Quoted in A. Mlambo, *A History of Zimbabwe*, 198.
29. Ndlovu, *Crocodile*, 6, 7. Italics added.

9

Judging Empire

To history has been assigned the office of judging the past, of instructing the present for the benefit of future ages. To such high offices this work does not aspire: it wants only to show what actually happened.
                                                            Leopold von Ranke[1]

We need to know what is real as opposed to what's false . . . the best obtainable version of the truth.
                                                            Carl Bernstein[2]

What, finally, are we to make of it all, this episode of White colonial rule in the heart of Africa?

We have seen in previous chapters what this settler colony looked like; the impact of a host of uninvited foreign immigrants spread over nine decades; and the unfolding relations between the races there beginning in 1890, in a world very different from that of 1980, when Rhodesia gave way to Zimbabwe.

All historians write in the shadow of Leopold von Ranke, the nineteenth-century German founder of the modern discipline who, dismissive of the condescension applied to the past by philosophers such as Voltaire, focused instead on presenting what he had learned of the past without making judgments on it. Seemingly leading us in a similar direction is the guiding principle of two celebrated investigative American journalists, Carl Bernstein and Bob Woodward. They have seen their role as setting the truth before the public, leaving the latter to make their own judgments.

In such a light, this study should perhaps stop here, having nothing more to say. But the issues are more complicated. Von Ranke went further than his fictional literary contemporary, Mr. Gradgrind, the central figure of Charles Dickens's novel *Hard Times,* who advocated a schooling based on nothing but the acquisition of dry, hard facts. He argued that the historian should try to understand "the facts" and share this understanding with his readers. He was opposed to "the wrong kind" of judgments, though: in short, "the past could not be judged by the standards of the present. It had to be seen in its own terms."[3] For their part, Woodward and Bernstein clearly displayed a less than entirely disinterested point of view when, as all journalists must, they originally chose their story of Watergate and Richard Nixon and then pursued it so assiduously. Conditioned in every case by their own times, historians (like journalists) have their own perspectives and purposes. It is best that each should be aware of and acknowledge this personal standpoint.

Meanwhile, forty or so years on from the collapse of White minority rule, a lively retrospective (and heavily judgmental) discussion of "empire" in Britain and elsewhere in the West is a context that cannot be ignored in any individual case study such as this. Southern Rhodesia was always distant in space from the metropolis; it is now sufficiently distant in time, too, for a dispassionate reappraisal.

Therefore, a final chapter follows, for readers who are inclined to make judgments about people in the past and what they did. Its purpose is to proceed beyond the narrative and analysis of earlier pages and to suggest a meaningful method for criticizing those who shaped this history: not just well-known individuals such as Cecil Rhodes and Ian Smith, but the thousands of mostly anonymous White settlers from successive generations.

Here follows a moral yardstick; a glance at the broader current context; a template for making meaningful judgments; an extended examination of the RF; a consideration of the relationship of Rhodes's reputation with the colony he founded; and some African perspectives on aspects of their colonial experience.

* * *

For the study of any period since 1945, there is no more persuasive reference point than the Universal Declaration of Human Rights, adopted by the newly formed United Nations in Paris on December 10, 1948. Articulating core aspirations of the US and French revolutions, this document encapsulated the Enlightenment. More immediately, it was humanity's response to World War II, the horrors of which had given birth to new categories of international law: genocide, illegal warfare, and crimes against humanity. These added up to a historic, previously unimaginable moral landmark. Since that moment in Paris, mankind has had both a reference point and a progressive agenda.

No Easy Generalizations

Empire, at heart the rule of one person or group of people over others, has been a recurrent state of affairs throughout human history and across the globe. The nineteenth century was marked by a fresh surge of imperialism, which straddled several continents. The westward expansion of Manifest Destiny in the United States, as well as the Zionist project in Palestine, entailed not so much rule over other peoples as their displacement and dispossession, later termed "ethnic cleansing." By contrast, the late century "scramble for Africa," involving several European states, brought about an ongoing relationship between colonizers and the colonized—between races, that is—such as the relationship that evolved in Britain's African colonies, including Southern Rhodesia.

To understand prevailing British views at that time, we should recall that many saw their own imperialism—powered though it unquestionably was by economic interests—as the instrument by which an advanced civilization could raise people out of "backwardness." As the secretary of the Rhodes Trust put it a little later, in 1927, "modern civilization, even modern capitalism" could "lift the mass of men and women into independence and self-respect and give them that competence with which they can afford to think of something other than the satisfaction of urgent physical needs."[4] Such a viewpoint might strike us today as patronizing, even racist, but it was not malevolent.

In the nineteenth century, the British were brought up to admire, not to deplore, the Roman Empire. The Indigenous peoples of Britannia had been among Rome's subjects . . . even victims, as one might infer from the statue on Westminster Bridge, London, which commemorates Boudicca's resistance to Roman rule. Yet overall, and over time, the British came to associate the Pax Romana with advances in industry, commerce, and technology; the benefits of an infrastructure of roads and water supply; the development of towns and urban life; and "as much self-government as was compatible with orderly administration."[5] Centuries later, Rome was flattered by imitation. The Pax Britannica provided what the British claimed was good government, associated with order, the rule of law, and material progress.

British colonies, in turn, could prove tolerable or more than tolerable: for some Africans at least, for some time, and in some places. In 1958, that pivotal year in Southern Rhodesia's history, the White liberal Hardwicke Holderness offered an informed assessment of emergent Africans in the colony. He wrote of "the sort of moderate African who holds down a responsible job in a modern firm; is busy building himself a house in town; has to support his family without hidden subsidies from the reserves; has a lot to lose if there is any 'trouble'; sincerely believes in Christian principles and co-operating, and has no ambition to be a radical or a demagogue."[6] This "moderate middle-class" was a potential partner of White reformers in a nonracial future. Holderness's view of such Africans was shared at the time by the academic Lewis Gann, perhaps surprisingly, given his advocacy of White settlement. "It would be a serious mistake to suppose that a wealthy bus-owner in Southern Rhodesia or a successful fish-trader on Lake Bangweulu [Northern Rhodesia] is now particularly anxious to mount the barricades."[7]

Comparisons from the period of World War II confirm that empire came in many forms. Then, the two most brutal, ideologically driven empires of all time, Nazi and Soviet, were fighting each other to the death. Meanwhile, in the White settler colony of Southern Rhodesia, a debate took place in the national legislature as to whether Africans should be compelled to do work—*paid* work, that is—on White farms to ease the local food crisis.[8] As Nigel Biggar advises in *Colonialism: A Moral Reckoning*, "The whole truth is morally complicated and ambiguous."[9]

In her recent novel, Hafsa Zayyan has the African girlfriend of a third generation Ugandan Asian seek to reassure him regarding his family history of colonizing East Africa. "There's nothing to be sorry about. Everything your grandfather thought or did was a result of his personal experiences, his own personal circumstances. He was a product of his time. Just like we're a product of ours."[10] If people in the past were just as likely to have been conditioned by their community and times as we are by ours today, yet were far less likely to have had opportunities for encounters, reflection, and choices than we have, we might hesitate, as advised by Leopold von Ranke and others, before judging them by our standards. As recently as the first half of the twentieth century, communities were much more isolated, and so were more ignorant of alternative ways of looking at the world. This was especially true of peoples living in far flung corners of a globe that was far from globalized. Settlers in remote landlocked colonies, for example, could remain secure in views which for lengthy periods remained, as far as they were aware, largely unchallenged. Those regions included the closed world of southern Africa—from which Rhodes wished his Oxford-bound scholars for a while to escape. Andre Maurois wrote several biographies, including one of Cecil Rhodes. In *Ariel,* he advised his readers against pontificating about the thoughts and deeds of their predecessors: "The minds of different generations are as impenetrable, one by the other, as are the monads of Leibnitz."[11]

A Template

Chris Patten, the accomplished British politician, knew something about latter-day British colonialism through his experience as the last governor of Hong Kong: a colony, incidentally, where thousands of mainland Chinese risked their lives to flee to and settle in after the revolution of 1949. In his 2017 memoir, Patten reflects on his own family history and poses a rhetorical question: "How can we pronounce from our vantage point and from a contemporary moral stance about behaviour in the past?"[12] This deserves an answer.

Let us imagine a three-stage framework—a grid for tracking any historic moral issue. It comprises an age of *consensus*; a period of *challenge*; and a time of *choice*. Of course, such a skeleton is crude, since retrospective periodization is only neat and tidy when it ignores the complexity and exceptions of reality. But it should not be rejected for that reason alone. As with light, when we seek something in the dark, some assistance is better than none, and may be enough to find what we are looking for. The framework can be illustrated and tested on slavery.

Consensus

Slavery was at the heart of countless civilizations over many centuries. In the Western World (Europe, Central America, and North America), slavery and the slave-trade were widely regarded as acceptable until well into the eighteenth century. The British played the leading part in the transatlantic slave trade from the mid-seventeenth century onward. The founding fathers of the United States were inspired in 1776 by the fine words of Thomas Jefferson. "We hold these truths to be self-evident, that all men are created equal." But the US Constitution, formulated a little later, did not recognize hundreds of thousands of enslaved Black plantation workers as equal. George Washington, after whom the new capital city was named, was himself a slave-owner. So too was William Penn, Quaker leader, whose statue today rises high above Philadelphia, the de facto pre-independence capital he founded in 1682. Slavery came in various forms, but the institution itself was largely taken for granted.

Challenge

The great age of encounter began in Britain, where in the later eighteenth century a broad based slave-trade abolition movement gathered pace, driven by an assortment of individuals. Among the campaigners were African writers such as Olaudah Equiano and Ottobah Cugoano, both former slaves. Prominent Englishmen such as Thomas Clarkson and William Wilberforce challenged slavery and the slave trade on moral grounds, strongly influenced by a heartfelt personal Christian conviction. From the 1780s onward, practices formerly considered acceptable, even Biblically endorsed, were increasingly called into question. Consensus was challenged, erstwhile moral certainties were shaken. A great moral-historical-political debate was played out.

Only when an established practice has, in such a way, become a moral issue *in the period which we are studying* may we as students of history intervene, as it were, by offering our own judgments. The historian and journalist Ben Macintyre offered an illustration of this point when in May 2023 he wrote about another infamous British transgression. For over 170 years, Charles Edward Trevelyan had been blamed for the huge death toll in Ireland arising from the mid–nineteenth century potato famine. A believer in laissez-faire economics and divine providence, Trevelyan had refused to ease the crisis through direct food and monetary aid. "Judging the past by the ethical standards of the present is an easy though often pointless exercise," Macintyre wrote, echoing von Ranke. But, he added, in the case of Trevelyan, many voices were raised at the time. "The judgement on Trevelyan that really matters," Macintyre concluded, is that of his own contemporaries who witnessed the horrors of the famine but urged him in vain to prevent it.[13]

Choice

"Forgive them, for they know not what they do."[14] But once they did know? Encounter opens up alternatives and requires choice. In the case of slavery, if owners and traders were confronted by a grounded moral challenge to their accustomed ways yet chose to continue as before, those of us today who adhere to the principles of the Enlightenment (from which, in part at least, that challenge sprang) may reasonably add our own "guilty" verdict to that of their contemporaries. William Wilberforce's stricture in the first parliamentary abolition debate of 1789 has enduring power. "The nature and all the circumstances of this trade are now laid open to us; *we can no longer plead ignorance*, we cannot evade it, it is now an object placed before us."[15] Slave owners and traders could choose to look the other way, but they could never again say that they did not know. In this way, what we think now was being put to them then; in that encounter they lost the moral argument and so may be judged.

Consensus in Southern Rhodesia

This was a settler colony, functioning in the interests of its master caste. As we saw in Chapter 3, from the turn of the century into the 1940s there was, unsurprisingly, a high level of consensus there, among the Whites of the territory, regarding the character and purposes of imperialism. Those who went to acquire land and those went to save souls could agree that the territory carved out by the British South Africa Company (and governed by the settlers since 1923) provided them with the opportunities they sought. There were differences of opinion and emphasis, of course, but even Arthur Shearly Cripps, something of a lone voice when he published *An Africa for Africans* in 1927, was critical of certain White attitudes and practices more than the colonial principle itself. In Southern Rhodesia before World War II, few Europeans questioned the beneficence of colonial rule in general or, specifically, the tripod legislation, restrictive franchise, and racial segregation. This small, remote colonial outpost remained for the time being undisturbed by any changing attitudes or expectations in the world beyond. Nor were the Whites yet under pressure from their colonial subjects. In the aftermath of a defeated revolt, Africans had no choice but to adapt and adjust: to acquiesce in the new order, albeit in a wide variety of forms and degrees. While it has been asserted as a generalization that "insurgencies were frequent during British colonial rule," in this White settler colony there was no insurgency between the primary resistance of the 1890s and the liberation struggle against the (RF) in the 1960s.[16] But as a perceptive White South African noted of the changes being wrought on Africans by White rule as early as 1918, "The present generation is not like their fathers, and the next will differ more widely."[17]

Challenge in Southern Rhodesia

World War II called into question colonialism as never before. In this new world, were aggrieved and frustrated Africans to be seen as a threat by

White settlers, or as potential partners in economic and political development? This was the challenge, as depicted in Chapters 4 and 5. "We could write volumes on the good things that European powers brought to Africa." These are the words not of Ian Smith but of Ndabaningi Sithole.[18] The tragedy for Southern Rhodesia was that increasing numbers among the growing African population felt denied "the good things" that they increasingly and earnestly sought. Among these, high in importance were personal security and land rights in town or country; a meaningful vote, which would enable them to share equitably in the determination of their own future; and, perhaps above everything else, to be treated with dignity. Eventually, scarred by experience and inspired by what was going on elsewhere on the continent, many shook off deference and acquired the language of "nationalism," the goal of majority rule and the confidence to challenge White domination. The process took time. At thirty years old in the mid-1940s, even Joshua Nkomo "had still not started to make myself a political philosophy."[19] Now it was different.

By the 1950s, Southern Rhodesia faced two freshly articulated, overlapping, and value-loaded questions. The first was the imperial question. Should the British continue to be responsible for the fate of other peoples? Here was the principle of self-determination. The second was the race question. Was it reasonable or acceptable for any society to continue to sustain a discriminatory racial hierarchy of privilege and power? Here was the principle of equality. Of the two, the former—the rights and wrongs of ultimate authority residing in London—was almost peripheral to the latter. Once the Central African Federation (CAF), on which many Whites had pinned their hopes, began to implode, the increasingly urgent question was what *kind* of Southern Rhodesia would seek or could be granted independence from Britain. This was the context for the informal, spasmodic debate on race among the Europeans, which gathered momentum from the days of Godfrey Huggins through the days of Garfield Todd. Should political exclusiveness, industrial color bar, and social segregation continue?

Choice in Southern Rhodesia

In Chapter 6 we accounted for the turn to the right, for which a majority of Whites opted. The challenge to ongoing racial segregation was considered to be liberalism's last chance. It proved to be Hardwicke Holderness's *Lost Chance*. By the end of the 1950s, the "Livingstonian" tradition, which flickered with such promise for a few years in the middle of the decade, was in retreat. The Canadian political journalist Patrick

Keatley was struck by a "supreme irony." He wondered whether the region's greatest explorer and teacher "would fit in," if he were to return (in 1963) to the country he had helped bring into being. He sadly concluded that "if David Livingstone were to reappear . . . now, saying and doing the things he did in his lifetime, he would not last a week."[20]

The fork in the road had two prongs. This was a contest with just two possible outcomes, each heavy with moral as well as political significance. The liberal challenge to the status quo rested on the right of peoples of all colors and ethnicities to be treated as equals in the territory's social, economic, and political life. It required the Whites to adapt to a changing world, to compromise, and to abandon long-established privileges and patterns of behavior. Resisting this liberal critique, White diehards chose to argue, in some cases citing Rhodes, that it was they who stood not only for order and prosperity but also, as Ian Smith claimed on the day of the Unilateral Declaration of Independence (UDI), for "the preservation of justice, civilisation and Christianity."

Consequences for Rhodesia

Following consensus, challenge, and choice among the Whites of the colony came the consequences of the choice made: to retain and consolidate inequality, racial discrimination, and political exclusiveness. Chapter 7 explored how this led them down a cul de sac. In response, many Africans chose militancy: to resist by force White prejudices and practices no longer tolerable. Judith Todd detected how White racist attitudes had evolved over time. "Our philosophy moved progressively from the stage at which we said that Africans were different, to the stage at which we said they were different and inferior, and so to the final stage at which we tried to convince ourselves that they were different, inferior, and dangerous. In short, we made them our enemies although they were prepared to be our friends."[21] The 1959 state of emergency and accompanying repressive legislation closed down peaceful opposition to government and drove African nationalism underground.

It was not only the Africans' prospects that the Rhodesian Front (RF) was jeopardizing but the Whites' prospects too. Doris Lessing detected an "unreasoning spirit of self-destruction."[22] Nowhere was this more in evidence than in the obdurate, intransigent leadership provided by Smith. He more than any other individual took Rhodesia into a crisis that threatened not only White supremacy but White lives as well. But he was not alone. In 1976, his RF minister of defense, Reg Cowper, tried to explain, in tragicomic terms, why the war was being fought. "We in Rhodesia are fighting to create a stable country where Black and White can live side by side." In fact, he was a key figure in causing violent instability, whereas Blacks fought Whites for political mastery. It is sadly ironic that the best chance of realizing such a vision of multiracialism had been destroyed by men like him, twenty years earlier, when genuine partnership had had a far greater chance of success.

In Rhodesia itself the essential error of White reactionaries was to believe that they were living in a time warp, on a detached planet. Smith said in 1976: "Any premature handover to black rule will inevitably lead to chaos and internal strife."[23] And yet delay was already generating "chaos and internal strife." Furthermore, a handover in the late 1970s would not have been premature if steps cautiously taken toward it had not been blocked by White diehards in the 1950s, of which he had been one. In December 1974, Des Frost, the inflexibly diehard chairman of the RF, was claiming that "the Africans prefer a European government."[24] He was indulging in wishful thinking, then, though twenty years earlier many of 'the Africans" had been ready to give conditional support to Garfield Todd.

Consequences for Zimbabwe

The UDI did lasting damage, as noted in Chapter 8. All transitions from colonial rule to independence were difficult. It is ironic that the RF years made it considerably harder in (Southern) Rhodesia, where twenty years earlier there had been some potential for a manageable, staged transfer of power. Instead, the right-wing won the local political struggle; convinced that they were in the right, they defied the late twentieth-century global consensus that they were wrong. Predictably, reinforced White minority policies damaged the country and all its peoples, if not beyond repair then beyond the capacity of successor African majority rule to fully make good. We may conclude, from looking again at "how it all began," that "what went wrong" owed less to the Whites' record over the first half of the century than to the inflexibility of reactionary Whites when challenged, and their near fatal miscalculations thereafter. It was those later choices which rendered the early days of Zimbabwe so challenging, their own fate more vulnerable—and themselves more culpable.

Peter Godwin provides a most interesting concluding comment on White opinions in 1979/1980, as Rhodesia ceded to Zimbabwe. Few

Rhodesians could admit that the fighting had been a mistake, he wrote, and, in reference to a political party of which previously he had been dismissive, "Certainly there would be no acknowledgement that the reviled Centre Party liberals, and their predecessors and successors, had been right all along."[25]

The Right Was Wrong

> *Outcasts . . . rebels . . . dispossessed*
> *That is what we are today,*
> *But good old Smithy, he knows best!*
> *Three cheers for Smith! Hip, hip, hooray*[26]

During the years of the UDI, the White community in Rhodesia continued to be differentiated by background, educational achievement and occupation, political preferences, and attitudes toward race relations. There were liberals among them still, as well as the "swivel-eyed fanatics on the Rhodesian right."[27] Yet this was a community that, when offered an electoral choice, repeatedly maintained the RF in power and endorsed their policies. A broad core of Europeans shared prejudices, and an outlook toward the millions of Africans whose territory they shared, that was largely incurious, unimaginative, and unsympathetic. No doubt many of their beliefs and values resembled those of contemporary conservatives who lived in Britain rather than Central Africa. But the responsibility these Whites bore for the lives of others gave their views major significance. The stakes were far higher in Salisbury, Rhodesia, than in Salisbury, England.

European ignorance of Africans persisted. This arose largely from a continued reluctance or refusal to talk (and listen) to Africans in general and, especially, to African political leaders. Europeans did not collectively heed the surprisingly frank and prophetic admission of Todd's predecessor as prime minister, Godfrey Huggins, in 1952: "There is a much larger group of partially educated Africans," he observed. "These . . . set us a problem because we have a rather contemptuous outlook towards them. We forget to take them seriously; they must be treated seriously, and we must try to help them to sort out their ideas, otherwise . . . we shall be creating trouble for ourselves, our heirs and successors."[28] Huggins showed little interest in acting on his own insight. Liberal, moderate, and radical Whites, such as those associated with the Interracial Association (IA) and the Capricorn Africa Society (CAS) later in the decade, were too few in number to break the bonds of segregation.

Fueled by ongoing segregation was White grievance at the ingratitude of the natives. As one White correspondent put it in a letter to the press in January 1976, in sub-Churchillian prose, "Where else in Africa, or the world for that matter, have so few people done so much for the underprivileged and emerging people?" The reality was that the Whites had indeed done much—primarily for themselves, and to the Africans—and that they had depended very heavily on African manpower to do so. As Doris Lessing observed, "It is taken for granted by white citizenry that all the wealth of the country is created by them and that whatever is 'done' for the Africans is a favour on their part."[29] Keatley noted, a little later, that the Whites "say that they are doing all they can for the blacks; white taxes, they say, are paying for black education. The African answer is, simply: Who asked you to?"[30] By the mid-late 1970s, Africans were no longer grateful for favors; they wanted to make their own policy decisions.

Whites' misunderstandings led to an alienating condescension toward Africans. Proprietary and patronizing, Whites tended to talk of "our African tribesmen." This was doubly offensive to Rhodesian Africans, whose response was, in short, "We are not *yours*, and we are not *tribesmen*."[31] Delusory wishful thinking flourished. In 1972, Ian Smith famously claimed "of course, we have the happiest Africans in the world," just as the Pearce commission was finding that this was not the case. As self-servingly patronizing as any of Smith's views was his assertion that if Africans had indeed rejected those settlement proposals, it could only be because they had not properly understood them. Many of his fellow Whites took comparable proprietorial pride in the exceptionalism of "their" Africans. Company director Alex Maddocks, for example, in 1976 said, "In my opinion our black Africans are the finest in Africa, they're fine people and I'm proud of them."[32]

Complacency was nothing new. After Smith became leader of the RF in 1964, Nkomo described him as one who "publicly talked a lot of nonsense about the excellent race relations of Southern Rhodesia."[33] Smith himself described his return to Southern Rhodesia after the war. "I had never had a problem living with and getting along with our black people." He could write of Southern Rhodesia at that time that "we were a small country with a small population, and no problems of any consequence." He wrote, too, of "gradually bringing our black people in, as and when they were prepared to accept change." There were some "mischief makers" about, "but our average black was not interested."[34] In a nutshell, and as for so many Whites, Smith convinced himself that he and his followers understood "our" Africans and thus knew what was good for them. Vividly if acerbically, Hills summarized this prevailing

White outlook in the late 1970s; it seemed to him to be one of smug, indifferent detachment. "I am left, after my first exposure to Rhodesia's rebel capital, with an impression of people who have in the past given more loving care to their roses, their South African syringas, their Currie Cup cricket and rugby and their dogs, than to the black people on whose land they live. . . . By Salisbury standards, being good to blacks amounts to paying the houseboy regularly and giving him one's cast-off clothes and aspirin when he has a headache."[35]

The White settlers failed to see how their assumption that Rhodesia was *their* home was provocative. Though many were indeed born there, or descended from people who had been, this could not cancel out a history of conquest and dispossession. The claim was more clearly bogus when uttered by postwar immigrants who readily settled into the segregation of their newly adopted country. For many postwar immigrants, authentic "home"—home to identify with, and even return to—was far away. Hills colorfully caught the reality of the situation. "Whites who have refused to accept the black man as neighbour and friend, or his 'offspring' as playmates for their own children, have forfeited the right to call Rhodesia their 'home.' How can it be their home, if they have erected racial barriers, wire fences and noticeboards to keep Africa out, and employ dogs and watchmen to see that their separateness is enforced?" Many Whites sought to create tropical versions of the homes they had left behind. "Here in Ridgemont, on the road to Salisbury," Hills noted, "a section of the white race have gone to ground in a garden suburb where they hide from each other, and from Africa, in numbered plots behind gravel drives, hedges and name-boards that, despite the flaming bracts of poinsettia and the wild fig trees, strive to reproduce the illusion of Pinner."[36]

On November 21, 1977, to the backcloth of an escalating liberation war, Mrs. H. Knight of Salisbury wrote to the *Rhodesia Herald*. "I'm Rhodesian born. This is my country. Here I stay. Let every white man and woman stay put. This way we will keep Rhodesia."[37] As in so many ways, White attitudes fostered their mirror image. The paper's December 20 edition carried a response from L. A. B. Mudzane, also of Salisbury. "Those whites who cannot live with Africans can pack their bags and go. This is our country, and we must be equals."[38]

Because they continued not to talk to or to listen to Africans, Whites continued to harbor and act on serious misunderstandings. In September 1964, before the UDI but with African parties banned and their leaders in detention, Smith was asked, in London, about African opinion. "My assessment of the position is this," he replied. "Sithole has the support of the more educated, enlightened African, but on the other hand Mr. Nkomo quite obviously has the support of the masses."[39] But he would talk to neither. The RF did not want to listen to, and Whites generally did not want to hear, what Africans really thought and wanted. They closed one African newspaper after another. One of these was the *Gonakudzingwa News*, produced by Nkomo and others while in detention. In it, Nkomo wrote at length of the continuing role of Whites in a country that was envisaged by African nationalists. White civil servants, for example, were necessary; their services would not be dispensed with. More generally, "people are being told that we, the African leaders . . . do not want a parliamentary form of government; that we want to chase away all whites from this country. . . . There can be nothing further from the truth."[40] Determined White self-isolation and perpetuation of ignorance blocked awareness of true African feelings and aspirations.

Moreover, Whites "lacked the imagination to understand the anger that comes from not being allowed to govern your own lives."[41] They could not bring themselves to accept that Africans had legitimate ambition and that their grievances were genuine, spontaneous, and homegrown, rather than, as Whites claimed, the product of communist-inspired agitation. Smith grumbled that "the free world was bluffed into believing that the terrorists—who were in fact a group of Marxist-Leninist gangsters—had justice and the ideals of freedom as their objective."[42] Here, typically, was no recognition that the uncompromising policies of White supremacy might have brought about the opposition. Having so little contact with Africans or understanding of their general thirst for reform rather than revolution, White governments failed to see how their own policies fostered African opposition: indeed, turned it from nonviolent argument toward violent confrontation (and association with communists). They themselves created the very enemy they previously and wrongly accused the politically articulate, representative African elite of being.

The Whites' arithmetic had always belonged in cuckoo-land, but it was only after their decisive 1960s turn to the right that their assumptions were shown to be disastrously wrong. They had assumed it would always be necessary to keep the races apart, and that their own race could continue to direct the affairs of the colony as an exclusive caste. But the sums did not add up. Given the steep increase in size of the African population during the years of the self-governing colony, the minority White regime always did what it could to attract ever increasing numbers of European immigrants to settle in the country. But this policy emphasis owed more to faith than reason. Despite the surge after World War II, there would never be "enough" Whites to perpetuate White political ascendancy or to service a developing economy. The proportion of

Africans to Europeans was always growing. It was not just a matter of numbers. White immigration could never provide all the skilled manpower the country needed. Yet Smith and the RF kept believing in, and relying on, White immigration. By the late 1970s, when Whites were emigrating to an unmanageable extent, the regime had long since spurned the alternative strategy, which would have required imagination and courage, of promoting social and economic advancement while working with Africans in a political partnership of substance.

Smith and the RF were seriously wrong, too, in their timing. They had torpedoed 1950s attempts to find a peaceful compromise. Thereafter, their own policies and attitudes hardened African opposition to White rule, and as such made their own superficially similar attempts at resolution pointless. It was an error for Smith to allow fourteen months to elapse after the Pearce commission had reported before he first had talks with Abel Muzorewa, who had done so much to determine the outcome of that consultation. Very belatedly, in 1973 the RF sanctioned talks with Black political leaders, but Smith remained adamant that he would not talk to "murderers." However, 1974 did see him talk to the recently released Joshua Nkomo for the very first time. At this meeting Nkomo told Smith, "You cannot stand against the forces around you today. You haven't got time to buy."[43]

Smith ignored this advice. Throughout the continent, African nationalism was a political tsunami, and liberation from colonial rule was unstoppable. Reactionary White Rhodesians were seriously mistaken to think that somehow "their" Africans would not demand the freedoms being won elsewhere. Liberals had been far more realistic. They had recognized in the 1950s that no social or political system that caused justifiable grievance to a majority of its people could ultimately prevail. This view was endorsed in 1972 by Lawrence Vambe. "I believe that the African people have remarkable physical, psychological and moral stamina, which I think Mr. Smith and the ideology he espouses in Rhodesia will find indestructible, however hard he and his supporters try to perpetuate racialism and white supremacy."[44]

Smith's personal misjudgments included his demonization of Robert Mugabe. Later, Smith commented on the aftermath of the February 1980 election, in which victory was claimed by Mugabe and Zimbabwe African National Union—Patriotic Front (ZANU-PF). Blithely unaware that he could no longer determine the country's future, Smith wrote: "For some time, I had been in the invidious position of having to decide between Nkomo and Mugabe. The thought of siding with Nkomo was particularly repulsive. On the evidence before us, however, he seemed to be the lesser of the two evils." Nevertheless, as the days and weeks of 1980 passed, Smith had to accept that Mugabe had won. His assessment of Mugabe thereafter, having met with the new president—the greater of "the two evils"—makes for fascinating reading. Of Mugabe in March: "He behaved like a balanced, civilised, Westerner, the antithesis of the communist gangster I had expected." In May: "Once again I pondered to myself over the man's maturity, reasonableness and sense of fair play."[45] There was no recognition here that for years, Smith had been mistaken in not talking to all the main African political leaders, nor was there recognition that it was his own regime that had demonized Mugabe as a gangster.

Mugabe was seen by most White Zimbabweans as the opposite of "reasonable and fair." But such an assessment can only add poignant weight to the verdict of Denis Norman. A White farmer who lived and worked in Rhodesia throughout this period, Norman castigated Smith's decision to declare unilateral independence. "This action more than any other, I am convinced, brought Robert Mugabe to power fifteen years later." Based on his experience of working with him in government, Norman's own portrait of Mugabe is telling. Of the new prime minister's visit to White farms soon after independence, Norman writes of Mugabe: "He impressed everyone with his friendliness and the ability he had to communicate with all he met."[46]

At first after the 1980 election, Mugabe surprised everyone with his statesmanlike moderation. But by this time White intransigence had brought into being its eventual nemesis. Mugabe had eventually supplanted Sithole as head of Zimbabwe African National Union (ZANU) to become the most intransigent adversary of the White regime, ready to authorize acts of terror against opponents and rivals in the late 1970s (and again in the mid-1980s). But this African Robespierre had not been a figure of note in the Southern Rhodesia of the 1950s. For much of that decade he was abroad, and he became involved in radical African nationalist politics only in 1960. To be sure, he had already by then adopted an uncompromising ideological stance. But he was on the margins of a movement that, for a short while yet, sought dialogue and accommodation with the Whites, not Black power through socialist revolution, as he later would. By the later 1970s, Whites made Mugabe a pivotal figure. As Bishop Muzorewa observed in 1978, "There is no logic in the oppressive acts of an enemy desperate to stay in power."[47]

Notwithstanding sunshine and a material standard of living unattainable elsewhere, the experience of the White settlers does not seem to have made them, to borrow Ian Smith's formulation, the happiest Europeans in the world. There are more than a few hints in the literature of a malaise among the Whites: that their determinedly preferred lifestyle had its shortcomings. "The other day," recorded Hills, "when one of the African teachers stopped in town to give me a lift and I got into his van, I heard a voice call after me 'You bastard!' I looked round to see two white women scowling at me for accepting a favour from a black man. They had wrinkled, unhappy faces like chows."[48] Doris Lessing recorded meeting a White inspector of African schools who seemed disturbed when he described to her a recent tour:

> In all the Reserve, there is no telephone, there is nothing. Neither telephone, nor radio, nor electric light, nor running water, nor books, nor newspapers. Nothing, nothing. They might as well be on the moon. There is a choice of churches, and mealie-porridge to eat, and a whole lot of visiting government officials telling them they must become civilised. So I inspect the school, very efficient and uplifting, and I leave that Reserve accompanied by a million happy kids, waving and shouting good-bye. . . . What right have they got to be so bloody happy living like that?[49]

An old school friend of Lessing's was finding life a struggle. "Sometimes I think we are worse off than the natives. They don't seem to worry as much as we do. And they are such a *cheerful* lot—I envy them."[50] Whites, consciously or not, faced a particular dilemma. Philip Mason posed the question in 1958: "Shall they teach freedom and provoke revolt? Or shall they suppress the lesson of their own history and themselves become as miserable and as leaden eyed as is usually the fate of conquerors who are slaves to their own fears?"[51] For many Whites in the 1970s, there was a somewhat grim reality. The Rhodesian republic of Smith and the RF was a weird mixture: a sunny world of White standards and happy African acquiescence, yet a world menaced by alien shadows comprising unsympathetic foreigners and, at home, malevolently ungrateful Blacks.

If there are global tides of history, Smith and the RF were swimming against one. Their UDI of November 1965 must be seen in the context of what was happening elsewhere.

Historic changes were being introduced in the United States under President Lyndon Johnson. In July 1964, the Civil Rights Act banned racial discrimination in employment and public places; in August 1965, the Voting Rights Act banned discriminatory practices associated with elections. This was the America of James Baldwin, whose *The Fire Next Time* was published in 1963: that is, just after the RF came to power in

Southern Rhodesia but before the UDI. He wrote of his own experience, but he could have been describing that of Blacks in Southern Rhodesia. "One did not have to be abnormally sensitive to be worn down to a cutting edge by the incessant and gratuitous humiliation and danger one encountered every working day." Again, of the White majority, "most people guard and keep. . . . What they are actually guarding and keeping is *their system of reality* and what they assume themselves to be."[52] It was a fatal misjudgment of Smith to assume that the United States, deeply troubled by intractable race relations of its own, having to adjust to Black grievances at home as well as overseas, would give material support to his regime as an ally in the Cold War. First, Henry Kissinger, committed to a realpolitik indifferent to the preferences of a self-beleaguered White minority in Rhodesia, cannily persuaded Smith to make concessions. Then, in 1976, Jimmy Carter prioritized his own human rights agenda.

The White regime made an even more serious error in putting its faith in the Republic of South Africa, a key Cold War ally of the West. There, the apartheid barrier to African national liberation did hold up for a while. Two years after the Sharpeville massacre, Nelson Mandela was convicted at the Rivonia trial of 1962 and sentenced to twenty-seven years in prison. But what disturbed the White regime in South Africa was not so much internal African dissent, which they could control for the time being, but the imploding of the Portuguese African empire, which they could not. In both their huge neighboring Portuguese colonies, nationalist movements took to guerrilla warfare. In Angola, the People's Movement for the Liberation of Angola (MPLA) was born in 1956, and the National Liberation Front of Angola (FNLA) in 1961. In Mozambique, Frelimo took shape in 1964, and by the time of the UDI was well established in the region, Tete, where ZANU would establish bases for their incipient war against the White regime in Rhodesia.

In a piece of political myopia and self-pity extraordinary even for him, Ian Smith later wrote of the Portuguese president, Antonio Salazar: "Had he stayed on for an extra decade, Rhodesia would have survived."[53] After 1974, the long permeable border with Mozambique, now friendly, offered African nationalist fighters a far better opportunity for damaging the White regime in Rhodesia than the geographically more challenging border with Zambia had done, or could do. The priority for South Africa in this new and unwelcome context was for Rhodesia to have an early and orderly transition to a "moderate" African regime, which would tolerate South Africa and thus prevent the establishment of another hostile, extremist one.

For Smith, however, the betrayal greater than that of either the United States or South Africa was that of Britain. The British granted independence to all its West and East African colonies by 1963; and then in 1964, in the wake of the break-up of the CAF, to Northern Rhodesia and Nyasaland. Smith and his colleagues never fully grasped that the British were not free agents at this time: in particular, that successive British governments could not ignore the wishes of the Commonwealth. Smith thus failed the first test of diplomatic competence, the ability to understand a protagonist's position and what has formed it. So, of the Labour Party after the war, a bemused Smith wrote: "Those socialists certainly had some strange principles and philosophies." He could not put himself in conservative shoes. Of Britain's changing policies in colonial Africa, he wrote that "the most outrageous thing of all was that it was not the Labour Party but the Conservatives, our 'trusted' friends, who were the architects." For Smith, everything in politics, morality, and history was simple—cut and dried, a matter of absolutes. His outlook on public affairs seems to have been profoundly shaped by the uncomplicated moral certainties of World War II. Never one for nuance, in domestic Rhodesian politics he was content to accuse liberals among his fellow Whites of "blatant treason" in 1964, just a year before he committed the blatant treason of the UDI.[54]

He returned to the treason theme on a later occasion. After the post–Lancaster House elections in 1980, Smith insisted they be challenged as having not been free and fair. Other prominent Rhodesian Whites, however, were prepared to accept the outcome, along with the British government, as representing the people's will—notwithstanding any intimidation that had taken place. Smith was incensed. "First it was the British, then the South Africans. Those we managed to resist, but now it was a combination of Britain, South Africa, and some of our own Rhodesians . . . traitors working with your enemies and undermining your foundations from within." There was no room in Smith's thinking for any standpoint other than his own. "If only people would come and see," lamented Smith.[55]

But he and his colleagues could not see. Indeed, their core weakness was that of all reactionaries: not being able to recognize and adjust to *change*. After decades of self-conditioning and having found no means of breaking out from the mental and physical confinement of segregation, the diehard Whites who dominated Rhodesia in the UDI years were unable to change their attitudes toward Africans or to question their own right or competence to rule. In September 1976, Garfield Todd concluded that "the Rhodesian government no longer has the solution within its own grasp. It has lost the political kingdom and won't face up to that reality."[56] That same year, during the Geneva conference fiasco, a British journalist offered his own assessment of the former premier. "Todd strikes one not just as a very nice guy, so much as the nice guy who was saying all or most of this 15 years ago. By shutting him up, the stupid settlers lost the years in which decent and peaceful plans might have been made for majority rule."[57]

Although they had defiantly taken the path of their choice, it is tempting but arguably unfair to condemn all Whites who voted for the RF, or every member of that party and government, as incorrigible racists. In 1960, before the UDI but after the fall of Todd, Mason wrote generously of Whites as "kindly people whose only fault is that they have been too slow about waking up to the tide of events overtaking them."[58] Shortly afterward, Keatley was bemused to find "apparently sensible, logical, White people . . . operating on the basis of sheer fantasy."[59] Lord Pearce reported in 1972 that many Europeans supported the settlement proposals of that year. "They did not really welcome majority rule," his report explained, "but realised it had to come, so that the more gradual and peaceful the road the better."[60] Of these, we can only guess what proportion had consciously missed the opportunity ten years earlier to support the progressive alternative road when African nationalists, since then held in detention under Smith, had been free men.

At the end of the decade, Hills judged that "white Rhodesians as a whole are a decent lot: confused by Christian precepts which they dare not or will not implement in their dealings with the black people . . . but not deliberately cruel to them."[61] It seems clearer in retrospect that what such Whites lacked, however "kindly, sensible, or decent," was principled, clear-headed, far-sighted political leadership. Regarding such leadership, the RF surprisingly presents us with two rather different characters, Winston Field and Ian Smith. We may depict the former, the tobacco farmer who came to public prominence reluctantly, as a "pragmatic" racist: his view was that Africans were not ready or capable of running their own country. Ian Smith, the ambitious dogmatic politician, we may more readily classify as an "ideological" racist: it was certainly true of many of his ministers and others who supported him that they regarded Africans as people of a lower order whose interests would always be best served by the rule of White men.

Having been challenged, most White Rhodesians were beguiled by the myopic promises of the RF, and, with varying degrees of enthusiasm, followed Smith, ignoring African hopes for justice and dignity. This was a historic mistake. We may agree with Hills. Smith "diddled everyone, including his own White people."[62] In 1978, at a by-election meeting in Salisbury, Smith announced: "We have had fifteen of the most wonderful years in our history."⁶³ But this time he was met by derisive (White) laughter. His claim was hollow as well as shameless. "Good old Smithy, he knows best"? He did not.

Responsibility for what occurred in the 1960s and 1970s—and thus for the situation inherited by the new state of Zimbabwe in 1980—lay with those diehard settlers who in the late 1950s responded to the aspirations of a still law-abiding African nationalism by closing the door on it and breaking with Britain to secure the maintenance of exclusive White rule. Defiant in the face of liberal criticism, they dismissed moderation and compromise and made their choice: to go further along the route of privilege and racial discrimination. For progressives, there had appeared to be an alternative future. We cannot be confident, let alone sure, that multiracial partnership would have worked. But there is no doubt that the diehards' alternative could not and did not. They brought their fate upon themselves. The core claim of Smith's political autobiography, *The Great Betrayal*, is that the Whites of Southern Rhodesia were betrayed by Britain. It is more convincing to argue that they were betrayed by the racism of the RF and the short-sighted intransigence of Smith himself. Today's opprobrium is better directed at them than on former generations of White settlers.

A Reputation: Cecil Rhodes and Zimbabwe

John Lonsdale once observed that "the questions which historians ask keep changing . . . reflecting their contemporary preoccupations."⁶⁴ Subsequent generations make what they choose of history's "great men," including Rhodes. Nothing can alter what each did or said, but reputations can rise and fall in subsequent years and centuries, according to the changing predispositions of the day. In 1946, for example, the writer Stuart Cloete presented Rhodes in *African Portraits* as having been a forerunner of Hitler, thus associating him with the latter's unspeakable excesses. This was an excellent illustration of the extent to which judgments can be distorted beyond evidence and reason by the preoccupations of one's own day.

In Rhodes's own time, his British contemporaries saw things differently. Certainly, there was some moral criticism of the consequences of British imperialism: for example, from the Aborigines' Protection Society. In 1902, the year of Rhodes's death, J. A. Hobson's *Imperialism: A Study* proved to be an influential critique, though its focus was on capitalists whose conspiracies dragged Britain into financially costly adventurism overseas, not on the sufferings of Indigenous peoples. Criticism of Rhodes personally tended not to associate him with either racism or imperialism in any general sense. It highlighted instead two other specific matters. First, his support of the Jameson Raid, the reckless attempt over the 1896 new year to seize power from the Boers in the Transvaal. Second, and bearing directly on the history of Southern Rhodesia, the duplicitous dealings with King Lobengula of the Ndebele, described in Chapter 2, which were designed to legitimize his pioneers' advancement.

In this light, the contemporary attitude of the Ndebele has a special relevance. Lobengula was indeed deceived; the Ndebele army was beaten in the war of 1893 (and Matabeleland occupied); and the revolt of 1896/1897 was quelled. For years afterward, the Ndebele sought to recover lost land. But they admired Rhodes. Rhodes died in South Africa in 1902. He had expressed a wish to be buried in the Matopo Hills of Matabeleland, in the colony that bore his name. His body was duly taken by train to Bulawayo and then to the large granite hill that was his chosen resting place. J. G. McDonald, a friend of Rhodes, later described what he saw and heard on the day of the burial. By the time the coffin arrived, "the hills were already lined with thousands of the Matabele who came to do honour to Rhodes as to the greatest of white men." After the burial, "mourners sadly retraced their steps to the sound of the Matabele warriors chanting, as is their custom, the praises of the departed chief. Thus," McDonald concluded, "the grave of Rhodes is watched over and guarded" by the Africans whose resistance he had overcome.[65]

It is difficult to review the story of Southern Rhodesia thereafter without taking account of the role of its founder and trying to measure any lasting significance. Yet Rhodes died in 1902, more than twenty years before it acquired (as he had hoped) its status as a self-governing colony. To what extent should Rhodes's reputation be adjusted in the light of what happened there, half a century later?

On the one hand, there was no predetermined linear course of events from the days of Rhodes and his pioneers to the RF, the UDI, and the liberation war. Rhodes did no more than set in motion a train of events: events that had more than one possible direction and outcome. The colony was in its infancy when he died. He did not govern or guide it through the subsequent decades. It would thus be as unreasonable to judge Rhodes by the aims and deeds of the RF. government of 1964 to 1979 as it would be to blame Karl Marx and Frederick Engels for the excesses of Stalinism and Mao Zedong. We are looking here at consequences, certainly, but not necessarily at consequences that were either intended or inevitable. Decisions were made fifty years after Rhodes's death by other people, in new circumstances, and after protracted consideration of alternatives.

On the other hand, half a century on, Whites in Southern Rhodesia in the 1950s were generally proud to associate themselves with the man who had given his name to what they regarded as their home. Rhodes was respected (alongside David Livingstone) as a giant of a heroic age. Rhodes had carved out this territory, had seen it incorporated into the empire which many admired, and had given a generation of resourceful, pioneering settlers the opportunity to make their homes in a viable colony. Each generation of White settlers could identify with him and what they interpreted as his legacy. This, many believed, was benign imperialism, in which Rhodes and other Anglo-Saxons brought progress to Africans through race relations, which distinguished them from the apartheid gestating to the south.

We see something of these attitudes expressed in 1953. For three months, Bulawayo staged a Rhodes Centenary Exhibition. Given royal approval (it was opened by the Queen Mother), it was planned as a celebration of the British empire and of interracial harmony. "Civilization" was manifest in exhibits on the export of raw materials, as well as on agriculture, industry, and transport. Alongside these pavilions, a reconstructed African village pictured the dwellings, music and dance, and arts and crafts of the Africans. This was more than a birthday party for the colony's founder. The exhibition had political propaganda purposes, too. Freshly arrived postwar White immigrants could learn the founding myths of Southern Rhodesia, while the Britishness of the occasion could serve to distance the territory from Afrikanerdom. The African village, though bogus, might nonetheless persuade visitors that while only a few hundred Africans had a vote, they were included in that famous dictum attributed to Rhodes, "equal rights for all civilised men."

Overall, however, the influence of Rhodes was limited and uneven. The colony's founder could be useful as a means of shaping the settlers' own view of themselves. Even so, some Whites were not awed by his memory. While many respected Rhodes for one reason or another, they did not all fall under the spell of the RF ten years later. In 1978, Denis Hills described the Rhodes statue in the centre of Salisbury. "Cecil Rhodes, in a baggy stone suit, bareheaded, round-shouldered, looks from a plinth down Jameson Avenue. . . . To some he is a hero; to others, a greedy bore, a non-hero who hired others to do the soldiering for him."[66]

Tens of thousands of immigrants from a range of backgrounds poured through Southern Rhodesia's open door to a new life in Central Africa after World War II. They were not so much inspired by Rhodes as simply attracted to a "Rhodesian way of life" founded on continuing racial privilege. It was these latecomers to Southern Rhodesia (who doubled the number of Whites) who eventually had to confront unwelcome issues in a context Rhodes would not have anticipated. It is unsurprising that these new settlers mostly strove to maintain exclusive White power. Individual exceptions aside, they had not left their homes to participate in a bold and challenging experiment in racial partnership. "Smithy" would be their man.

We cannot know how Rhodes would have responded to critical phases of Southern Rhodesia's growth. But we do know that it was not he who declared a state of emergency in 1959 when there was no emergency, or removed Africans from the common voting roll, or pretended in the mid-1960s that a handful of emasculated chiefs were the true voice of millions of Africans while many of their genuine representatives were held in detention. For all his ruthlessness, Rhodes was at heart a pragmatic businessman who might have come to conclude that a thriving economy required skilled African labor along with an entrepreneurial African middle class who had a stake in stability and continuity. He would not have been alone in this respect among long-term members of the privileged White community. During the premiership of Edgar Whitehead, for instance, many businessmen recognized the need to move toward liberalizing both the economy and the politics of the colony.

Indeed, it is easy to picture Rhodes among the White business executives who, from the late 1950s, prioritized economic development over political concession while advocating, too, a loosening of qualifications for the franchise. Perhaps the latter-day career of "Tiny" Rowland gives us a hint of Rhodes's likely preference. A man with huge interests in Rhodesia's farming, mining, services, and press, Rowland backed Joshua Nkomo during the 1960s and 1970s out of hard-headed, nonracial pragmatism. Although a settler-run colony free of interference from London appears consistent with Rhodes's resentment of metropolitan interference in the affairs of "Zambesia," we cannot know whether Rhodes, after careful consideration of the circumstances, would have done such "a very silly thing" in 1965 as to unilaterally declare independence.

Perhaps the most remarkable public acceptance in sub-Saharan Africa of Rhodes's legacy occurred in South Africa in 2002. President Nelson Mandela approved setting up a hybrid Mandela Rhodes Foundation. The Rhodes Trust would pour £10 million into the Mandela Foundation over ten years to fund scholarships and to promote education, health, and sporting facilities for disadvantaged South Africans. Here was an echo of the earlier Rhodes scholarships. Rhodes's fortune had funded not a secret imperialist confraternity, but a new international elite of less sinister, more admirable characters. In this we see that Rhodes still has a legacy—and a multilayered reputation—but it is probably sounder to base whatever judgments we choose to make of him on what he did during his lifetime.

African Perspectives

"Nothing has become more controversial now than the question of the nature of the impact of colonialism on Africa."[67] So wrote Adu Boahen, subsequently professor of history at the University of Ghana in 1985. Thirty years or so later, the question has arisen again, and there are no signs that it is going away. In concluding this reappraisal of Southern Rhodesia, such a context invites us to consider what some Africans have said by way of judgment: first, on British imperialism in Africa in general (which may warrant application to Southern Rhodesia) and, second and in particular, on that settler state itself.

It is no surprise that a range of opinions have been aired. Over the last fifty years or so, numerous African scholars have sought to explain to Europeans that it is inappropriate to portray Africans in colonial situations, even in those of White settlement, as mere victims. Yet within the frame of that consensus, there have been considerable differences of emphasis. By way of illustration, we may look at the views of two late eminent West African academics. Adeniyi Ajayi was a distinguished historian at the University of Ibadan. He advised us to see colonial rule in Africa as just one episode in the long course of African history, the significance of which should not be exaggerated. Ajayi's main purpose was to stress African agency and choices, albeit within a new restrictive framework. He did not underplay the initial shock and lasting subjection of colonial rule. However, he showed that to present it exclusively in terms of a clash, in which one set of human beings dominated another, is to belittle African involvement. Thus over time, Western-educated Africans found opportunities in business and commerce and a range of white-collar jobs. They welcomed schools and hospitals, roads and railways, as well as ports that linked their countries with the wider world "and other features of European technological civilization, as the necessary infrastructure of the nations of their dreams."[68] For some at least, Ajayi acknowledged, Western "civilization" could be accepted by Africans as a modernizing, ultimately liberating force.

While Ajayi's conclusion may be characterized as largely positive, that of his contemporary fellow West African, the Ghanaian Adu Boahen, was (on balance) negative. Boahen explicitly placed himself between European historians who were arguing that colonial rule's credit balance far outweighed its debit account, on the one hand, and mainly African historians who held that colonialism represented only exploitation and repression and made no positive impact, on the other hand. Influential among the latter was Walter Rodney, who denounced European rule in Africa for exclusively serving its own imperial economic needs and neglecting those of Africans. Boahen's own forensic approach was to take the political, social, and economic fields separately, identifying positive and negative legacies in each. Among his positives were the decades of peace and stability; the provision of an infrastructure of roads, railways, and harbors; the establishment of bureaucracies and judicial systems; and urbanization, along with new class formation. His negatives included the uneven spread of education, which led to an educated elite becoming detached from the mass of people, and the disparagement of African traditional culture by both colonial rulers and the African elite they had cultivated.

This balance sheet approach adopted by Ajayi, Boahen, and others, can be a productive analytical tool. But its use as a means of making meaningful value judgments about empire is at best limited and at worst open to manipulation. It makes no distinction between intended and unintended legacies. It is, moreover, loaded with ambiguities: in many instances the same "legacy" can be regarded as both positive and negative. An example from Boahen illustrates the unacknowledged point. As a positive, he mentions "the very appearance of the independent states of today . . . in place of the existing innumerable lineage and clan groups, city-states, kingdoms and empires without any fixed boundaries"—an interesting acknowledgment, in passing, that Africa had its own empires before the Europeans arrived. Yet, as Boahen rightly observes, this was also a negative: in some respects, "the creation of the states has proved to be more of a liability than an asset to the present independent nations."[69]

There are weightier problems and limitations. First, it is too easy for interested parties to pick and choose their own imperial legacies to sustain a critique shaped by a pre-existing personal bias. It was not chance that the advocates of empire identified by Boahen in 1985 were primarily European, and the critics mainly African and/or Marxist. All history relies on selection and omission: those personally inclined to look favorably on colonialism will prioritize what they regard as positive, and those of an anticolonial predisposition vice versa. Second, the balance-sheet approach is essentially *unhistorical*: it freezes the colonial moment

Judging Empire 215

and the legacies; it recognizes neither context nor the complexities of continuity and change over time. Third, and most seriously, it focuses on an all-embracing "ism," a concept, rather than on the individuals who were, consciously or unconsciously, the agents of empire. There was no empire without imperialists; no colonialism without colonists. If we wish to make moral judgments about the past, it makes much more sense to focus on people—human beings like ourselves, who happened to live in other times and places and cultures—than on abstract concepts such as colonialism, which are so broad and so hard to define.

By way of illustration, we may look at two individuals whose personal perspectives (on slavery, in the first instance, and colonialism, in the second) changed or were changed during the course of long and active lives. Benjamin Franklin, an American, is widely regarded as a figure of the Enlightenment: writer, scientist, statesman, publisher, and political philosopher. But his relations with slavery are not easily summed up. In his early adult life, Franklin benefited financially from active participation in the slave trade. When he first arrived in London, he had with him two African slaves. As noted above, however, the latter half of the eighteenth century is when the consensus on slavery was challenged; by the 1780s, Franklin was a vocal abolitionist who not only condemned slavery but in 1790 urged the infant Congress of the United States to act against it, albeit in vain.

The life of Stewart Gore-Browne offers another illustration of how casual judgments of individuals, out of context, tend to break down. The other "Rhodesia" (northern) also attracted some White settlers, though these were fewer and less significant than across the Zambezi. Among them was Gore-Browne, an "imperialist" and "racist" of his day. He established an English-style house and garden there in the 1920s. A bad-tempered, monocled martinet, he routinely beat African workers on his estate with a long black stick. Later, however, in the 1930s and 1940s, he became a prominent member of the territory's legislative council—chosen to represent them, in that body, by a predominantly African electorate. While in that assembly, he deplored mistreatment of African workers on the Copperbelt and argued in favor of African advancement and easier access to the common voters' roll. Setting himself apart from most White settlers in both Rhodesias, he talked to and made friends with Africans. Among these were Harry Nkumbula and Kenneth Kaunda, of whom he presciently noted in his diary: "These are the shoulders on which the future of the country will depend, though they don't realise it themselves."[70] The times had changed, and Gore-Browne had changed with them.

To ensure our judgments are indeed historical, we should seek clues within the colonial and postcolonial past as to how Africans in the British

Empire have regarded their rulers. We have seen something of how Ajayi and Boahen judged a British colonial rule into which they were born, and which later they subjected to scrutiny. However, scholars are not our only guides. In Ghana, formerly the Gold Coast, an introductory poster exhibit at the museum of Cape Coast Castle (a grim relic of the trans-Atlantic slave trade) states with some passion that while the slave trade had indeed been a centuries-long trauma for the people of the region, there followed from the mid-nineteenth century a colonial rule that brought benefits and can be seen overall as a period of progress. This anonymous statement is highly significant as an expression of how some Africans today can see their historic relationship with Britain. While castigating the slave trade, it adopts a measured analysis of what followed. Moreover, the poster echoes the judgment of Africans of the Gold Coast in the heyday of empire. Though the governor Hugh Clifford had to steer that protectorate through the disruptive years of World War I, this British imperialist was lauded in the African press (which could be highly critical of his government) upon his retirement in 1919 as "our popular governor" who had "a real and genuine interest in the welfare of the people."[71]

For a perspective on the specific case of Rhodesia/Zimbabwe, we have both academic and non-academic insights. It has perhaps been easier for Nigerians and Ghanaians to find positive aspects of imperialism, because none of Britain's West African colonies experienced the impact of White settlers. The verdict of an eminent African historian of Zimbabwe is thus of particular interest and relevance. In 2014, Alois Mlambo's single volume overview (covering precolonial, colonial, and postcolonial times) offered a sober account of the colonial period, which emphasized the complexity that marked interracial (and intraracial) relationships. Colonial rule was no mere episode, in this interpretation. Mlambo devoted well over half of his study to the "tremendous economic and political changes that established a modern state" between 1890 and 1980. This was no mere clash, either. Though defeated and resentful, Africans were resilient and enterprising; and the results of colonial rule "were, of course, not all despondent for the African people."[72] In the six decades between the 1890s revolt and the emergence of militant nationalism, colonial rule exposed Africans to new ideas, as well as to Western schools and medicine. African beneficiaries, he noted, included clerks, teachers, preachers, social workers, journalists, nurses, lawyers, and doctors. Mlambo's assessment of a transformative period was dispassionate in tone and measured in judgment.

A balanced assessment of Whites associated with the settler colony is not unknown among today's Zimbabweans. In February 2020, the city council of Bulawayo, second city of Zimbabwe and historic heartland of the Ndebele, was considering road name changes. Before finalizing these, they adopted the motion of one of their councilors. "It is desirable," said Mr. Moyo, "to preserve the pre-colonial, colonial and post-colonial history and heritage of the local people of Bulawayo and promote national cohesion, healing, peace and tranquillity."[73] Emerging from this review there were, as one might have expected, roads named after precolonial kings Mzilikazi and Lobengula. Robert Moffat Drive honors that respected White missionary, friend of the Ndebele and father-in-law of David Livingstone. But also approved were Dr. Leander Starr Jameson Road, named after one of the Pioneer Column who in 1890 initiated the subjugation of both Ndebele and Shona (and, later, the aforementioned raid); Charles Patrick Coghlan Avenue, commemorating the first prime minister of the White self-governing colony (1923–1927); and Cecil John Rhodes Avenue, named after the man whose statue in Oxford has been the subject of so much excited controversy. For many years, meanwhile, Harare has had a Bishop Gaul Avenue and Theological College. The manner in which Mr. Moyo and his fellow city councilors carry their history is a challenge to the West's more sweeping critics of colonial rule.

* * *

In his detailed study of White liberals, moderates, and radicals in this period, Ian Hancock of the Australian National University suggested that they had two brief opportunities to lead the colony away from an entrenchment of White racism: the first, from 1956–1958; the second, from 1960–1962. It is no accident that each of these short periods ended with the fall of a prime minister who had assumed office as a relatively pragmatic conservative yet, by total immersion in the tide of events, came to conclude that only a progressive option made sense. In this light, the cases of both Todd and Whitehead warn us once more against generalizing about individuals, let alone groups.

Of the two opportunities, the former is perhaps more credible as a real (albeit lost) chance, as it was marked by the prominence of Garfield Todd and Joshua Nkomo: representatives of cautiously progressive European and broadly moderate African political opinion, respectively. The later opportunity, 1960–1962, appears to have had rather less potential. By this time there was a state of emergency, the African National Congress (ANC) was banned, and African nationalists were proscribed. More prosperous Whites, notably in the business community, still advocated change. As a senior White mining executive declared in the pages of an African newspaper, "Practically every industrialist is a liberal."[74] However, latent class differences among the Whites were exposed now. The growing electoral success of the Dominion Party (DP) demonstrated that White artisans, Whites on the lower rungs of the civil service, and poorer White farmers all regarded segregation and the color bar not as a barrier to progress but as essential protection for their jobs and their way of life. In 1960 and after, progressive Whites experienced in business and politics continued to talk to some prominent Blacks—among them Robert Mugabe and Ndabaningi Sithole—but before long too large a proportion of diehard Whites, and too many prominent dissident Blacks, rejected compromise and conciliation.

Shortly after spending two years in Rhodesia at the University College of Rhodesia and Nyasaland in Salisbury, Larry Bowman conceded that the 1960s had been a time of "heated White political controversy"; but he concluded that no political party with a hope of success offered any real choice to the electorate. Garfield Todd's small party proposed "a vague possibility" in 1958; but in 1962, "on the question of permanent White control and the destruction of the nationalist movement, there was only one choice."[75] There is strength in this argument, but it is too narrow. It fails to note that choices—moral and political—had to be made by individuals at a personal level, and that it was those choices that were reflected in two phases of electoral politics. By contrast, Hancock argued that there was still a real choice before the electorate in December 1962. Indeed, a bigger African turnout might have seen Whitehead's United Rhodesia Party (URP), which had tried to reason with the electorate, scrape back home. But Black disillusionment with the pace and potential of reform through White rule was enough to strangle that possibility.

In the flow of politics, timing is everything. While in retrospect there appear to have been grounds for Nkomo and Todd to work together effectively, a couple of months in late 1957 illustrate just how tiny a window there was for them to explore possibilities of doing so. On September 12, the Southern Rhodesia branch of the ANC was reborn, with Nkomo at its head. Before this organizational rebirth, Nkomo lacked formal status and authority to represent the African population; afterward, it was not certain that he could speak both for the educated African elite and for City Youth League (CYL) radicals. Black radicalism was already looming as an alternative to interracial forums such as the Inter-racial Association (IA) and the Capricorn Africa Society (CAS). Moreover, Todd's standing in his own party was seriously threatened by late November. He was brought down in the new year.

Many years later, in 1991, Todd, eloquent as ever, poignantly encapsulated what had gone wrong. "The whole African population was ready to negotiate . . . would have been prepared to take what I would offer. . . . *That was the time*, because Blacks were ready. . . . Whites never were ready to negotiate and that was the key time, and they missed their opportunity."[76]

Nothing in history is as simple as it looks, or as we might want it to be. If we today are looking for culprits among White Rhodesian settlers, it is Smith and hard-line ideologues within the RF who qualify, rather than the earlier settlers or those who, after World War II (and the Universal Declaration of Human Rights) argued against views like Smith's and continued to oppose him in the cul-de-sac years after the UDI. Smith and his colleagues were accountable to the White electorate then; they are accountable, too, to the generations that have followed.

Notes

1. Leopold von Ranke, in the introduction to his first published work: quoted in Evans, *In Defence*, 17.
2. Carl Bernstein, "Watergate to Trump," BBC 2, May 16, 2023.
3. Evans, *In Defence*, 17.
4. Philip Kerr, preface to Cripps, *An Africa for Africans*, viii.
5. Scullard, *Roman Britain*, 49.
6. Quoted in Hancock, *White Liberals*, 19.
7. Gann, *White Settlers*, 131.
8. Kenneth P. Vickery, "Wars and Rumours of Wars: Southern Rhodesian Africans and the Second World War," unpublished paper, North Carolina State University, 1984.
9. Biggar, *Colonialism*, 7.
10. Zayyan, *We Are All Birds of Uganda*, 262.
11. Maurois, *Ariel*, 51.
12. Patten, *First Confession*, 17.
13. Ben Macintyre, "It's Right to Revile the Man Who Let Ireland Starve," *The Times*, May 6, 2023.
14. Luke 23:34, *King James Bible*.
15. Quoted in Hague, *William Wilberforce*, 183. Italics added.
16. Gopal, *Insurgent*, 448.
17. M. Evans, quoted in Cripps, *An Africa for Africans*, xiii.
18. N. Sithole, *African Nationalism*, 68.
19. Nkomo, *My Life*, 38.
20. Keatley, *The Politics of Partnership*, 466, 467.
21. Judith Todd, *The Right to Say No*, 11.
22. Lessing, *Going Home*, 71.
23. Quoted in Meredith, *The Past*, 244.
24. Quoted in Meredith, *The Past*, 170.
25. Godwin and Hancock, *Rhodesians Never Die*, 280.
26. The Ballad of UDI, quoted in Weiss, *Sir Garfield Todd*, 188.
27. Moorcroft and McLaughlin, *The Rhodesian War*, 11.
28. Quoted in Leys, *European Politics*, 288.
29. Lessing, *Going Home*, 70.
30. Keatley, *The Politics of Partnership*, 256.

31. Hills, *Rebel People*, 85. Italics in original.
32. Quoted in Caute, *Under the Skin*, 27, 28.
33. Nkomo, *My Life*, 118.
34. Smith, *Betrayal*, 25, 31.
35. Hills, *Rebel People*, 71.
36. Hills, *Rebel People*, 140–141, 174.
37. Hills, *Rebel People*, 119.
38. Quoted in Hills, *Rebel People*, 121.
39. Quoted in Todd, *The Right to Say No*, 128.
40. Quoted in Todd, *The Right to Say No*, 100.
41. Nkomo, *My Life*, 67.
42. Smith, *Betrayal*, 6.
43. Quoted in Meredith, *The Past*, 208.
44. Vambe, *An Ill-Fated People*, 232.
45. Smith, *Betrayal*, 342, 348, 363.
46. Norman, *The Odd Man In*, 32, 107.
47. Muzorewa, *Rise Up*, 167.
48. Hills, *Rebel People*, 234.
49. Quoted in Lessing, *Going Home*, 136, 141.
50. Quoted in Lessing, *Going Home*, 136, 141. Italics added.
51. Mason, *The Birth of a Dilemma*, 317.
52. Baldwin, *The Fire Next Time*, 26, 75. Italics added.
53. Smith, *Betrayal*, 73.
54. Smith, *Betrayal*, 32, 40, 62.
55. Smith, *Betrayal*, 344, 374.
56. Quoted in Hills, *Rebel People*, 85.
57. Christopher Hitchens in *The Listener*, November 1976, quoted in Woodhouse, *Garfield Todd*, 413.
58. Mason, *Year of Decision*, 251.
59. Keatley, *The Politics of Partnership*, 305.
60. Report, Appendix 4.
61. Hills, *Rebel People*, 169, 170.
62. Hills, *Rebel People*, 129.
63. Quoted in Meredith, *The Past*, 343.
64. John Lonsdale, Foreword to Boahen, *Perspectives*, vi.
65. McDonald, *Rhodes*, 371, 372.
66. Hills, *Rebel People*, 67.
67. Boahen, *Perspectives*, 94.
68. J. F. A. Ajayi, "Colonialism: An Episode," in Gann and Duignan, *Colonialism in Africa*, 497–508.
69. Boahen, *Perspectives*, 95.
70. Quoted in Lamb, *The Africa House*, 234.
71. *The Gold Coast Leader*, quoted in Wrangham, *Ghana During the First World War*, 258, 262.
72. A. Mlambo, *A History of Zimbabwe*, 51, 52.
73. *The Zimbabwe Mail*, February 6, 2020.
74. Colin Kirkpatrick of RTS, *African Daily News*, August 25, 1960, quoted in Hancock, *White Liberals*, 88.
75. Bowman, *Politics*, 3, 32, 44.
76. Quoted in Woodhouse, *Garfield Todd*, 278. Italics added.

Timeline

1890	Pioneers cross the Zambezi and enter Mashonaland
1893	War against the Ndebele
1896–1897	Revolt by Mashona and Ndebele
1898	Southern Rhodesia created under British South African Company rule
1923	Southern Rhodesians vote to become a self-governing Crown colony
1930	Land Apportionment Act
1934	Industrial Conciliation Act
1946	Native (Urban Areas) Accommodation and Registration Act
1953	Birth of Central African Federation (CAF)
	Garfield Todd becomes prime minister (PM) of Southern Rhodesia
1957	Rebirth of Southern Rhodesia African National Congress (ANC)
1958	Edgar Whitehead replaces Todd as PM
1959	Declaration of a state of emergency
1962	Election: Winston Field of the Rhodesia Front (RF) replaces Whitehead as PM
1964	Ian Smith replaces Field as PM
1965	Unilateral Declaration of Independence (UDI)
1972	Arrival of Pearce commission
	Start of the liberation war

1978 Internal Settlement agreed to in Rhodesia
1979 Abel Muzorewa becomes PM of Zimbabwe-Rhodesia
1979 Start of Lancaster House conference
1980 Robert Mugabe becomes PM of Zimbabwe

Acronyms

ANC	African National Congress
ANC	African National Council
BSAC	British South Africa Company
CAF	Central African Federation
CAS	Capricorn Africa Society
CYL	City Youth League
FNLA	National Liberation Front of Angola
FRELIMO	Front for the Liberation of Mozambique
FROLIZI	Front for the Liberation of Zimbabwe
IA	Inter-racial Association
ICU	Industrial and Commercial Workers' Union
MDC	Movement for Democratic Change
MPLA	People's Movement for the Liberation of Angola
MP	Member of Parliament
NC	Native Commissioner
NDP	National Democratic Party
PF	Patriotic Front
RBVA	Rhodesia Bantu Voters' Association
RF	Rhodesian Front
RICU	Reformed Industrial and Commercial Workers' Union
UANC	United ANC
UDHR	Universal Declaration of Human Rights
UDI	Unilateral Declaration of Independence
UFP	United Federal Party
UN	United Nations

URP	United Rhodesia Party
ZANLA	Zimbabwe African National Liberation Army
ZANU	Zimbabwe African National Union
ZANU-PF	Zimbabwe African National Union—Patriotic Front
ZAPU	Zimbabwe African People's Union
ZIPRA	Zimbabwe People's Revolutionary Army
ZUPO	Zimbabwe United People's Organisation

Sources

ANY STUDENT OF THE CONTRASTING OPINIONS HELD BY SOUTHern Rhodesians during the crucial period of the late 1950s and early 1960s is fortunate. A good number of participants wrote at the time or a little later about what they thought and what they did. So did several foreign (mainly British) visitors and close observers of the momentous political and moral debate of those years. Unsurprisingly, more was written by progressive White Rhodesians (who were likely to own, read, and write books) than their reactionary rivals; but the substantial, bitter memoir of Ian Smith, *The Great Betrayal*, clearly spoke for many and redresses the balance, as does Frederick Cleary's biography of Winston Field (his predecessor as prime minister), co-authored by Field's wife, Ann.

Of the participants, key witnesses include Guy Clutton-Brock, who fostered a multiracial community at St. Faiths's Mission east of Salisbury and played a central role in drawing up policies and the constitution for the revived African National Congress (ANC) in 1957; Hardwicke Holderness, who founded the Inter-racial Association (IA) in 1953 and was a member of parliament (MP) in Garfield Todd's government from 1954; Judith Todd, daughter of Garfield Todd and a politically active student who campaigned against White minority rule; and Robert Tredgold, minister of justice and defense during World War II and then federal chief justice until resigning in protest at the passage of the Law and Order (Maintenance) Act in Southern Rhodesia in 1960. We may include in this company, too, Doris Lessing, the Nobel Prize–winning novelist who spent her childhood years and other time in Southern Rhodesia before she was banned. As for Garfield Todd, in 2018 his former secretary, Susan Woodhouse, published a substantial volume including much of what he thought and stood for, in his own words.

A range of Southern Rhodesia's Africans at that time wrote valuable accounts of their political ideas and involvement. Bernard Chidzero took up a teaching appointment at the University College of Rhodesia and Nyasaland in Salisbury only to have the job offer withdrawn when it became known that he had a White (French-Canadian) wife; Eshmael Mlambo was a teacher, academic, and journalist who fled Rhodesia in 1966; Joshua Nkomo, a giant of African nationalism in the 1950s and beyond left us *The Story of My Life;* Nathan Shamuyarira, teacher and journalist, was active in the IA and was, in 1956, the first editor of the *African Daily News;* Ndabaningi Sithole, an ordained minister in the Methodist Church, was a pivotal figure in fractious nationalist politics after his *African Nationalism* was published in 1959; and Lawrence Vambe, trainee priest, teacher, and journalist, became the Central African Federation's (CAF's) press attaché in London in 1959 before writing *An Ill-Fated People*.

Several well-informed foreign academics and journalists wrote and published their views and thus give us an extraordinarily rich window into the events and, particularly, the debate that divided Whites. Richard Gray was a founding father of African history as an academic study; Denis Hills, writer, journalist, and traveler, taught in Gwelo, Rhodesia, for six months between 1977 and 1978; Patrick Keatley, the London-based, widely traveled Canadian journalist, was commonwealth and diplomatic correspondent for *The Guardian*; Colin Leys, political economist, held a succession of university chairs in England, East Africa, and Canada; Philip Mason worked for the Indian Civil Service, and later became director of Chatham House and director of the United Kingdom's Institute of Race Relations. Terence Ranger, a pioneer of African history as experienced by Africans, moved as a young academic to Salisbury, Southern Rhodesia, in 1957 to become a lecturer at the university: a radical critic of the White regime, he was deported in 1963 to England, where he was appointed Oxford University's Rhodes Professor of Race Relations. Lewis Gann was something of an exception: a conservative academic and himself an immigrant (a refugee from Nazi anti-Semitism), his analysis of the state of Southern Rhodesia led him to conclude that the answer lay not in political concessions to Africans, but in the immigration of more White settlers.

This book owes much to all the above, and others, who chose to write and be published.

* * *

Ajayi, J. F. A. "Colonialism: An Episode in African History," in Lewis Gann and Peter Duignan, eds., *Colonialism in Africa 1870–1960: The History and Politics of Colonialism 1870–1914*, Vol. 1. Cambridge: Cambridge University Press, 1969.
Baldwin, James. *The Fire Next Time*. London: Penguin Random House, 1963.
Beinart, William. "Rhodes Must Fall: The Uses of Historical Evidence in the Statue Debate at Oxford, 2015–2016." https://oxfordandempire.web.ox.ac.uk/article.
Biggar, Nigel. *Colonialism. A Moral Reckoning*. London: William Collins, 2023.
Blake, Robert. *A History of Rhodesia*. New York: Alfred Knopf, 1978.
Boahen, Adu A. *African Perspectives on European Colonialism*. New York: Diasporic African Press, 2011.
Bowman, Larry W. *Politics in Rhodesia: White Power in an African State*. Cambridge, MA: Harvard University Press, 1973.
Brand, C. M. "Race and Politics in Rhodesian Trade Unions," in Vernie February, ed., *White Minorities, Black Majorities*. Leiden: Afrika-Studiecentrum, 1976.
Casey, Michael W. *The Rhetoric of Sir Garfield Todd*. Waco: Baylor University Press, 2007.
Caute, David. *Under the Skin: The Death of White Rhodesia*. London: Allen Lane, 1983.
Chidzero, Bernard. "The Meaning of Good Government in Central Africa," in Colin Leys and Cranford Pratt, eds., *A New Deal in Central Africa*. London: Heinemann, 1960.
Cleary, Frederick, and Ann Field. *Kamoto: The Life of Winston Joseph Field, 1904–1969*. St. Arnaud, Victoria: Private publication, 1998.
Cliffe, Lionel. "Zimbabwe's Political Inheritance," in Colin Stoneman, ed., *Zimbabwe's Inheritance*. London: Macmillan, 1981.
Clutton-Brock, Guy. *Cold Comfort Confronted*. London: Mowbrays, 1972.
Coltart, David. *The Struggle Continues: 50 Years of Tyranny in Zimbabwe*. Auckland Park, South Aafrica: Jacana, 2016.
Cripps, Arthur Shearly. *An Africa for Africans*. London: Longmans, 1927.
Dangarembga, Tsitsi. *Nervous Conditions*. London: Faber and Faber, 2021.
Dorman, Sara Rich. *Understanding Zimbabwe: From Liberation to Authoritarianism*. London: Hurst, 2016.
Dungani, Paul. "The Mission School as Locus of Evangelisation of Children in Zimbabwean Historiography (1859–1969)." https://www.academia.edu.
Eldridge, C. C. *Victorian Imperialism*. London: Hodder and Stoughton, 1978.
Evans, Richard J. *In Defence of History*. London: Granta, 1997.
Fage, John and Roland Oliver. *The Cambridge History of Africa, Volume 8, 1940–1975*. Cambridge: Cambridge University Press, 1984.
February, Vernie, ed. *White Minorities, Black Majorities*. Leiden: Afrika-Studiecentrum, 1976.
Fieldhouse, D. K. *Economics and Empire, 1830-1914*. London: Weidenfield and Nicolson, 1973.
Flint, John. *Cecil Rhodes*. London: Hutchinson, 1976.
Freeth, Ben. *Mugabe and the White African*. Oxford: Lion, 2011.
Gann, Lewis. *A History of Southern Rhodesia: Early Days to 1934*. London: Chatto & Windus, 1965.
Gann, Lewis, and Peter Duignan, eds. *Colonialism in Africa 1870–1960: The History and Politics of Colonialism, 1870–1914*, Vol. 1. Cambridge: Cambridge University Press, 1969.

Gann, Lewis, and Peter Duignan. *White Settlers in Tropical Africa*. Harmondsworth, London: Penguin, 1965.
Godwin, Peter. *Mukiwa: A White Boy in Africa*. London: Picador, 1996.
Godwin, Peter, and Ian Hancock. *"Rhodesians Never Die": The Impact of War and Political Change on White Rhodesia, c.1970-1980*. Northlands, South Africa: Pan Macmillan, 1993.
Gopal, Priyamvada. *Insurgent Empire: Anticolonial Resistance and British Dissent*. London: Verso, 2019.
Grant G. C. *The Africans' Predicament in Rhodesia*. London: Minority Rights Group, 1972.
Gray, Richard. *The Two Nations: Aspects of the Development of Race Relations in the Rhodesias and Nyasaland*. London: Oxford University Press, 1960.
Gray, Richard. *Black Christians and White Missionaries*. New Haven, London: Yale University Press, 1990.
Gunther, John. *Inside Africa*. London: Ebenezer Baylis, 1955.
Hague, William. *William Wilberforce*. London: Harper Collins, 2007.
Hancock, Ian. *White Liberals, Moderates and Radicals in Rhodesia 1953-1980*. London: Croom Helm, 1984.
Hills, Denis. *Rebel People*. London: George Allen and Unwin, 1978.
Holderness, Hardwicke. *Lost Chance. Southern Rhodesia, 1945-1958*. Harare: Zimbabwe Publishing House, 1985.
Huddleston, Trevor. *Naught For Your Comfort*. London: Fontana, 1956.
Kavanagh, Robert Mshengu. *Zimbabwe: Challenging the Stereotypes*. Harare: Themba Books, 2014.
Keatley, Patrick. *The Politics of Partnership: The Federation of Rhodesia and Nyasaland*. Baltimore: Penguin, 1963.
Lamb, Christina. *The Africa House: The True Story of an English Gentleman and His African Dream*. London: Penguin, 1999.
Landes, David. *The Wealth and Poverty of Nations: Why Some Are So Rich and Some Are So Poor*. London: Abacus, 1998.
Lapsley, Michael. *Neutrality or Co-option?* Gweru, Zimbabwe: Mambo Press, 1986.
Lessing, Doris. *Going Home*. London: Flamingo, 1968.
Leys, Colin. *European Politics in Southern Rhodesia*. Oxford, Oxford University Press, 1959.
Leys, Colin, and Cranford Pratt, eds. *A New Deal in Central Africa*. London: Heinemann, 1960.
Loney, Martin. *Rhodesia: White Racism and Imperial Response*. Harmondsworth, UK: Penguin, 1975.
Lovell, Julia. *Maoism: A Global History*. London: Bodley Head, 2019.
Luthuli, Albert. *Let My People Go*. London: Fontana, 1962.
Martin, David, and Phyllis Johnson. *The Struggle for Zimbabwe*. London: Faber and Faber, 1981.
Mason, Philip. *The Birth of a Dilemma: The Conquest and Settlement of Rhodesia*. London: Oxford University Press, 1958.
Mason, Philip. *Year of Decision: Rhodesia and Nyasaland in 1960*. London: Oxford University Press, 1960.
Maurois, Andre. *Ariel*. London: Penguin, 1936.
Maurois, Andre. *Cecil Rhodes*. London: Collins, 1953.
Maylam, Paul. *The Cult of Rhodes: Remembering an Imperialist in Africa*. Claremont, South Africa: David Philip, 2005.
McDonald, J. G. *Rhodes: A Life*. London: Philip Allan, 1927.

Meredith, Martin. *The Past is Another Country: Rhodesia, 1890–1979.* London: Andre Deutsch, 1979.
Mlambo, Alois S. *A History of Zimbabwe.* New York: Cambridge University Press, 2014.
Mlambo, Eshmael. *Rhodesia: The Struggle for a Birthright.* London: Hurst, 1972.
Moorcraft, Paul, and Peter McLaughlin. *The Rhodesian War: Fifty Years On.* Philadelphia: Pen and Sword, 1982.
Moore, David B. *Mugabe's Legacy: Coups, Conspiracies, and the Conceits of Power in Zimbabwe.* London: Hurst, 2022.
Morris-Jones, W. H., ed. *From Rhodesia to Zimbabwe: Behind and Beyond Lancaster House.* London: Frank Cass, 1980.
Muzorewa, Abel. *Rise Up and Walk.* London: Sphere, 1979.
Ndlovu, Ray. *In the Jaws of the Crocodile: Emmerson Mnangagwa's Rise to Power in Zimbabwe.* Cape Town: Penguin, 2018.
Ndlovu-Gatsheni, S. J., ed., *Joshua Mqabuko Nkomo of Zimbabwe: Politics, Power, and Memory (African Histories and Modernities).* London: Palgrave, 2017.
Nkomo, Joshua. *Nkomo: The Story of My Life.* London: Methuen, 1984.
Norman, Denis. *The Odd Man In: Mugabe's White-Hand Man.* Harare: Weaver, 2018.
Oates, C. G., ed. *Matabeleland and The Victoria Falls: The Diaries and Letters of Frank Oates 1873–1875.* London: Kegan Paul, 2007.
Palmer, Robin. *Land and Racial Domination in Rhodesia.* Berkeley: University of California Press, 1977.
Patten, Chris. *First Confession: A Sort of Memoir.* New York, Penguin Random House, 2018.
Popper, Karl. *The Poverty of Historicism.* London: Routledge and Kegan Paul, 1957.
Raftopoulus, Brian, and Alois Mlambo, eds., *Becoming Zimbabwe: A History from the Pre-colonial Period to 2008.* Harare: Weaver, 2009.
Ranger, Terence. "African Politics in Twentieth-Century Southern Rhodesia," in Terence Ranger, ed., *Aspects of Central African History.* London: Heinemann, 1968.
Ranger, Terence. *Are We Not Also Men? The Samkange Family and African Politics in Zimbabwe, 1920–1964.* London: James Currey, 1995.
Ranger, Terence. "Traditional Authorities and the Rise of Modern Politics in Southern Rhodesia, 1898–1930," in Eric Stokes and Richard Brown, eds., *The Zambesian Past: Studies in Central African History.* Manchester: Manchester University Press, 1966.
Ranger, Terence. *Peasant Consciousness and Guerrilla War in Zimbabwe.* Oxford: James Currey, 1985.
Reynolds, Reginald. *Beware of Africans: A Pilgrimage from Cairo to the Cape.* London: Jarrolds, 1955.
Roberts, Andrew. *Salisbury: Victorian Titan.* London: Phoenix, 1999.
Rodney Walter. *How Europe Underdeveloped Africa.* Washington, DC: Howard University Press, 1982.
Scullard, H. H. *Roman Britain: Outpost of the Empire.* London: Thames and Hudson, 1979.
Segal, Ronald. *African Profiles.* Harmondsworth, UK: Penguin, 1962.
Shamuyarira, Nathan. *Crisis in Rhodesia.* Nairobi, Kenya: East African Publishing House, 1967.
Shepherd, Robert. *Iain Macleod: A Biography.* London: Pimlico, 1994.
Shutt, Allison K. *Manners Make a Nation: Racial Etiquette in Southern Rhodesia, 1910–1963.* Rochester, New York: University of Rochester Press, 2015.

Sithole, Masipula. *Zimbabwe's Struggle Within the Struggle*. Harare, Zimbabwe: Rujeko, 2019.
Sithole, Ndabaningi. *African Nationalism*. Cape Town: Oxford Univeristy Press, 1959.
Smith, Ian. *The Great Betrayal: The Memoirs of Ian Douglas Smith*. London: Blake, 1997.
Stokes, Eric, and Richard Brown, eds. *The Zambesian Past: Studies in Central African History*. Manchester: Manchester University Press, 1966.
Stoneman, Colin, ed. *Zimbabwe's Inheritance*. London: Macmillan, 1981.
Summers, Carol. *Colonial Lessons: Africans' Education in Southern Rhodesia, 1918–1940*. Oxford: James Currey, 2002.
Thompson, Gardner. *African Democracy: Its Origins and Development in Uganda, Kenya and Tanzania*. Kampala, Uganda: Fountain, 2015.
Todd, Judith. *Rhodesia*. London: Panther, 1966.
Todd, Judith. *The Right to Say No*. London: Sidgwick and Jackson, 1972.
Todd, Judith. *Through the Darkness: A Life in Zimbabwe*. Cape Town: Zebra, 2007.
Tredgold, Robert. *The Rhodesia that Was My Life*. London: George Allen and Unwin, 1968.
Vambe, Lawrence. *An Ill-Fated People: Zimbabwe Before and After Rhodes*. London: Heinemann, 1972.
Verrier, Anthony. *The Road to Zimbabwe, 1890–1980*. London: Jonathan Cape, 1986.
Weiss, Ruth. *Sir Garfield Todd and the Making of Zimbabwe*. London: British Academic Press, 1999.
Welch, Pamela. *Church and Settler in Colonial Zimbabwe: A Study in the History of the Anglican Diocese of Mashonaland/Southern Rhodesia, 1890–1925*. Leiden: Brill, 2008.
West, Michael O. *The Rise of an African Middle Class: Colonial Zimbabwe, 1898–1965*. Bloomington: Indiana University Press, 2002.
West, Richard. *The White Tribes of Africa*. London: Jonathan Cape, 1965.
Wilson, Francis. "Southern Africa," in John Fage and Roland Oliver, *The Cambridge History of Africa: 1940 to 1975, Vol. 8*. Cambridge: Cambridge University Press, 1984.
Woodhouse, Susan. *Garfield Todd: The End of the Liberal Dream in Rhodesia*. Harare: Weaver, 2018.
Wrangham, Elizabeth. *Ghana During the First World War: The Colonial Administration of Sir Hugh Clifford*. Durham, NC: Carolina Academic Press, 2013.
Zayyan, Hafsa. *We Are All Birds of Uganda*. San Francisco: Merky Books, 2021.
Zvogbo, C. J. M. "The Influence of the Wesleyan Methodist Missions in Southern Rhodesia, 1891–1923," in J. A. Dachs, ed., *Christianity South of the Zambezi*. Harare: Mambo Press, 1973.

Index

abolitionism, 194–195; British abolition and imperialist expansion, 13–14; Franklin's shifting view of slavery, 215
accommodation: African response to White settlement, 34–36
An Africa for Africans (Cripps), 195
African Daily News, 119–120
African Demonstrators, 57
African National Congress (ANC), 1; growth and support for, 145; independent church movement, 41–42; lost opportunities for political change, 217–218; NDP and, 112; Pearce commission finding, 145–146; Pretoria Agreement, 148–149; revival and manifesto, 91–94; uniting urban radicals, farmers and elites, 58; Whitehead's refusal to engage with, 105–106; Whites' reaction to the emergence of, 95. *See also* National Democratic Party
African Portraits (Cloete), 209
African Workers' Trade Union, 57
Afrikaners/Boers, 10, 60, 210. *See also* South Africa
agriculture. *See* farming
Ajayi, Adeniyi, 213–216
Amin, Idi, 172, 186
Anglo-American plan, 151–152
Anglo-Saxon hegemony, 12–13
Angola, 150; rise of African nationalism, 206

apartheid. *See* South Africa
artisan class: postwar White immigrants, 64–65
atrocities: African revolt, 19; ZANU-PF control of the media, 175

Baldwin, James, 205–206
Bantu Education Act (1953), 97–98
Bashford, Pat, 146
Belgian Congo: independence and violence, 104
benign imperialism, 211
Bernstein, Carl, 189–190
Biggar, Nigel, 3, 192
Black Lives Matter: Rhodes Must Fall campaign, 9
Blake, Robert, 6–7, 34, 117, 143
Boahen, Adu, 213–216
Boers. *See* Afrikaners/Boers
Bottomley, Arthur, 131
Bowman, Larry, 218
boycotts: bus boycott, 91; replacing strikes, 58
Britain: abolitionist movement, 194; approval of the 1961 constitution, 110–111; colonial history, 2–3; constitutional settlement, 145; demise of the CAF, 54; domestic politics and colonial independence, 113–114; expansion into Africa, 13; the importance of empire, 191–192; the Internal Agreement, 155;

232 Index

Lancaster House negotiations, 173–174; Nkomo's request for intervention, 107; Owen-Young plan for majority rule transition, 153–154; postwar federation of Central Africa, 49; postwar immigration to South Africa, 60–61; postwar shrinking of the Empire, 47–48; pressuring Smith for political concessions, 151–152; Rhodes's imperialist ambitions, 10–11; Smith's perceived betrayal by, 206–207, 209; Zimbabwe's land redistribution, 183. *See also* Central African Federation; independence from Britain; Unilateral Declaration of Independence

British East Africa, 74, 77, 169–170

British South Africa Company (BSAC): African response to White settlement, 34–36; church reliance, 31–32, 41; lack of intellectuals and professionals, 29; Livingstone's vision, 30; morality of White supremacy policies, 79; provoking the Ndebele war, 19

Bulawayo, 18; acknowledging the colonial history, 216–217; native land purchase areas, 24–25; provenance of the White population, 29; railway strikes, 57–58; Rhodes Centenary Exhibition, 211

bus boycott, 91

business community: economic and political pragmatism, 212; White stratification, 29–30

Capricorn Africa Society (CAS), 77–78, 199–200, 218

Carter, Jimmy, 206

Carter, Morris, 23–24

Carter commission, 23–24, 35–36

Central African Federation (CAF), 48–55, 196; accusations of failure, 114–115; coal miners' strike, 75; drive for secession and independence, 104–105, 121–132; effect on Todd's ouster, 87; election shambles of 1962, 115–117; Rhodes's ambitions for global domination, 16; White vision for, 5

Centre Party, 143, 145–146

challenge phase: framework for tracking moral issues, 193–197

Chidzero, Bernard, 27–28, 88, 134, 185

Chikerema, James, 78, 91, 122, 145, 155

Chikerema, Robert, 105–106

Chinese population, 74

Chitepo, Herbert, 93–94, 160–161

Christians and Christianity: the African view of missionaries, 39–43; ANC revival, 92; British view of modern Africans, 192; criticism of Smith and the RF, 150; expansion into Central Africa, 30–32; failure to improve Africans' lives, 162; materialism in Whites' "civilizing" mission, 139–141; mission school curriculum replacing African faith, 40; opposition to RF segregation, 145; political fissures among White Christians, 85–86; Rhodes's imperialist vision, 14–15

Churchill, Winston, 21

City Youth League (CYL), 86, 91, 122, 218

Civil Rights Act (US; 1964), 205–206

civilizing mission of colonialism: British view of the importance of empire, 191–192; early White settlers' views of Africans, 18; emergence of the African middle class, 5; material priorities of White settlers, 137–141; Rhodes's imperialist vision, 14–15; Smith's defense of White rule, 124–125

class: government by etiquette, 62–63; Industrial Conciliation Act, 26–27; Lessing's historical and political analysis, 6; postwar demand for African inclusion, 55; postwar fissures in White society, 64–66; White Southern Rhodesian speech, 59; White stratification, 29; working class Whites supporting segregation, 218. *See also* educated Africans; labor; middle class, African

Clements, Frank, 125

Cloete, Stuart, 209

Clutton-Brock, Guy: ANC manifesto, 91–92; criticism of the RF, 118–119; interracial dialogue, 78; liberal bent, 62; 1961 constitution voting areas and qualifications, 110; postwar fissures in the White population, 64, 67–68; Whitehead's state of emergency, 105; ZANU-ZAPU split, 121–122

Coghlan, Charles, 38

Cold War: colonial powers' fears of communism, 172–173; global context of empire, 47; refusing to grant Rhodesia independence, 126

Index

colonialism: Boers in South Africa, 10–11; British history in Southern Rhodesia, 3; evaluating the impact from the African perspective, 213–217; framework for moral issues, 193–197; justifying British rule, 21; White settlers claims of home, 201–202. *See also* White minority rule

Colonialism: A Moral Reckoning (Biggar), 3, 192

color bar: effect on poor Whites, 65–66; fear driving, 66–67; IA agenda, 77–78; industrial, 26–27, 161; racial etiquette as, 62–64. *See also* segregation

Coltart, David, 110, 132

common voter roll, 68–69, 79–83, 117

Commonwealth Heads of Government meeting (1979), 158

communism and communists: ANC manifesto, 91–92; influencing the Black African majority, 47–48; Maoist support for the liberation war, 162–163; Nkomo's prosecution for union activity, 58; Whites' attributing African nationalism to, 202

Confederate Party, 104

"Confession of Faith," Rhodes's, 11–15

consensus: institutionalization of slavery, 193–194

conservative Whites: character of postwar White immigrants, 62; consolidation of power, 98–99; increasingly punitive policies in the CAF, 114; lost opportunities for political change, 217–218; reaction to increasing nationalism, 96–98; RF reversing Todd's policies, 120–121; Whitehead's rightward shift, 105. *See also* Rhodesian Front; Smith, Ian; Unilateral Declaration of Independence

constitutionalism: acquisition of, 172; lack of plan for, 169–170

constitutions: African National Congress, 78; CAF benefiting Whites, 51; 1961 constitution, 109–115; RF's racist constitution, 142–143; UDI revisions of the 1961 constitution, 132; White leaders manipulating, 176

corruption, 139, 172

coups d'état, 178

Cowper, Reg, 197–198

Cripps, Arthur Shearly, 26, 195

Dangarembga, Tsitsi, 142

decolonization, the failure of, 169–170

democratic governance: political interference in elections, 178–180; post-independence legacy, 175. *See also* elections

desegregation: class fissures in White society over, 65–67; creating an African-White partnership, 54–55

detention camps, 1

diamonds: Rhodes's wealth, 10

Dickens, Charles, 190

discontent, African, 36, 113–114; Africans' bearing the status quo, 163–164; increasing African to White ratio, 48; increasing nationalist feeling, 94–95; intra-African violence, 164; Ndebeles' postwar resentment over land, 56–57; revival of the ANC, 91–92; segregation increasing, 89–90; UDI suppressing, 132; White authorities explaining African nationalism, 112; White privilege in land acquisition and use, 37; Whitehead's intransigence increasing, 105–108; Whites' failure to see or understand, 134–135, 146. *See also* liberation, war of; nationalism, African

Dominion Party: increasing conservatism, 97; increasing electoral support, 98; programs and membership, 117; Quinton Report recommendations, 108; Whitehead's leadership, 103–104

dominions office, 22

Dorman, Sara Rich, 180

Douglas-Home, Alec, 126, 145

Dupont, Clifford, 125, 133–134

Dutch Reformed Church, 42

economic development and interests: the goals of the liberation war, 161; the importance of empire, 191–192; pressure for political concessions, 147–148; RF encouraging increased White immigration, 118; Rhodes's and Livingstone's vision of race relations, 4–5; transformation under UDI, 142–143; White minority rule, 20–21

economic status: franchise qualifications, 69; postwar White immigrants, 64

educated Africans: *African Daily News* support, 119–120; failure of African-White partnerships, 93–94; failure to break color bars, 161–162; the impact of

colonialism, 213–214; increasing militancy, 55–56; persistent White ignorance toward, 199–202; radicalization of, 92; religious preaching against racism, 30–31; reviving the ANC, 91; White settlers' views of, 22–23. *See also* middle class, African
education: the connection to colonialism, 42; mission school curriculum, 40; missionaries' opposition to educating Africans, 31; RF reversing Todd's policies, 120–121; Todd's political agenda, 77; University College of Rhodesia and Nyasaland, 84, 97–98, 118, 143–144
elections and referenda: April 1979, 160, 178–180; coalition against ZANU-PF, 186; Huggins's political tenure, 28–29; Lancaster House, 207; postcolonial manipulation, 171–172; under the Rhodesian Front, 142–143; right-wing Whites increasing fear, 104; the shambles of 1962, 115–117; Smith raising support for UDI, 126–129; Smith's 1965 general election, 130; Smith's unwillingness to cede to Mugabe, 203–204; South Africa's consolidation of apartheid, 98; transition to majority rule, 157–158. *See also* franchise, African
electoral systems: incorporating Africans into the CAF, 52
emigration, White, 147–148, 160
enlightened despotism, British colonial rule as, 170
entrepreneurship: agricultural competition, 36–37
ethnic cleansing, 21
ethnic divisions: the liberation war intensifying, 164–165; Mugabe's violence against the Ndebele, 185–186; ZANU-ZAPU friction, 147
etiquette: creating obstacles to social mixing, 89; government by, 62–63; Todd's reforms, 84
eviction, 27

farming, 19; economic "underdevelopment," 171; Land Apportionment Act, 23–26; mission schools' curriculum, 40; Native Land Husbandry Act, 69–71; peasant support for the war of liberation, 162–164; White stratification, 29–30. *See also* land ownership and occupation
fearfulness of White settlers: the African revolt instilling, 32–34; as conservative electoral strategy, 104; creating obstacles to social mixing, 88–89; fear of desegregation, 66–67; Whitehead's state of emergency, 105–106
HMS *Fearless,* 142
federation. *See* Central African Federation
Field, Winston, 117–118, 123–124, 208–209
The Fire Next Time (Baldwin), 205–206
Fletcher, Patrick, 49, 86–87
food crises, 192, 194
Fox, Wilson, 79
franchise, African, 195–196; ANC revival and agenda, 92; CAF formation and design, 51; consequences of colonialism, 197–198; DP program, 117; Huggins's legislative constraints, 68–71; incorporating Africans into the CAF, 52–53; 1961 constitution voting areas and qualifications, 110; RBVA, 38–39; representative government restricting, 20; Smith quashing reforms, 153; Smith tying majority rule to, 131; Smith-Home proposals, 145–146; Todd's reform agenda, 79–83, 97–99; Todd's unconventional perspective, 75; universal, 91; Victoria Falls Conference, 149; White businessmen's pragmatism toward, 212
Franchise Act (1951), 68–69, 79
Franklin, Benjamin, 215
Freedom Charter (South Africa), 98
Frost, Des, 146, 198

G40 political faction, 187
Gabellah, Elliot, 155
Gann, Lewis, 117–118, 192
Gaul, William, 30–32, 40–41
gender roles: mission school curriculum, 40
Geneva Conference (1976), 152–153, 159
genocide: suppression of African rebellion, 19
Ghana: independence and self-government, 104; legacy of colonialism and the slave trade, 216
Glendenning, David, 179
globalization: expanding perspectives of community and individual, 192–193

Godwin, Peter, 165, 198–199
gold: Rhodes's wealth, 10; Whites' northward movement from South Africa, 17–18
Gopal, Priyamvada, 3, 13–14
Gore-Browne, Stewart, 215
governance: lack of a plan for decolonization, 169–170; Rhodes's vision of CAF rule, 16. *See also* majority rule; White minority rule
gratitude, White minority expectations of Africans', 200–202, 205
The Great Betrayal (Smith), 209
Grey, Richard, 61
grievances of White settlers, 200–202
Group Areas Act (1950), 97
guerrillas: April 1979 elections, 158; competition for land, 182; election interference, 179–180; internal security crisis, 157; Mugabe's triumphalism, 174; pressuring Smith for political concessions, 151–152; RF violence against ZAPU, ZANU, and ZIPRA, 175–176. *See also* liberation, war of
Gunther, John, 73, 95–96

Hancock, Ian, 217
Hard Times (Dickens), 190
hegemony, British, 12–13
Hills, Denis: evaluating White Rhodesians, 208–209; fear of desegregation, 66; RF deporting Bishop Lamont, 150; social mixing, 205; the war of liberation, 164; White attitudes and outlooks in the 1970s, 200–201; Whites' view of Rhodes, 211–212
History of Rhodesia (Blake), 6–7
Hobson, J.A., 209–210
Holderness, Hardwicke, 196; character of postwar White immigrants, 62; consequences of social mixing, 89; emergence of modern Africans, 192; industrial color bar, 161; power sharing with Africans, 22; Whites' "civilizing" mission, 139
home, White settlers' claims of, 201–202
Hong Kong: British colonization, 193
Hove, Byron, 155
Huddleston, Trevor, 120
Huggins, Godfrey: appeasing White fear of Africans, 67; background, 22; CAF formation and design, 50–51; constraining the franchise, 68–69; criticism of the UDI, 130; persistent White ignorance, 199–202; racial franchise, 39; tenure, 28
Hyam, Ronald, 21

identity: African response to White settlement, 34–36; characterizing postwar European immigrants, 59–68
ideological racism, 208–209
ideology: the rural guerrilla war, 162–163; ZANU-ZAPU split, 122
immigrants, White: DP and RF programs encouraging, 117–119, 202–203; growing fissures in the White population, 67–68, 85–86; postwar increase, 48–49; self-identification of postwar immigrants, 59–68. *See also* White settlers
imperialism: the benefits of, 213–217; benign, 211; historical perspectives, 190–192; League of Nations modified version, 20; moral criticism of, 209–210; Rhodes's vision of British global hegemony, 12–13, 15
Imperialism: A Study (Hobson), 209–210
indaba for UDI support, 127–129, 131
independence from Britain: failure of the CAF, 99; fate of White settlers in Africa, 104–105; lack of a plan for decolonization, 169–170; lack of political and economic growth, 170–172; the lasting damage of the UDI, 198–199; multiracialism as requirement for, 109; self-determination and equality for Africans, 196; Smith ignoring the rise of African nationalism, 203–204; Smith's negotiations, 121–132; Smith's perception of betrayal by Britain, 206–207; Smith's rationale, 130–131; Whitehead's agenda, 105. *See also* Unilateral Declaration of Independence
independent church movement, 41–42
Indian population, segregation of, 74
Industrial and Commercial Workers' Union (ICU), 38–39, 43
Industrial Conciliation Act (1934), 26–27, 107
Industrial Revolution, 12–13
industrialization: the importance of empire, 191–192
Insurgent Empire: Anticolonial Resistance and British Dissent (Gopal), 3

integration: RF campaign to stop, 116
intellectuals, lack of, 29
Internal Settlement (1978), 151–152
Inter-racial Association (IA), 77–78, 82, 199–200
interracial dialogue: Europeans' lack of interest in, 88; fear stemming from the lack of, 90; Holderness's hope for, 96; interracial criticism of, 85–86; legacy of the lack of, 180–185; Mugabe's willingness to engage, 204; race issues dominating, 5; Smith's rejection of, 141; under Todd's URP, 78; Whitehead and Nkomo, 115; Whitehead's refusal to engage in, 105–106; ZANU-PF coalition with White settlers, 183–185
interracial forums, 218
Ireland: potato famine, 194
It's Our Turn to Eat (Wrong), 172

Jameson Raid, 210
Jefferson, Thomas, 193–194

Kaunda, Kenneth: Anglo-American Agreement, 152; Gore-Browne and, 215; international recognition of Rhodesia, 158; pressure for Smith's political concessions, 147–148; Pretoria Agreement, 148–149
Keatley, Patrick: *African Daily News* ban, 119–120; on Africans' lack of gratitude, 200; consequences of segregation, 90; on Livingstone's tradition, 196–197; ongoing segregation, 133; Rhodesia's founding fathers, 29; White attitudes toward majority rule, 138, 208; White liberals, 65
Kenya: land disputes, 182
Kissinger, Henry, 151–152, 155–156, 173, 206
Knight-Bruce, George, 30, 32, 140

labor: African farmers' refusal to work for Whites, 36; coal miners' strike, 75; compelling Africans to work for Whites, 192; Industrial and Commercial Workers' Union, 38–39, 43; industrial color bar, 161; Industrial Conciliation Act, 26–27; native reserves providing, 23–24; pass law legislation, 27; peasant support for the war of liberation, 162–164; postwar discontent, 48; postwar radicalization of Africans, 55; postwar White immigrants, 64; railway strikes, 57–58; shifting views of African rights, 215. *See also* class
Labour Party (Britain), 207
Lamont, Donal, 142, 145, 150
Lancaster House conference, 166–167; land issues, 181–183; successes and failures, 180–185; the war as priority, 173–174
Land Apportionment Act (1930), 39; Native Land Husbandry Act, 69–71; overpopulation of native reserves, 57; Quinton Report recommendation, 108; RF campaign to retain, 116; RF replacement, 144–145; Sithole's intent to abolish, 181–182; terms and actions, 23–26; Todd commission and Quinton reports, 107–109; Todd's multiracial amendments, 83–84; White paternalism, 93–94; Whites' refusal to repeal, 185
Land Husbandry Act (1951), 69–71, 79, 92, 94, 113, 127, 181–182
land ownership and occupation, 196; African response to White settlement, 34–36; ANC revival and agenda, 92; colonial boundaries and ethnic diversity, 170–171; exclusion of Indians and Chinese, 74; Industrial and Commercial Workers' Union, 38–39; Mugabe weaponizing the land question, 187; post-independence hostility over, 181–183; postwar eviction of Africans, 56–57; RF Land Tenure Act, 144–146, 153, 181–183; turn of the century land seizures, 185. *See also* Land Apportionment Act
Land Tenure Act (1969), 144–146, 153, 181–183. *See also* Land Apportionment Act
Lardner-Burke, Desmond, 143
Law and Order (Maintenance) Act (1960), 99, 107, 114, 175
League of Nations: modified imperialism, 20
left, political. *See* liberal Whites
Lessing, Doris: on Africans' lack of gratitude, 200; denial of dignity for Africans, 90; Land Apportionment Act, 26; Native Land Husbandry Act, 69; obstacles to social mixing, 88; poor Rhodesian Whites, 64–65; postwar White immigrants, 61; RF destruction of White prospects, 197; social mixing,

205; University College of Rhodesia and Nyasaland, 84; White liberalism, 126
Leys, Colin, 28, 83, 123
liberal Whites: Centre Party, 143; challenging prevailing race relations, 90; diehard Whites countering multiracial policies, 78–79; ignorance toward educated Africans, 199–200; increasing challenges to reactionary Whites, 98–99; political agenda, 77–79; relative security of educated Whites, 65; Todd's ejection from office, 86; Todd's franchise reform, 79–83; understanding African nationalism, 203–204; Whitehead's state of emergency, 105–106. *See also* multiracialism; Todd, Garfield
liberation, war of, 6–7; April 1979 elections, 157–158; defining Zimbabwean politics, 187–188; effect on the people, 177–178; the goals of, 161–162; Lancaster House objectives, 173–174; NDP declaration of violence policy, 113; peace talks, 159–160; peasant support for, 162–164; political choice for Whites and Africans, 165–166; take-off event, 147; White strategy, 163; Whites' failure to understand, 181; Whites' failure to understand Africans, 201–202; ZANU-PF land seizures, 185. *See also* Mugabe, Robert; ZANU-PF
literacy: mission schools curriculum, 40; voter qualifications, 81
Livingstone, David: British abolition and imperialist expansion, 13; the Rudd Concession, 11; Southern Rhodesia's political shift to the right, 196–197; Tredgold's connection, 80; vision of race relations, 4
Lloyd, Edgar, 32
Lobengula (Ndebele king), 10–11, 18, 210
Lonsdale, John, 209
Lovell, Julia, 174
Luthuli, Albert, 98

Macdonald, Hector, 177
Macintyre, Ben, 194
Macleod, Iain, 126
Macmillan, Harold, 114, 125
Maddocks, Alex, 200–201
maize controls, 36–37
majority rule: conformist African perspectives, 55–56; interracial dialogue and cooperation, 141; land redistribution issues, 181–183; Nyasaland, 105; pressure on Smith for political concessions, 150–151; proposed transition, 153–158; UFP election defeat over, 116–117; White settlers' failure to work with Africans, 181; ZANU-ZAPU agreement over, 123. *See also* liberation, war of; Mugabe, Robert
Malan, D.F., 47, 49
Mandela, Nelson: South Africa's internal dissent, 206
Mandela Foundation, 212–213
Manifest Destiny, 13, 191
Maoists, 162–163, 174–175
martial law, 160, 179
Marxism: Lessing's historical and political analysis, 6
Mashona people: agricultural competition, 37; early White settlers' views of Africans, 18; liberation war, 164–165; native land purchase areas, 24–25; revolt against White settlers, 18–19; Rhodes's imperialist ambitions, 10–11
Mason, Philip, 6, 14, 53, 59, 64, 205, 208
Matabele people: European perceptions of, 18; grain markets, 36–37; postwar territorial politics, 56–57; RBVA, 38–39; respect for Rhodes, 210–211. *See also* Ndebele people
material success, White settlers prioritizing, 137–141
Maurois, Andre, 193
media: *African Daily News* ban, 119–120; ZANU-PF politicizing, 175
middle class, African: British view of modern Africans, 192; economic "underdevelopment," 171; emergence of, 5; lack of social acceptance by Whites, 89; mission school education, 43–44; opposition to the general labor strike, 57–58; White liberal agenda, 76–79. *See also* educated Africans
migrant labor, 36–37
military action: NDP protests and riot, 106–107
military service of Africans, 131
minority rule. *See* White minority rule
miscegenation, 66, 84
missionaries: the African point of view, 39–43; expansion into Central Africa,

30–32; political fissures among White Christians, 85–86. *See also* Christians and Christianity
Mlambo, Alois, 19, 165, 216
Mlambo, Eshmael, 104, 122, 134–135
Mnangagwa, Emmerson, 178, 186–187
modernization: the African perspective of colonialism, 213–214
Moffat, Robert, 11, 18, 217
Monckton Report (1960), 54, 105
Moore, David, 177
morality. *See* values
Movement for Democratic Change (MDC), 186–187
Mozambique: rise of African nationalism, 206
Mugabe, Grace, 187
Mugabe, Robert, 218; African and White views of, 203–204; Anglo-American Agreement, 152; CAF criticism, 58; election upset of 1962, 116; NDP ban, 111–112; patterns of political violence, 177–178; peace negotiations, 160; Smith's demonization of, 203–204; Victoria Falls Conference, 149–150; violence against the Ndebele, 185–186; White cabinet members, 183–185; ZANLA violence against the Smith regime, 157
Mugabe's Legacy (Moore), 177
multiracialism: character of postwar White immigrants, 62; Mugabe's cabinet, 183–185; the noble aims of colonialism, 6–7; RF jeopardizing, 197–198; Todd's franchise reform, 83; White liberal agenda, 76–79. *See also* liberal Whites; majority rule
Mundy, H.G., 96
Muzorewa, Abel, 203–204; ANC leadership, 145; coercive governance, 176; Lancaster House land negotiations, 182; nationalist leadership, 141; opposition to RF segregation, 145; political interference in democratic processes, 178–180; Pretoria Agreement, 148–149; proposed transition to majority rule, 155; Smith's compromise failure, 203; Victoria Falls Conference, 149
Mzingeli, Charles, 39, 77, 86

nation building: postcolonial dysfunction, 172

National Democratic Party (NDP): policy of violence, 113; referendum for the 1961 constitution, 111–112; renaming the ANC, 95; Whitehead's violence against, 105–107. *See also* African National Congress
nationalism, African: Africans' desire for racial, political, and economic equality, 196; emerging African middle class, 5–7; postwar Matabeleland, 56–57; revolts in Portuguese colonies, 206; the role of Whites under majority governance, 202; Whites framing as intimidation, 112–113; Whites' growing intolerance of, 145–147; ZANU-ZAPU political split, 121–123. *See also* African National Congress; liberation, war of
nationalism, White. *See* Dominion Party
nation-building, 180
Native (Urban Areas) Accommodation and Registration Act (1946), 27, 39
Native Commissioners (NC), 21, 23, 57, 69–70, 94, 127
Native Land Husbandry Act (1951). *See* Land Husbandry Act
native reserves: government pressure on native land use, 36–37; growth of the nationalist movement, 92; Land Apportionment Act, 23–26; Native (Urban Areas) Accommodation and Registration Act, 27, 39; Native Land Husbandry Act, 69–71; postwar overpopulation, 56–57; Quinton Report recommendations, 108; remoteness from the war of liberation, 165. *See also* land ownership and occupation
Ndebele people: the appeal of Christianity, 40; criticism of Rhodes's treatment of, 210; early White settlers' views of Africans, 18; grain markets, 36–37; liberation war, 164–165; Mugabe's state-sponsored violence, 185–186; native land purchase areas, 24–25; response to White settlement, 34–36; revolt against White settlers, 13, 18–19, 32–36, 56, 71, 210; Rhodes's imperialist ambitions, 10–11. *See also* Matabele people
Ndhlovu, Masotsha, 38–39
Nkomo, Joshua, 196; *African Daily News* support, 119; Anglo-American Agreement, 152; arrest and detention,

133–134; CAF election, 51; creation of ZAPU, 113; death threats against, 176; detention camp, 1; impending revolt, 150; lost opportunities for escaping White racism, 217–219; Mugabe's violence against the Ndebele, 185–186; nationalist priorities, 66; Pretoria Agreement, 148–149; proposed transitional government, 155–156; prosecution for union activity, 58; relationship with South African Whites, 50; revival of the ANC, 91; Smith ignoring the rise of African nationalism, 203–204; Smith's assessment of Sithole and, 201–202; Smith's condescension toward Africans, 200–202; Smith's *indaba* for UDI support, 131; UN address, 106–107; ZANU-ZAPU split, 122–123; ZIPRA and ZANLA violence, 157
Nkumbula, Harry, 215
Norman, Denis, 127, 183–184, 203–204
Northern Rhodesia, 19, 48–49, 215
Nyandoro, George, 92, 105–106
Nyasaland, 19, 48–49, 51, 53, 104–105. *See also* Central African Federation

Oates, Frank, 18
Official Secrets Act, 175
ordinary voters, 81
Owen, David, 154
Owen-Young plan, 153–154
Oxford University: Rhodes Must Fall campaign, 9

Palley, Ahrn, 116
partnership, CAF as, 49–52, 87
pass law legislation, 27–28
paternalism, White: Africans challenging, 94; depersonalization of Africans, 55; Douglas-Home, 126; of liberal Whites, 77; postcolonial states' unpreparedness, 170; White expectations of African gratitude, 200–202; White missionaries educating Africans, 31; White settlers' views of Africans, 22; Whites' failure to see and understand, 134–135
Patriotic Front (PF): Lancaster House conference, 173; proposed transitional government, 153–155; Smith's political concessions, 152; Zimbabwean land redistribution, 183. *See also* ZANU-PF

Pax Britannica, 172, 191–192
peace negotiations. *See* Lancaster House conference
Pearce, Edward, 145–146
Pearce commission, 145–146, 152, 178–179, 200–201
Penn, William, 193–194
police, 112–113; Judith Todd's arrest, 120, 146; torture of Mnangagwa, 178
political consciousness, African, 55–58
political exclusion of Africans. *See* franchise, African
political participation, 21–22; educated Africans questioning, 41; incorporating Africans into the CAF, 52–53; RBVA, 38; the religious connection, 42–43. *See also* franchise, African
Popper, Karl, 3
population demographics: British colonial history, 3; colonial boundaries and ethnic diversity, 170–171; increasing discontent in a growing African population, 71; land distribution, 24–25; postwar European migration, 202–203; the White population of Southern Rhodesia, 28–30
Portuguese colonies, collapse of, 148, 206
postcolonialism: failure of nation-building, 180
potato famine, Irish, 194
pragmatic racism, 208–209, 212
Pretoria Agreement (1975), 148–149
progressiveness: missed opportunities to soften White supremacy, 217–218
Protestant work ethic, 41
Public Order and Security Act (2002), 187
purity, racial, 96

Quenet, Vincent, 153
Quinton, Jack, 89, 108
Quinton Report, 108, 185

race relations, 3; colonial domination driving, 32–34; deference requirements, 70; dominating political dialogue, 5–7; downfall of the CAF, 50–51; incorporating Africans into the CAF, 52; intra-White arguments over, 107–109; Livingstone and Rhodes's falling out, 11; postwar White immigrants, 61–63; Rhodes's and Livingstone's visions and influences, 4–5; Todd's unconventional

attitude, 74–76; White community under UDI, 199; White liberals challenging, 90; White missionaries' treatment of Africans, 30–32
racial discrimination: conformist African perspectives on majority rule, 55–56; consequences of colonialism, 197–198; Lamont's criticism of RF governance, 150; Muzorewa's failed leadership, 158; the political economy, 71; Quenet commission investigation, 153; US Civil and Voting Rights Acts, 205–206. *See also* franchise, African; land ownership and occupation; segregation
racism: CAF formation and design, 51–53; early White settlers, 18; guide to racial etiquette, 62–64; Indian and Chinese people, 74; moral criticism of British imperialism, 209–210; pragmatic and ideological, 208–209; Rhodes's imperialist vision, 12–13, 15–16; White attitudes toward majority rule, 208; White fearfulness driving, 32–34; White missionaries' opinions of Africans, 30–32; Whites defending racial purity, 96
radicalism, Black, 218
railways: BSAC investment in, 19; carrying religion through Central Africa, 32; racial inequity, 73; workers' strike, 48
Ranger, Terence, 36, 57, 128, 162
Rebel People (Hills), 165–166
recognition of Rhodesia, 158
Reformed ICU, 39
religion, African: the importance of land, 26
religion, European. *See* Christians and Christianity
representative government, 20; lack of plan for, 169–170. *See also* majority rule
resource wealth: Rhodes's wealth, 10, 15; the Rudd Concession, 11; Whites' northward movement from South Africa, 17–18
revolt, Ndebele and Mashona, 13, 18–19, 32–36, 56, 71, 210
Reynolds, Reginald, 25
Rhodes, Cecil: African revolt against White settlers, 19; ambitions for global domination, 15; background, 9–10; "Confession of Faith," 11–15; death and burial, 210–211; missionary expansion into Central Africa, 30–32; negotiating the end of revolt, 33; noble aspirations of colonialism, 6–7; northward movement of White settlers, 17–18; past and current perceptions and criticisms, 209–213; vision of race relations, 4; Whites' view of, 211–212
Rhodes Centenary Exhibition (1953), 211
Rhodes Must Fall campaign, 9
Rhodes Trust, 26, 212–213
Rhodesia Bantu Voters' Association (RBVA), 38–39, 43
Rhodesian Front (RF): *African Daily News* criticism, 119–120; character of postwar White immigrants, 61; consequences of colonialism, 197–198; election upset of 1962, 115–117; encouraging increased White immigration, 117–119; far-reaching consequences of White policies, 198–199; investigating racial discrimination, 153; Lamont's criticism of, 150; Land Tenure Act, 181–183; Mugabe's patterns of political violence, 177; the noble aims of colonialism, 7; racist constitution, 142–143; reversing Todd's liberal policies, 120–121; violent approach to governance, 175–177; White attitudes toward majority rule, 208; White stratification, 199; Whites' "civilizing" mission, 138–140; working toward an internal settlement, 153–158; ZANU-PF's coercive regime, 174–176, 188; Zimbabwean land redistribution, 183. *See also* Smith, Ian
Richard, Ivor, 152–153
right, political. *See* conservative Whites; Rhodesian Front; Smith, Ian
riots, 78, 106–107
Rolin, Henri, 33
Roman Empire, 191–192
Rowland, "Tiny," 212
Rudd, Charles, 11, 18
Rudd Concession, 11
rural areas: postwar eviction of African farmers, 56–57; rise of nationalism, 92. *See also* farming; land ownership and occupation
Ruskin, John, 12
Russia: global political and economic expansion, 13

Sadoma, Ronnie, 146
Salazar, Antonio, 206

Samkange, Thompson: combining religion and politics, 42–43; territorial politics, 55–56; White paternalism, 94; Whites' fear of desegregation, 67
sanctions, 142–143, 147, 151, 180–181
Savanhu, Jasper, 114–115
scramble for Africa, 170, 191
secret society: Rhodes's imperialist vision, 12, 14–15
security forces: failure of the Owen-Young plan, 154–155; the war of liberation, 160
segregation, 195; continuing after UDI, 133; evolution of social distancing, 33; increasing obstacles to social mixing, 88–91; Indian and Chinese people, 74; Industrial Conciliation Act, 26–27; Land Apportionment Act providing, 24, 26; 1950s society, 73; persistent White ignorance, 199–202; post-independence persistence, 184; RF differences over, 143; RF program, 118–119; RF's Land Tenure Act, 144–145; social segregation of postwar immigrants, 62–64; support by working class Whites, 218; University College of Rhodesia and Nyasaland, 84; White liberal criticism, 79; White settlers' claims of homeland, 201–202; Whites' "civilizing" mission, 139–141. *See also* color bar
self-determination, 47, 50, 69, 95, 196
self-government. *See* majority rule; White minority rule
Selous, Frederick, 19
Shamuyarira, Nathan, 37, 61, 70–71, 85–87
Sharpeville shootings, 107
Shimmin, Isaac, 40
Sithole, Masipula, 122
Sithole, Ndabaningi, 218; the benefits of European colonialism, 196; chiefs' loss of authority, 127–128; creation of ZAPU, 113; land legislation, 181–182; Mugabe replacing, 204; political interference in democratic processes, 178–179; proposed transition to majority rule, 155; Smith's assessment of Nkomo and, 201–202; Smith's *indaba* for UDI support, 131; status in the Christian community, 140–141; Todd's franchise reform, 82–83; Todd's liberalism, 76; Victoria Falls Conference, 149; ZANU founding, 121

Skelton, Kenneth, 140
skilled labor: Industrial Conciliation Act, 26–27; White immigration failing to bring, 203
slavery: British abolition and imperialist expansion, 13; framework for tracking, 193–195; historical shift in attitudes toward, 215–216
Smith, David, 183–184
Smith, Ian, 142; assessment of Sithole and Nkomo, 201–202; coal miners' strike, 75; condescension toward Africans, 200–202; defense of UDI, 137; delaying Black rule, 197–198; ideological racism, 208–209; ignoring the rise of African nationalism, 203–204; international pressure for political concessions, 151–153; justice, civilization, and Christianity, 141; Land Apportionment Act amendment, 108–109; maintaining "civilized standards," 120–121; the noble aims of colonialism, 7; peace talks, 159–160; Pearce commission, 145–146; perception of betrayal by Britain, 206–207; postwar White immigrants, 60–61; pressure for political concessions, 147–153; proposed settlement, 153–158; Southern Rhodesia's political shift to the right, 197; University College of Rhodesia and Nyasaland, 143–144; US race relations and foreign policy, 206; Victoria Falls Conference, 149; ZANU-ZAPU split, 123. *See also* Rhodesian Front
social distancing, 32–34, 62–64
societal degeneration, 178
South Africa: Boer settlers, 10–11; Britain's postwar dependence, 49; collusion against Mugabe's regime, 184; influence of the Dutch Reformed Church, 42; northward movement of White settlers, 17–18; peace talks with Smith, 159–160; postwar adoption of apartheid, 47–48; postwar British immigration, 60–61; pressuring Smith for political concessions, 151–152; provenance of the White population, 29; Rhodes Trust funding, 212–213; Rhodesia's increasing political dependence, 147–148; Rhodes's political and financial connections, 10–11; Smith's perceived betrayal by, 206–207; White ignorance,

120; White Rhodesians' sympathies with, 94–95, 97–98
special voters, 81–82
state of emergency, 76, 85, 95, 105–106, 119, 147, 180, 197, 212, 217
state-sponsored violence: Mugabe's regime, 174–180, 185–186; NDP policies and practices, 113–114; RF deporting Bishop Lamont, 150; targeting the MDC, 186–187
strikes, labor, 48, 57–58, 75
student protest: Judith Todd's arrest, 120; Rhodes Must Fall campaign, 9
suffrage, White, 53
suicide, 22

Takawira, Leopold, 78, 95, 123
taxation: governmental accountability, 171–172; negotiating the end of revolt, 33
terrorism: Mugabe's radicalism, 203–204; RF violence, 177
Thatcher, Margaret, 158
HMS *Tiger*, 142
Todd, Garfield: arrest and detention, 120, 146; British sympathy with the policies of, 114; consequences of social mixing, 89; ejection from office, 78, 85–88, 93; entry into politics, 74–76; franchise reform, 79–83, 99; Land Apportionment Act, 25, 83–84; lost opportunities for escaping White racism, 217–219; Native Land Husbandry Act, 70; placating conservative Whites, 97; political position, 76; RF reversing Todd's policies, 120–121; the White government's loss of power, 207–208; ZANU-ZAPU split, 122
Todd, Judith, 1, 197; *African Daily News* ban, 120; arrest and detention, 120, 146; criticism of the 1961 constitution, 111; on Edgar Whitehead, 103; postwar White immigrants, 61; Smith's *indaba* for UDI support, 129; Whites' "civilizing" mission, 138–139
Tongorara, Josiah, 174
torture, 178
totalitarianism: post-independence legacy, 174–175
trade: grain markets favoring White farmers, 36–37
traditional culture, integrating Christianity into, 40–42

transition to majority rule: Africans' demand for inclusion, 55–56; proposed internal settlement, 153–158
treason, Smith's accusations of, 207
Tredgold, Robert: *African Daily News* criticism of the RF, 119; coercive majority rule, 176; consequences of segregation, 90; franchise reform, 53–54, 80–83, 86, 93; 1961 constitution voting areas and qualifications, 110; resignation over racist legislation, 99, 107, 138; revised franchise system of 1958, 53–54; RF negotiation for independence, 125; on segregation, 79; Smith's *indaba* for UDI support, 129; on White Africans, 59; Whitehead's state of emergency, 105; Whites' reaction to the ANC, 96
Trevelyan, Charles, 194
tribalism, political, 121–123, 128–129, 171, 180
tripod legislation, 23–28, 62, 89, 107, 115, 195. *See also* Industrial Conciliation Act; Land Apportionment Act; Native (Urban Areas) Accommodation and Registration Act
Tsvangirai, Morgan, 186

Uganda: Black-on-Black violence, 186; colonial boundaries and ethnic diversity, 170–171; postcolonial tyranny, 172; protectorate status, 3
underdevelopment, 171
Unilateral Declaration of Independence (UDI): early policies and criticisms, 142–146; increasing White emigration, 147–148; justice, civilization, and Christianity, 141; lasting damage, 198–199; RF negotiations for independence from Britain, 121–132; Rhodes's vision of CAF rule, 16; Smith raising supporters for, 126–129; Smith's defense of, 131, 137; White attitudes toward majority rule, 208; White stratification, 199. *See also* Rhodesian Front; Smith, Ian
union labor: ICU, 38–39; Industrial Conciliation Act, 26–27, 107; Todd's reforms, 84; White stratification, 29–30
United Federal Party (UFP), 99; election disaster of 1962, 115–117; Quinton Report recommendations, 108. *See also* Todd, Garfield

United National Federal Party, 158
United Nations, 47; Nkomo's address, 106–107; pressure on Smith's regime, 125–126; Todd's address, 75–76; Universal Declaration of Human Rights, 190–191
United Rhodesia Party (URP), 218; African representation, 78; hampering Todd's authority, 75; Todd's ejection from office, 86. *See also* Todd, Garfield
United States: British global hegemony, 12–13; Civil and Voting Rights Acts, 205–206; the Internal Agreement, 155; Lancaster House conference, 182; Owen-Young plan for majority rule transition, 153–154; pressuring Smith for political concessions, 148, 151–152; slavery, 193–194; westward expansion, 13, 191
Unity Agreement (1987), 186
Universal Declaration of Human Rights (1948), 97, 138, 190–191
University College of Rhodesia and Nyasaland, 84, 97–98, 118, 143–144
Unlawful Organisations Act (South Africa), 106
urbanization: Industrial Conciliation Act, 26–27; Land Apportionment Act, 25; Native (Urban Areas) Accommodation and Registration Act, 27, 39; postwar migration, 48; postwar urban protest, 57–58

vaccinations, 165
values: consequences of White racial policies, 3–4; framework for tracking moral issues, 193–197; moral criticism of British imperialism, 209–210; postwar militancy of educated Africans, 55–56; RF's racist constitution, 142–143; Smith's rationale for independence, 130–131; UDI defense of, 137–141; Whites' material priorities, 137–140; Whites' treatment of Africans, 1
Vambe, Lawrence: African resilience, 203; defining the CAF, 49–50; effect of the UDI, 134; material considerations of White settlers, 138; relative security of educated Whites, 65; White appropriation of African land, 35–36; White missionaries, 31–32
van der Byl, P.K., 119, 143, 176–177

Vermeer, Anthony, 60
victims, framing Africans as, 213–214
Victoria Falls conference (1975), 149
violence, NDP policy of, 113–114
von Ranke, Leopold, 189–190, 192
Vorster, John, 148–149, 151, 159–160
voting rights. *See* franchise, African
Voting Rights Act (US; 1965), 205–206

wages: Industrial Conciliation Act, 26–27
Wankie Colliery strike, 75
Washington, George, 193–194
Watergate, 190
Welch, Pamela, 31
Welensky, Roy, 5, 51, 54, 114, 138
West, Richard, 133
westward expansion in the US, 13, 191
White economy, 4–5
White minority rule: consequences for Zimbabwe, 198–199; establishment of, 19; intra-White arguments over, 109; Smith's faith in the success and superiority, 147–148; state violence under majority rule, 186–187; tripod legislation supporting, 23–28; White intransigence destroying, 209. *See also* franchise, African; majority rule
White privilege: attracting immigrants, 211–212; character of postwar immigrants, 61–63; driving African opposition to White rule, 160–161; enlightened despotism, 170; fear of desegregation, 66–67; intractable defense of, 95–96; maize controls, 36–37; materialism over moral values, 137–141
White settlers: coalition with ZANU-PF, 183–185; complacency of, 200–202; excluding Black interests, 19–23; fall of the CAF, 53–55; northward movement from South Africa, 17–18; provenance and character, 28–30; religious control over, 31; Rhodes's ambitions for global domination, 15–16. *See also* immigrants, White
White supremacy: educated Africans questioning, 41; identity of postwar immigrants, 60; liberal-conservative divide over the political future, 5–7; 1950s society, 73; postwar consolidation through federation, 48–55; RF differences over, 143; RF

jeopardizing, 197–198; strengthening African nationalism, 93; Whites' failure to understand Africans' grievances, 202
Whitehead, Edgar: African chiefs' loss of authority, 128; election and lack of power, 103–105; election disaster of 1962, 115–117; fear of Africans, 66; increasing African discontent, 105–108; Land Apportionment Act amendment, 108–109; Smith's contempt for, 124; state of emergency, 105–106; Todd's franchise reform, 82–83; White liberals' optimism toward, 93
Wilberforce, William, 195
Wilson, Harold, 123, 130
women: growth of the nationalist movement, 92
Woodward, Bob, 189–190
work ethic, Protestant, 41
World War II: African chiefs' loss of authority, 128; Africans' military service, 131; questioning empire, 47–48
Wrong, Michaela, 172

Young, Andrew, 154, 173

Zambesia, 11, 17, 212
Zambia: Victoria Falls conference, 149
ZANU-PF, 203; the conflict shaping the party and regime, 174–177; election fraud and intimidation, 179; election victory over Smith, 203–204; ethnic rivalries during the conflict, 165; intolerance of opposition, 186–188; land redistribution, 182–185. *See also* Mugabe, Robert; Nkomo, Joshua
ZANU/ZANLA, 203–204, 206; competition for leadership, 147; formation of ZANU-PF, 152–153; interracial dialogue, 141; the liberation war intensifying ethnic divides, 164–165; Maoist support and influence, 163, 174–175; political split with ZAPU, 121–123; Victoria Falls Conference, 149–150; war against White settlers and the transitional government, 156–157; ZANU-PF violence against, 175–176. *See also* liberation, war of; Sithole, Ndabaningi
ZAPU/ZIPRA, 37–38, 175–176; creation of, 113; generational commitment to, 164; interracial dialogue, 141; leadership, 147; the liberation war intensifying ethnic divides, 164–165; political split with ZANU, 121–123. *See also* Nkomo, Joshua
Zayyan, Hafsa, 192
Zimbabwe, 180–185; far-reaching consequences of White policies, 198–199; political interference in democratic processes, 178–179; post-independence land redistribution, 183. *See also* Lancaster House conference; Mugabe, Robert; ZANU-PF
Zimbabwe African National Liberation Army (ZANLA). *See* ZANU/ZANLA
Zimbabwe African National Union–Patriotic Front (ZANU–PF). *See* ZANU-PF
Zimbabwe African People's Union (ZAPU). *See* ZAPU/ZIPRA
Zimbabwe United People's Organisation (ZUPO), 156
Zionists: global political and economic expansion, 13
ZIPRA. *See* ZAPU/ZIPRA

About the Book

GARDNER THOMPSON OFFERS A FRESH HISTORY OF BRITISH rule in Southern Rhodesia, from the first colonial settlements in Mashonaland in the 1890s to the establishment of the country's sovereignty as Zimbabwe.

After tracing developments in the early decades, Thompson turns to the post–World War II debate about the colony's future direction—which pitted progressive settlers against the increasingly racialist conservative core—the impact of the Unilateral Declaration of Independence in 1965, and the many damaging consequences of the choices that were made. Not least, he assesses the legacy of Rhodesian colonialism in postcolonial Zimbabwe.

Gardner Thompson is a historian of British imperialism, with a focus on Africa and the Middle East. His previous publications include *Uganda: British Colonial Rule and Its Legacy* and *Legacy of Empire: Britain, Zionism and the Creation of Israel* (short-listed for the Middle East Monitor's 2020 Palestine Book Awards). Dr. Thompson is a fellow of the Royal Historical Society.